The
COURT-MARTIAL
of PAUL REVERE

The Court-Martial of Paul Revere

A SON OF LIBERTY *and*

AMERICA'S FORGOTTEN

MILITARY DISASTER

Michael M. *Greenburg*

ForeEdge

ForeEdge
An imprint of University Press of New England
www.upne.com
© 2014 Michael M. Greenburg
All rights reserved
Manufactured in the United States of America
Designed by Richard Hendel
Typeset in Merlo and Letterpress Text by
Tseng Information Systems, Inc.

Hardcover ISBN: 978-1-61168-535-0
Ebook ISBN: 978-1-61168-650-0
Library of Congress Control Number: 2014935089

5 4 3 2 1

In loving memory of my father, Allen Greenburg.

If his deeds would but shine, as he wishes to tell,

It would please us to read, but we know the man well.

—Excerpt from an anonymous poem appearing

in the *Boston Gazette* on April 15, 1782

Contents

Illustrations follow page 110.

Prologue The Castle

The Rebel guns on Dorchester Heights were trained squarely on the British occupiers of Boston below. Henry Knox had completed his fifty-six-day journey through the winter snows from Ticonderoga, and by March 5, 1776, the sixth anniversary of the massacre at Boston, an impressive battery of mortar and cannon had been silently hauled into place and bore down on His Majesty's forces. "I know not what I shall do," reported General William Howe. "The rebels have done more in one night than my whole army would have done in one month."[1]

The consequences of inaction were painfully clear to Howe—either the guns had to be removed, or the British would be forced to evacuate the town. Wishing to avoid the consequences of another Bunker Hill—a nominal victory, but at terrible cost to his troops and morale—Howe attempted only a meager naval effort to dislodge the continental positions from the heights. As severe weather and high winds moved into the harbor, however, navigation became treacherous and the attacking fleet was forced aground. As one historian aptly noted regarding the turn of events, "Leaving or not leaving was no longer a matter of choice."[2]

Boston found herself in the crosshairs of a vanquished army in full and frustrated retreat. Though General Howe and the earlier departed governor, Thomas Gage, each had long understood the folly of permanent occupation in the hotbed of American rebellion, exit from Boston was anything but orderly. Despite vague and conflicting orders not to destroy the town, hordes of British personnel accompanied by Tory sympathizers looted and devastated private homes and businesses, leaving the streets and harbor docks littered with barricades, animal carcasses, and tree limbs.[3]

By the early morning hours of March 17, 1776, General Howe had begun the final evacuation of his forces from the shores of Boston. Under the escort of Admiral Molyneux Shuldham of the Royal Navy, the departing fleet skirmished its way through the mesh of harbor shoals, pausing specifically to engage the fort at Castle Island. British engineers mined strategic sites within the garrison and ultimately burned every structure on the island. They summarily spiked the cannons serving the fort and tore the trunnions, which allowed aim and maneuverability, from their mounts to further hinder any thought of repair. As the flotilla exited the harbor, Boston Light, the first lighthouse established in the American colonies, was blown up as a parting nod.[4]

Within days of the British departure, General George Washington entered the town and scanned the wreckage left behind. He visited the Common, Fort Hill, Faneuil Hall, and other prominent locales within Boston and promptly ordered that the houses and streets be "cleansed from infection" to avoid an influx of diseases such as smallpox.[5]

On March 20, the Continental Army reentered Boston and took control of the town's defensive positions.[6] Recognizing the strategic importance of the now burned fortress on Castle Island, Washington quickly commissioned the refortification of the site and ordered the swift repair of the armaments damaged during the British departure. Though the task of general reconstruction would ultimately fall on two military engineers, Richard Gridley, who oversaw the bulwark of Dorchester Heights,[7] and William Burbeck, who was then keeper of the ordnance on Castle Island,[8] the Town of Boston would turn to "that ace of versatility,"[9] Paul Revere, to assist in the immediate repair of the island's cannon.

Neither statesman nor soldier, by 1776 Paul Revere nonetheless had earned the reputation as a talented artisan and an ardent champion for the cause of American liberty. Though he had served briefly in the French and Indian War, Revere had become known more for his political, creative, and entrepreneurial talents than for battlefield prowess. As a resolute envoy among the colonies through Boston's Committee of Correspondence, Revere was well-known throughout the town, and therefore it was not surprising that this "Messenger of the Revolution"[10] would be relied on for the weapons restoration work at Castle Island.

Originally constructed in 1634 as a small stone and mud redoubt designed to protect the burgeoning Town of Boston, "the Castle," as it was simply known, had undergone a period of renovation, and by 1701 a more comprehensive structure had been erected on the island, to be christened "Castle William" in honor of King William III.[11] As revolution brewed in the streets and taverns of Boston in the 1770s, the island had become a place of safe haven for weary British officers against unruly and rebellious citizens.[12] With the evacuation of the British from Boston, however, and Washington's eventual removal of the Continental Army to New York, the task of defending the town would fall on her populace, and Castle Island would be seen as an important element of that defense.

Upon the British departure, the strategic garrison was renamed "Fort Independence" by the colonials and the project of restoration began in earnest. The island's fortress guns were, in fact, badly damaged during the exodus, but not beyond preservation. Revere's talents as a silversmith and engraver may have served him well as he and others fashioned repairs and even employed a newly designed gun carriage specifically invented to suit the need.[13] Revere's appointment to the restoration work on Castle Island would be the earliest in his long and often chaotic engagement at the site.

Though posted without a formal military commission, it would not be long before Revere would serve Massachusetts in a more official capacity. Recognizing the grave and immediate need for the defense of Boston and its harbor upon the departure of the Continental Army in March of 1776, the General Court of Massachusetts—the legislative body of the colony—soon began raising companies of militia to defend its ground. Revere ultimately would be commissioned as an officer in the local artillery regiment called the "Massachusetts State's Train,"[14] and by the fall of 1776, he would find himself in full command of Castle Island.[15]

Though clothed with an air of authority, Revere's post would quickly dissolve into a source of bitter frustration, providing little if any opportunity for distinction and merit. Life at the Castle would prove repetitive and uneventful. The regiment would face only insignificant military action, and Revere's position, it seemed, served merely to magnify the otherwise mundane existence within the confines of the bleak and isolated fort.

There can be no doubt that Paul Revere had played a pivotal role in the birth of the American Revolution. "He had the keen zest of the citizen whose patriotism is of the lusty type that causes him to . . . take an active part in all movements that make for civic progress," wrote one historian.[16] Yet he was recognized neither as an educated "gentleman" nor as an esteemed military authority. He had collaborated bravely with many leaders of the revolutionary movement in the prelude to war, and he had adapted his skill as an adroit craftsman and entrepreneur for the Patriot cause; yet as hostilities with Britain erupted, he would find himself conspicuously overlooked for service as an officer in the more prestigious Continental Army. "I have never been taken notice . . . [of], by those whom I thought my friends," Revere wrote to his trusted acquaintance, John Lamb, in April of 1777. "[I] am obliged to be contented in this State's service."[17] As Esther Forbes noted in her Pulitzer Prize–winning biography, *Paul Revere and the World He Lived In*, "He could learn a new trade as fast as most men turned around, yet his military record is undistinguished. He certainly had no liking for army life."[18]

Despite the undeniable esteem he had earned for his bold exploits in support of the Patriot cause, Revere appeared restless and generally unsuited for service in the local militia regiment and, over time, developed a somewhat restive and truculent disposition.[19] Circumstances for Revere's men at the Castle were difficult, and the often surly temperament of their commander led to some enmity in the ranks. A heightened scrutiny by the soldiers and officers in his regiment began to follow his official actions and, in time, political rancor would envelop the unit. Fellow officers began eyeing Revere with rising antagonism, and soon conspiracies began to stir.

In colonial days, the expansive territory of Maine was actually the eastern province of Massachusetts, governed and controlled by the political structures of Boston.[20] In 1775 Benedict Arnold had carried the battle to British-controlled Quebec using this wilderness as his staging headquarters, in an attempt to thwart the possibility of British maneuvers in the areas west of the colonies. The campaign failed, but the strategic importance of Maine to the Crown, as a buffer between British-controlled Nova Scotia and the rebellious colonies to the south, was unmistakable.[21] Though General Howe had departed from the shores of Boston several months earlier, the Crown would continue to eye the rocky coastline of northern New England with eager and covetous eyes.

Early in the summer of 1779, word came to the Massachusetts Council, acting as the interim executive of the colony prior to the adoption of a state constitution, that a British fleet finally had landed in Penobscot Bay, Maine, and had begun work on a fortress on the peninsula known, through its Native American appellation, as Majabigwaduce.[22] Such a defensive post would serve not only as a point of refuge for colonial loyalists and a ready source of timber for British warships, but also as protection for the enemy from American invasion of the north.[23] The fort, angry Massachusetts officials resolved, could not stand.

On June 26, 1779, Paul Revere, at long last, received the orders that he had hoped would rescue him from military obscurity:

> *Ordered*—That Col°. Revere hold himself and one hundred of the Matrosses under his command including proper Officers in readiness at one Hour's Notice to embark for the Defense of this State and to attack the Enemy at Penobscot, under the Command of General Lovell and make Return to this Board upon their being so prepared.[24]

Revere and his Castle Island artillery train would be part of a combined naval and marine expeditionary force designed to disengage the British from their Maine outpost.

Though a complex and expensive undertaking, the attack was calculated to be massive in force and would most certainly result in victory. Indeed, even Brigadier General Francis McLean, the commanding officer of the British forces at Majabigwaduce, would lament as the battle ensued that surrender of the garrison was all but assured.[25]

The sober and salient facts spoke otherwise. The Penobscot Expedition, as it would come to be known, would later be described by a noted Maine historian as "[a] prodigious wreck of property—a dire eclipse of reputation—and universal chagrin."[26] The financial hardship and political embarrassment to Massachusetts created by the ill-fated exercise would leave in its ruinous wake a fiasco of finger pointing and political haranguing.

Soon, outrage would lead to inquiry—and inquiry, to arrest.

On September 6, 1779, Lieutenant Colonel Paul Revere, dedicated member of the Sons of Liberty, paladin of Concord and Lexington, active participant in the Boston Tea Party—Paul Revere, artisan, activist, and agitator for the revolutionary cause—was summarily relieved of his command at Castle Island and placed under house arrest, his salary and rations suspended.

The charge: "unsoldierlike behavior during the whole expedition to Penobscot, which tends to cowardice."[27]

The
COURT-MARTIAL
of PAUL REVERE

Chapter I "The Pride of New England"

"IN THIS LAND of bustling am I safe arrived, among the most social, polite and sensible people under heaven,—to strangers, friendly and kind,—to Englishmen, most generously so," wrote a traveler to Boston in 1774. "This is fine country, for everything that can gratify the man or please the fancy."[1]

In the mid-eighteenth century, Boston was a small yet clamoring town surrounded by salt marshes and seawater, and punctuated by small hills and wild-rose gardens. The misshapen peninsula comprising the burgeoning town was connected to the mainland by a small isthmus known as Boston Neck, which during periods of flooding or unseasonable weather temporarily washed out, converting Boston into an island in Massachusetts Bay.

The roughly seventeen thousand inhabitants of the densely settled community, almost all English,[2] lived in a warren of narrow, winding, and busy avenues. Church steeples and stone chimneys marked the Boston skyline, and countless wharfs, such as Rowe's, Long, and Hancock's, beckoned to the Atlantic with outstretched arms that provided the town with the seafaring industry from which all other commerce sprang.

On any given day, young ship hands dashed about the weather-beaten docks securing hawsers and taking on or offloading cargo, while grizzled fishermen prepared their catch of cod, lobster, and oysters for market. The pungent odors of receding tides and decaying fish permeated the brackish air and joined a rising cacophony of shipbells, seabirds, and excited voices.

Just beyond the cluttered seafront of Boston, the markets churned with trade, and the taverns warmed wary shipwrights, merchants, and artisans. Boston "was not only the metropolis of Massachusetts and the pride of New England," boasted one historian, "but it was the commercial emporium of the colonies."[3]

Into this world Paul Revere was born on December 21, 1734. The first surviving son of Apollos Rivoire and Deborah Hichborn, Paul would carry his father's French Huguenot thirst for freedom and his mother's provincial fortitude.[4]

Revere's father, Apollos, was born in 1702 and, at the age of thirteen, left his boyhood home just east of Bordeaux, France, at the insistence of his parents in order to elude possible French persecution of the Huguenots, and he immigrated to the Island of Guernsey in the English Channel, where his uncle Simon Rivoire resided. Recognizing the growing opportunities of the British colonies in North America, Simon soon dispatched his nephew to join a small but growing Huguenot population in Boston, where an apprenticeship under respected goldsmith John Coney had been arranged.

Learning the ancient mechanical art under Coney's watchful eye, young Apollos settled well in his new home, and eventually he became adept at forming gold and silver vessels and ornaments for his Boston patrons. In time, he changed his name to the more appropriately "English" Paul Revere, "on account the Bumpkins should pronounce it easier,"[5] and with Coney's death in 1722, he purchased the indenture of his remaining apprenticeship and ultimately set up his own goldsmith shop in town.

Emerging as an established and religiously devout citizen of Boston, the elder Revere joined the New Brick Church on Hanover Street—the Cockerel, as it came to be known for the brass weathercock set upon its spire—and in 1729, at the age of twenty-six, he married Deborah Hichborn, the twenty-five-year-old daughter of a prominent Boston entrepreneur and landowner. The Hichborns were a lively and well-descended Yankee family of merchants, seamen, and artisans, and it was Deborah who would provide her son with the rich New England legacy that would one day become synonymous with his name.

Young Paul Revere was part of an ever-expanding family. Twelve children would be born to the marriage from 1730 to 1745, though only seven would survive beyond infancy. Revere learned to manage within the cramped quarters of his parents' North End dwelling.

From an early age it became apparent that he would join his father in the goldsmith trade. He was thought to be properly suited for the mechanical arts, and he appeared to have little interest in a more "gentlemanly" education, as had been afforded to his cousin Benjamin Hichborn and others in Boston who displayed an aptitude for a more highbrow vocation. Though the typical eighteenth-century American artisan was respected in the community as the provider of a required service, he was, nonetheless, thought of as a tradesman—one who relied on physical rather than intellectual capabilities. In sharp contrast to the powdered wigs and imported clothing of the colonial gentleman, the artisan's plain unadorned shirts and breeches were adapted more for utility than appearance, and his home generally would be simple in style and furnishings. He was, as a rule, less erudite and less inclined to engage in the deep political or philosophical ponderings of the upper classes, and he rarely extended his education beyond grammar school. The artisan, or "mechanic" as he was often called, served the affluent of his community, and though he may have attained a level of wealth and success, he seldom joined their social rank.[6]

As a boy, Paul Revere attended North Writing School, where he learned to read and write, but by the age of thirteen he joined his father's business as an apprentice goldsmith, as would surely have been expected of him. He would come to recognize the undeniable eighteenth-century distinction between artisan and gentleman, and though he did not continue his formal education as others in his extended family had, he developed a love for books and reading that would inform and challenge him far into his life.

By his mid-teenage years, Revere began to display a bold penchant for individualism. The nonconformist views of the Calvinist-leaning Huguenots conflicted with the pious doctrines of Catholicism, which required ordination of priests in "apostolic succession" rather than the communal election of ministers. According to Huguenot belief, the Anglican Church was simply an adjunct of Catholic dogma.[7] Confronting his father's edicts of religious propriety, Revere entered into a pact along six of his friends to ring the bells of Christ Church, also known as North Church, an Anglican congregation—an act that angered the elder Revere, who had a clear preference for a Puritan-leaning church.[8] True proclivity for independent thought—and, perhaps, the birth of his political awareness—came, however, when Revere began frequenting the congregation of the radically preaching Reverend Doctor Jonathan Mayhew at West Church on Lynde Street. To the bitter consternation of his father, Revere listened with rising interest to Mayhew's fiery brand of civil disobedience and hostility to tyrannical authority, and he developed, perhaps, the first spark of the transformation that was destined to propel him into America's quest for independence.[9]

Though mildly defiant in the realm of religion, Revere was a dedicated and faithful student of his father's trade. As an apprentice, he displayed a vibrant talent for art and design and became proficient in the skill of engraving. As his abilities developed, his reputation for fine craftsmanship grew in Boston, and he serviced his father's customers with his own brand of artistic creativity. He learned to fashion spoons, bowls, tankards, ewers, buckles, and every sort of button and ornament from precious metals, and he often adorned his creations with detailed engravings that personalized and enhanced his work. Thus his chosen trade was the seamless marriage of art and mechanics, tightly woven within the world of business.

In 1754 Revere's father died, leaving his nineteen-year-old son in charge of a grieving family and a goldsmith business that, ironically, he was not legally authorized to conduct. Local regulations at the time prevented anyone who had not attained the age of twenty-one and completed a seven-year apprenticeship from conducting a trade in the Town of Boston,[10] but they did allow the *widow* of the tradesman to continue in his name.[11] It is probable that, in the face of losing the family breadwinner, Deborah Revere assumed the mantle of proprietor, with her son Paul employed as the skilled hand. The family thus endured, and Revere grew in stature and professional standing.

As Paul Revere labored at the family business, the long-simmering conflict between the French and the English in North America finally erupted again into war. Since the early part of the century, the vital interests of trade and territory had resulted in competing claims to the rich lands of the Ohio Valley and the Appalachian country to the west of the British colonies. An ever-increasing British population had expanded the reach of the Crown into these disputed areas and, in response, the French began construction of a series of forts along the major rivers of the region as well as at Lake Champlain between Vermont and New York. Soon the British erected several garrisons of their own and encouraged trade and migration into the region, further heightening tensions on the continent. The imperial strength of each country clearly depended upon these lands for settlement and resources, and in 1756 the bloody and prolonged conflict that would become known as the French and Indian War was declared. Merely the North American theater of a worldwide struggle called the Seven Years' War, the Ohio Valley front would provide many New Englanders with their first taste of formal military conflict and sow the seeds of the American Revolution to come.

With the looming threat of ambush from the north constantly endangering the families of New England during this time, a call to arms among the men of Massachusetts was enthusiastically answered. At the age of twenty-one, Revere joined His Majesty's forces, receiving a commission from Governor William Shirley to serve as second lieutenant for the train of artillery led by Richard Gridley in the campaign to dislodge the French from Crown Point on Lake Champlain under the overall command of General John Winslow.[12] Leaving the family goldsmith duties to his younger brother Thomas while in military service, Revere assumed a post at Fort William Henry on Lake George from May through November of 1756. Though bold in its initiative, the expedition was plagued immediately with political wrangling over status and organization, as well as social prejudices between British soldiers and provincial troops—a harbinger of trouble to come. With colonial volunteers scorned by the British as craven, inept, and untrustworthy, the alliance would prove testy and quarrelsome. While internal conflicts ensued, the French gained successive clandestine victories with the Battle of Fort Bull, the capture of Fort Oswego, and later the siege of Fort William Henry, and British morale crumbled. Revere would endure the hardships and privations of war during that summer and fall, but was afforded little if any opportunity to distinguish himself in battle.

In the previous year, a similar expedition had been launched against Crown Point that had ended in failure. Now, with the fall of Fort Oswego and the French construction of Fort Carillon (later called Fort Ticonderoga), the British force again was compelled to retreat and ultimately abandon its mission.[13] Revere would return to Boston in late 1756 with little more military experience than when he had left his goldsmith shop in the North End of town seven months earlier.

Serving with the men of Massachusetts on the Crown Point expedition, however, was a young first lieutenant from Weymouth by the name of Solomon Lovell, who would later play a pivotal role in the darkest chapter of Paul Revere's military life.[14]

As the Seven Years' War droned on without him, Paul Revere focused his attention once again on business and family pursuits. By the summer of 1757 he had fallen in love with a young Bostonian woman by the name of Sara Orne, and the couple was married in August of that year. Crammed into his mother's house on Fish Street near Clark's Wharf, which had been rented by the family since 1743, Revere and his bride began life amid the tumult of extended family and the racket of an active goldsmith's shop attached to the property. On April 3, 1758, Sara gave birth to their first child, a girl whom they named Deborah. During the next fourteen years, seven more children would be born to the Reveres.[15]

With the burdens of a growing family, Revere constantly endeavored to widen his trade skills and increase the array of customers that he served. In the coming years, his willingness to explore new methods of design, including the chic French-influenced rococo style of ornamentation, enhanced his reputation for creativity and artistic mastery.

Revere's list of patrons ranged from extended family members to the wealthiest merchants and mariners in town, and though his political leanings proved consistently faithful to the Patriot cause, he certainly was not averse to doing business with Tory Loyalists or British officers when profit was at stake as tensions with Great Britain escalated.[16] On many occasions he would provide specialized engraving or fashioning services on a subcontractor basis to other Boston goldsmiths who did not, perhaps, possess the same level of skill or proficiency as he did. Ever the businessman, Revere maintained careful records of every transaction in a *Waste and Memoranda Book,* in which he even recorded the monthly receipts of board paid to him by his mother after she took up residence at his North Square home upon its purchase in 1770, as well as a detailed accounting of goods supplied by her and monies expended on her behalf.[17]

Above all else, Paul Revere was an entrepreneur. The ever-inventive goldsmith capably expanded his interests and trade beyond his chosen profession and, in years to come, would engage in such pursuits as currency printing, copperplate engraving, powder mill designing, bell and cannon foundering—and even dentistry. Indeed, Revere would advertise his unique dental services in the *Boston Gazette and Country Journal* in 1768:

> WHEREAS, many Persons are so unfortunate as to lose their Fore-Teeth by Accident, and otherways, to their great Detriment, not only in Looks, but speaking both in Public and Private:—This is to inform all such, that they may have them re-placed with artificial Ones, that looks as well as the Natural & answers the End of Speaking to all Intents, by PAUL REVERE, Goldsmith near the head of Dr. Clarke's Wharf, Boston.[18]

And in a later advertisement, Revere would boast that he "continues the Business of a Dentist, and flatters himself that from the Experience he has had these Two years (in which time he has fixt some Hundreds of Teeth) that he can fix them as well as any Surgeon-Dentist who ever came from London."[19]

As Revere developed his professional endeavors, he also matured socially. His growing relationships with fellow mechanics and artisans would provide a welcome respite from the toils of daily trade and serve to mold his early political views. In the many social clubs, caucuses, and taverns of Boston, local tradesmen would gather over a mug of grog or ale, and the banter of business and politics would fill the air. Revere was a frequent patron at the Salutation Tavern and the Green Dragon near his home in the north part of town, and here, amid the raucous fellowship of workmen, tobacco, and brew, many of Revere's early beliefs and associations took root and flourished.

And here too, in the alehouses and taverns of Boston, another, more structured, social organization would thrive—the Masons. On September 9, 1760, Revere was inducted into St. Andrew's Lodge of Freemasons as an entered apprentice, and through the next several months, he would rise through the ranks to the respected position of master Mason. In the coming years, he would become actively involved with several other Masonic lodges, including the Rising States Lodge and the Massachusetts Grand Lodge, and would hold high and respected offices in each. For the remainder of his professional life, Freemasonry would provide Revere with the social standing and intellectual foundation that rose above the everyday interactions of Boston's North End. It would forever inculcate the man with aspirations of brotherhood, honor, and humanity, and it would serve to expand his personal perspective and view of the world.[20]

Freemasonry in Paul Revere's America had evolved from a fourteenth-century stoneworker's guild in Europe. A rigid hierarchy of master Masons, fellows, and apprentices joined in the construction of ornate buildings in accordance with the jealously guarded secrets of their Middles Ages craft and passed along these tenets through an intricate maze of Masonic ceremonies and rituals open only to the chosen few of the trade.

By the early seventeenth century, Freemasonry in England had broadened its scope and had begun admitting men of other professions to the organization. Masonic lodges gradually transitioned from trade guilds where the main focus was one of detail to craft, to more of a social or philanthropic function. Moral character and social values became the hallmark of these clubs, and members increased status and standing through a variety of elected offices.

The Grand Lodge of England, the formalization of the modern Freemasonic movement, was created in 1717 and, within fifteen years, its first American charter was officially sanctioned in Boston and named St. John's Lodge. Though various lodges would take root in the colonies, their diverse membership often produced dissent and dissatisfaction over rituals and precepts and consequently the splintering of chapters. St. Andrew's Lodge, which Paul Revere joined in 1760, was chartered by the Grand Lodge of Scotland in 1756 and had been born out of a dispute with the Grand Lodge of England over the interpretation of ancient Masonic principles. Its members, mostly comprised of artisans and tradesmen, considered themselves "Ancient Masons" because of their strict adherence to the traditional ideologies of original Freemasonry and condemned their English counterparts as "Modern Masons" who had corrupted the original precepts of the institution. For its part, St. John's Lodge labeled the members of St. Andrew's as "Irregular Masons," and antagonism between the two groups persisted until April of 1766, when St. John's conceded that its failure to recognize and admit members of the competing lodge was "directly Subversive of the Principles of Masonry."[21]

In 1792 a Masonic committee in Boston, of which Revere was a member, compiled its constitution and rituals and described the unified purpose of Freemasonry as "an institution for the promotion of the most extensive philanthropy, the most diffusive and disinterested benevolence and universal virtue."[22] Though perhaps limited by his own lack of formal education, Revere nonetheless was able to demonstrate the transcendent attributes of integrity and leadership that would allow him to rise to the highest levels of the Masonic order. Membership in the Freemasons not only strengthened Revere's bonds with his artisan brothers, but also allowed him to expand his personal and political affiliations with some of Boston's most educated and influential leaders of the day. It was through St. Andrew's that Revere befriended Dr. Joseph Warren and others who would shape the political world of Boston in the years to come, and it was in the back rooms and halls of Masonic gatherings that enlightened philosophies of liberty and organized dissent took hold. As whispers of rebellion filtered from elites, such as Otis, Adams, and Hancock, down through the town's working classes, Paul Revere would be seen as a fitting liaison between statesman and tradesman.[23]

Freemasonry allowed Revere to slice through the social strata of Boston. His professional and community standing greatly benefited from the wide diversity of newly developed relationships acquired through St. Andrew's Lodge, and his adaptive personality allowed him to interact comfortably with both the elite gentlemen of Boston and the more earthy patrons of the Green Dragon. Revere's Masonic dealings also led to the growth of his goldsmith business. Many of his lodge brothers sought him out for the purchase or repair of items such as belt buckles, rings, buttons, and the like, and he was often engaged by the lodges themselves to create Masonic jewels and to engrave certificates and notices of meetings.

Though he aspired to the high tenets of Freemasonry, Revere also wrestled with a level of feisty truculence that could, on occasion, demand the settling of a personal score. In May of 1761, he found himself in such a dispute with a hatter by the name of Thomas Fosdick, who was married to one of Revere's Hichborn cousins. The quarrel escalated into a physical brawl, and Fosdick filed criminal charges against Revere in the courts of Suffolk County, for "assaulting & beating ye complainant." Revere denied the charge and filed a plea of not guilty, but after a full hearing on the matter, Judge Richard Dana ruled, "[I]t appears he is guilty." The defendant was fined for his transgression and ordered "to keep ye peace & be of good behavior."[24]

As Paul Revere advanced in status and reputation (notwithstanding the Fosdick incident), larger events began to take shape around him.

By the early 1760s, for the first time in years, Parliament began to impose measures to prevent blatant violations of the Navigation Acts. These trade regulations, aimed at limiting colonial imports exclusively to British-made products shipped on British-made and manned vessels, and conversely limiting the export of certain raw materials from the colonies exclusively to England, remained relatively dormant for decades and violations were mildly tolerated.[25] Other than the duty on molasses passed in 1733, these measures did not unreasonably restrict natural market forces already in place and were largely followed. "The purpose of the acts was to promote the economic welfare of the empire in general and of the mother country in particular," wrote one historian.[26]

Beginning in 1760, however, a renewed effort to curtail smuggling, mostly of Dutch products, took hold in the colonies; and Francis Bernard, governor of Massachusetts from 1760 to 1771 and a loyal defender of the Crown, became the point man in the endeavor. With wide popular sympathy for and acceptance of Dutch smuggling in Boston, local inhabitants had made it difficult for local customs officials to gather evidence successfully in such cases, and accordingly it became clear that other measures of enforcement would be required.

In November of 1760, the head of Boston customs, Charles Paxton, applied to the Massachusetts superior court for the issuance of writs of assistance to aid in the enforcement of the Navigation Acts. In essence, the writs were broad, open-ended, unlimited, and perpetual search warrants that enabled British officials to search, by force or otherwise, private homes and businesses without specific duration or restraint.[27]

At about the same time, Governor Bernard filled a vacancy in the seat of chief justice of the superior court with the much-maligned Thomas Hutchinson, who already held multiple government titles in and around Boston, several of which presented clear conflicts of interest with the position of chief justice. The appointment, clearly intended as a measure to ensure approval of the writs by the court, inflamed the populace and particularly angered the feisty Boston lawyer James Otis, whose father had been given long-standing assurances that the position was his.[28] When a group of local merchants who had brought suit challenging the writs approached Otis to represent them in their cause, he was only too happy to accept the case.

The trial took place in the council chamber of the Old Town House in Boston before five judges including Hutchinson, each adorned in flowing white wigs and crimson robes. In the packed chamber, Otis delivered a protracted and impassioned exposition on the rights of man and the fundamental principles of law and liberty. "Otis was a flame of fire," wrote the young lawyer John Adams, who intently watched the oration from the gallery.[29]

Otis condemned the writs as "slavery" and "villany" and proclaimed that it would be "impossible to devise a more outrageous and unlimited instrument of tyranny, than this." His narrow eyes focused on Hutchinson's. "A man's house is his castle," he charged. "[W]hilst he is quiet, he is as well guarded as a prince in his castle. This writ, if it should be declared legal, would totally annihilate this privilege."[30]

The court would ultimately uphold the writs of assistance — and Boston would never be the same. Years later, John Adams wrote: "Then and there, was the first scene of the first act of opposition, to the arbitrary claims of Great Britain. Then and there, the child Independence was born."[31]

In 1763 England's prolonged war with the French finally came to an end with the Treaty of Paris. With the victory, Great Britain had expanded its influence through the Mediterranean, India, and North America — but the celebration was short-lived. The American colonies had prospered during the wartime economy through a succession of subsidies and advantageous military contracts for shipbuilding and the provision of British soldiers, but with the end of hostilities came a marked reduction in commerce and a tightening of mercantile credit. In England, the British government was dealing with economic problems of its own. The national debt had skyrocketed during the war, and now, with the acquisition of the vast lands of Canada, the military cost of defending that land would add to the burden.[32] The cash-strapped Crown naturally turned to the colonies for assistance. The era of salutary neglect had come to an abrupt end.

The regulatory posture of Parliament toward the colonies now shifted from the regulation of trade and the prohibition of smuggling to the raising of revenue. In April of 1764, the Sugar Act was passed, which extended and imposed duties on a variety of goods such as sugar, molasses, and lumber and placed strict burdens of accountability on shipping interests, in order to ensure that tariffs flowed to Great Britain. With the stated purpose of raising revenue openly stated in its preamble,[33] the act curtailed colonial trade at a time when the economy was already sagging.[34] In addition, the Currency Act, which regulated the use of undervalued colonial paper currency, was enacted as a means to protect British creditors and commercial interests by forcing the colonies to use British currency, as opposed to the rapidly fluctuating and inconsistently regulated colonial notes.[35]

Though the measures were relatively modest in extent, they had the immediate effect of galvanizing public opinion. Forecasts of grave injury to the rum trade in particular and of economic disaster in general spread throughout the region. "Our trade," wrote Samuel Adams, "has for a long time laboured under great discouragements; and it is with the deepest concern that we see further difficulties coming upon it, as will reduce it to the lowest ebb, if not totally obstruct and ruin it."[36] Though the initially spirited dissent of the Massachusetts assembly would be somewhat tempered at the request of Lieutenant-Governor Thomas Hutchinson, its members formally endorsed the united protest of the colonies against the measures as advocated by James Otis in his "memorial," *Rights of the British Colonies Asserted and Proved.*[37]

The conclusion of the Seven Years' War had signaled an economic decline in the colonies, and the introduction of confiscatory tax measures, it was feared, would only worsen the situation. Activist voices began debating the broader philosophical implications of the measures—and soon the heated rallying cry of Boston promised an end to the villainous scourge of "taxation without representation." This notion was premised on Reverend Jonathan Mayhew's fiery sermon of January 30, 1750, before the West Church in Boston and was echoed by James Otis as early as September of 1762 in his pamphlet entitled *A Vindication of the Conduct of the House of Representatives of the Province of Massachusetts Bay.*[38] Now, in his instructions to Boston's newly chosen representatives, Samuel Adams wrote, "If taxes are laid upon us in any shape without our having a legal representation where they are laid, are we not reduced from the character of free subjects to the miserable state of tributary slaves?"[39]

With questions of liberty and economic freedom uppermost in the minds of his more eloquent and educated acquaintances, Paul Revere appears to have been focused more on business, family, and Masonic brotherhood during this period. His talents as a goldsmith and copperplate engraver continued to evolve, and his remarkable flair for artistic elegance and range was clearly appreciated by his growing customer base. Respect and admiration for Revere also expanded among his lodge brothers, and in December of 1761, he was elected to the office of junior deacon. By November of 1763 he would hold the post of junior warden.

With the end of the war against France, however, Revere's business began to decline as the overall colonial economy weakened—and worse, by the close of 1763 an epidemic of smallpox struck the Town of Boston. At the time a crude form of inoculation that had been introduced during the outbreak of 1722 by the prominent Puritan minister and author Cotton Mather had been generally accepted by both clergy and physicians and put into limited use; however, fever and death stalked the sullen community, and houses were marked by flags where quarantined families languished in sickness.

In February, Revere's growing family was struck by the disease. As required by local law, he informed Boston selectmen that one of his daughters was suffering from fever and open skin blisters. The illness had progressed to the point where the officials ordered the child to be placed in one of the town's "pesthouses." Revere objected. He was not going to allow any of his children to be taken from the nurturing arms of their mother, who herself again was expecting. After an extensive argument with the officials, they agreed that the child would be allowed to remain in the house with the entire family under quarantine flag and posted guard.

In the coming months Revere's daughter bravely fought her illness and slowly recovered. Gradually the blight of smallpox eased its grip on the town and normalcy slowly returned. Sara delivered the couple's third daughter, and Revere's business began to show signs of improvement.

Boston's economic and political troubles, however, were just beginning.

In March of 1765, a series of destructive storms ravaged Boston Harbor, damaging ships and affecting commerce. The Sugar Act and rigorous enforcement of antismuggling laws had hampered trade, and now general economic conditions in Boston had deteriorated.[1] By the spring of 1765, bankruptcies and business failures began to mount throughout the town, and demand for goods and services declined in dramatic fashion.[2]

To add to Boston's economic malaise, word came from England that a stamp duty on the colonies had been approved by Parliament with little objection or debate. By November every newspaper, pamphlet, bill, note, bond, lease, license, deed, manifest, or other document printed on vellum or paper was subject to the Stamp Act, which levied a direct tax on colonists. According to one historian, this "fatal measure" was enacted with "arrogance and blind indifference [to] the sentiments and petitions of the colonists . . ."[3] The cost of doing virtually any business in Massachusetts and beyond would now greatly increase—at a time when the citizenry could least afford it. Even more galling than the actual sums collected was the nakedly avaricious intent behind it. Most of the prior acts had at least been made in the name of regulating trade or commerce: this act, like the Sugar Act, was created purely for the purpose of raising money for Great Britain. Though the duties demanded under the measure were in and of themselves rather small, many colonists saw a sinister and veiled meaning in their passage. Joseph Warren charged, in rather excessive fashion, that the design of the Crown was to "force the colonies into a rebellion, and from thence to take occasion to treat them with severity, and, by military power, to reduce them to servitude."[4]

As talk of the Stamp Act unfolded, Revere's youngest daughter, Mary, died. Though the pall of death was constant in colonial life, the family naturally mourned the loss of the thirteen-month-old child who was born just as Boston's smallpox epidemic receded. And to add to Revere's troubles, once again his business was reeling.

With crippling unemployment spreading throughout the town, the goldsmith trade had declined sharply even before the new duties were to take effect. The services of such an artisan were considered a luxury afforded only by the wealthy during these difficult times. To curb his growing expenses, Revere leased out a portion of his shop, yet he still found himself in financial difficulty. Indeed, a local merchant, Thomas Fletcher, sued Revere for nonpayment of a demand note and attached his property to secure payment.[5]

The Crown had fatally misjudged colonial reaction to the Stamp Act. The imposed taxes were far-reaching and would clearly hinder not only tradesmen such as Revere but also businesses of all kinds throughout the colonies. Immediately, a clear demarcation of loyalties led to the proliferation of political parties. The Whigs—or the party of organized opposition—and the Tories—the party of submission to the king—sprang to life and split the colonists into divided factions. Open and aggressive hostility to the measure, however, was clearly the majority view in Boston and among the colonies at large.[6]

In England, Benjamin Franklin, then a colonial emissary, testified before the House of Commons regarding the response of his countrymen to the act:

"What was the temper of America toward Great Britain before the year 1763?" he was asked.

"The best in the world . . ."

"And what is their temper now?"

"Oh, very much altered."[7]

Beginning with a set of unequivocal resolutions authored by Patrick Henry in Virginia that decried any person who supported the act as "an enemy to his majesty's colony,"[8] an organized effort against taxation without the consent of the people swept through the colonies. A groundswell of hostility in the form of angry town meetings, provincial assemblies, pamphlets, and broadsides created a sense of tension and antagonism to the British taxing authority. Across provincial America, private citizens banned together and forged nonimportation agreements aimed at the boycott of all British goods.[9]

In a measure intended to unify the colonial effort, the Massachusetts legislature adopted a letter to be circulated among the various provincial assemblies inviting delegates to a congress called for the purpose of enlightening the Crown to the grave state of affairs caused by the Stamp Act. Likewise, James Otis urged the creation of provincial committees to consider the overall effect of the measure on the colonies. "There ought to be no New England man, no New Yorker, known on the continent, but all of us Americans," wrote one member of the Stamp Act Congress.[10]

In Boston and beyond, newspaper publishers inflamed the public with acerbic declarations on the natural rights of Englishmen and the duty of all citizens to rise in opposition to the enslaving measure.[11] One New York newspaper irreverently proclaimed that with the passage of the Stamp Act, "Lady North American Liberty had died of a cruel stamp on her vitals but happily, she had left an only son, prophetically named Independence."[12]

Protest inevitably turned to violence. As word of the pending Stamp Act spread through Boston, an angry mob of mostly tradesmen and shopkeepers turned its sights on Thomas Hutchinson and his brother-in-law, Andrew Oliver, who had been appointed as the Massachusetts stamp master. On the morning of August 14, 1765, effigies of Oliver and another instigator of colonial tax measures, Lord Bute, were suspended from a sprawling elm tree near Boston Neck. A series of labels were slung around the shoulders of Oliver's dangling cloth corpse and on the left arm was written, "What greater pleasure can there be, than to see a *stamp man* hanging on a tree!"[13] The majestic elm upon which the effigies hung would soon come to be infamously known as the Liberty Tree.

Later in the evening a similar mob removed the lifeless figures and carried them to the Town House, chanting, "Liberty, property, and no stamps!"[14] The crowd loudly paraded through the building where the governor and council were reported to be meeting in evening session and then proceeded to Kilby Street, near Oliver's Dock, and dismantled a building that they believed to be the home of the coming stamp office. Using timbers and beams from the demolished structure for kindling, the mob ignited a fire in front of Oliver's Fort Hill home and burned the effigies amid chants and angry speeches. Finally, they shattered the windows of the house and ransacked the property. Andrew Oliver resigned his post as stamp master the following day.

On Sunday, August 25, Reverend Jonathan Mayhew delivered a sermon at the West Church, brazenly condemning the Stamp Act and inciting the congregation to further resistance. His flock listened with rousing fury and sprang into "God's service."[15]

The following day, another mob ransacked the Vice-Admiralty Court, where charges of trade violations were prosecuted without juries, and torched its records. The homes of several customs officers as well as the private mansion of Thomas Hutchinson met a similar fate. "The doors were immediately split to pieces with broad axes, and a way made there, and at the windows, for the entry of the mob; which poured in, and filled, in an instant, every room in the house," Hutchinson later recalled. "They continued their possession until daylight; destroyed, carried away, or cast into the street, everything that was in the house; demolished every part of it, except the walls, as far as lay in their power; and had begun to break away the brick-work."[16] Ironically, Hutchinson had stood in staunch opposition to the Stamp Act.

Though most of the mob violence in the summer of 1765 appeared to be spontaneous and haphazard in form, in reality, a small group comprised mostly of local artisans and tradesmen had overseen and organized most of the protest effort. The Loyal Nine, as they called themselves, were men whose lives would be directly affected by the untenable revenue-raising measures of the Crown. Paul Revere knew several of the Loyal Nine, but it is unclear whether he was a direct participant in the mob violence of August 14 and August 25. What is *very* clear, however, is that during the period in question, Revere's daybooks indicate a troubling lack of business activity.[17]

It would not be long before the Loyal Nine would develop into a more radical alliance that began appearing throughout the colonies with the goal of resistance—forcible if necessary—to the implementation of the Stamp Act. The Sons of Liberty, as they came to be known, advocated a more zealous and militant form of dissent that would one day morph into open rebellion. The rank-and-file members of the group, many recruited from the docks and sordid taverns of Boston, often resorted to violence and intimidation in furtherance of their rebellious objectives. The organization would cut through the social strata of the colonies, enlisting men such as Samuel Adams, statesman; Benjamin Rush, physician; James Otis, lawyer; Benjamin Edes, newspaper publisher—and Paul Revere, goldsmith.[18]

Though extreme in their beliefs, the Sons of Liberty recognized the need to leverage the political and social message of their cause. Enlisting the cooperation of sympathetic newspapers such as the *Boston Gazette*, they spread their message of opposition to tyranny across the colonies.

Satire and political caricatures soon became a critical tool of the Patriot movement. As an accomplished engraver, Paul Revere enthusiastically joined the resistance effort and adapted his trade to the creation of allegorical renderings of significant events.

In a copperplate engraving entitled "A View of the Year 1765," borrowed from a British satirist, Revere depicted, in cartoon format, an elaborate and macabre Armageddon against the Stamp Act. A fierce dragon that personified the dreaded tax measure is confronted by a band of charging colonists led by a brave Bostonian with drawn and pitched sword. In the background appears the body of a pitiable British official hanging by the neck from a branch of the Liberty Tree, and below, the following rambling descriptive verse expresses Revere's fiery sentiments:

America! see thy freeborn sons advance
And at thy Tyrant point the threatng Lance!
Who with grim Horror ope[n]s his Hell-like Jaws,
And MAGNA CHARTA grasps between his Claws.
Lo Boston brave! unstain'd by Placemen's Bribe
'Attack the Monster and his venal Tribe.'
See loyal Hampden to his Country true,
Present his Weapon to the odious Crew;[19]

It would be the first of many political expressions that would find life through Revere's skillful hand and solidify him as a respected member of the Sons of Liberty.

Through these antics and the other carefully coordinated efforts of Whig leaders, encouraging results soon followed. In May of 1766, the lower house of the Massachusetts legislature was captured by resistance-minded statesmen such as James Otis, John Hancock, and Thomas Cushing, who ousted nineteen legislators earlier denounced by the *Boston Gazette* as "Tools to the Governor."[20]

And on May 16, 1766, news that Parliament had repealed the Stamp Act arrived in Boston.

Through the streets of Boston, joyous cheering and festive gunfire filled the air. Church bells clanged with their song of victory and, in the harbor, ships unfurled their colors and saluted with cannon fire.

A more formal celebration three days later swelled to every corner of the town and marked the repeal with fireworks and bonfires that were viewed by jubilant and often inebriated celebrants. On the Boston Common the Sons of Liberty, almost assuredly assisted by Paul Revere, erected a "magnificent Pyramid illuminated by two-hundred-and-eighty lamps."[21] The translucent obelisk was decorated on each side with flowery verse and symbolic depictions of the fight against the British tax measures, and it became the unquestionable focal point of the town's merriment.

"The Great Illumination," as the celebration would be called,[22] was to culminate with the placement of the pyramid at the foot of the Liberty Tree as a commemorative shrine to the event. Late into the evening, however, the structure, which was made primarily of oiled paper, predictably burst into flames and was instantly destroyed. Fortunately, Revere had earlier replicated for posterity each side of the creation in a copperplate engraving that he entitled, "A VIEW of the OBELISK erected under LIBERTY-TREE in Boston on the Rejoicings for the Repeal of the Stamp Act 1766." And across the bottom, Revere decreed, "To every Lover of LIBERTY this Plate is humbly dedicated by her true born SONS in Boston, New England."[23]

Though repeal of the Stamp Act was cause for colonial celebration, Parliament ominously reserved the future right through the enactment of the Declaratory Act "to do what the treasury pleased with three millions of freemen," and it reasserted its authority to impose laws and statutes to bind the colonies as it saw fit.[24] The united opposition to the act had taught the colonists that unwavering effort and concerted resistance would yield positive results. It was evident, however, that Revere and his fellow activists would need to stand strong and vigilant as events unfolded.

Among Whig leaders such as Adams, Warren, and Molineaux, questions of law and the policy of determined opposition often were considered within the quiet confines of private homes such as that of William Cooper in Brattle Square.[25] The middling artisans and mechanics—the foot soldiers of the movement—however, carried on their business in the Green Dragon, once referred to as the "headquarters of the Revolution,"[26] the Salutation, and other spirited taverns of Boston.

Revere became an active participant in these societies, including, most notably, the North Caucus,[27] which held regular meetings at which minutes were kept and where support for designated political candidates and causes was solidified. He was known and respected among educated gentlemen, merchants, and artisans, and moved easily among each group, communicating ideas and unifying the parties in times of quarrel.

Though Revere returned his attentions to family and commerce following the repeal of the Stamp Act, he and his local brethren remained warily conscious of the political climate in Great Britain. In 1767 the colonial economy continued its sharp postwar decline, and Parliament persisted in its debate regarding responsibility for sharing England's financial burdens. Revere's business orders fell precipitously during the year, and by the fall his attentions would again be torn between diverse business pursuits and the cause of liberty.

The tone in Parliament toward the colonies had turned decidedly bitter. At the time there was a pervasive British attitude that His Majesty's colonial subjects had dissolved into a collection of petulant and ungrateful rabble. It was almost universally agreed that staunch measures aimed at reasserting dominance and control over the colonies was required.

In May of 1767, Charles Townshend, England's "vain and volatile"[28] chancellor of the exchequer, successfully argued for the enactment of a series of measures that would lay import duties on glass, lead, printer's paper, and tea, and also create a new board of customs commissioners in Boston with broad and sweeping trade enforcement powers, including expanded writs of assistance. Disturbingly, the revenue raised by the measures would be used, in part, to pay the salaries of colonial officials appointed by and beholden only to the Crown.[29] The Townshend Acts, as they would become known, were to take effect in November.

Again, the colonies were roused into action. Nonimportation agreements initiated by Boston merchant John Rowe were signed, and a series of resolutions, addresses, and caucus meetings ensued. The press condemned Townshend's measures as political subjugation and actively advocated the cause of opposition. "In the atmosphere of the late 1760s," wrote one historian, "these measures and proposals were not simply irritating; they were explosive."[30]

Though the colonial response to the measures was clearly hostile, the opposition movement maintained a posture of restraint and nonviolence, in contrast to its impulsive aggression against the Stamp Act. Now, the determined undertaking of dissent focused on public debate and democratic process.

On February 11, 1768, a circular letter drawn up by Samuel Adams and adopted by the Massachusetts House of Representatives, which set forth in detail the formal objections to the Townshend Acts, was disseminated among the various colonies to "harmonize with each other" in protest.[31] Though the letter clearly and vigorously advocated the importance of unity and concert of purpose, it freely admitted the supremacy of Parliament and disclaimed all thought of independence.[32] Nonetheless, the secretary of the colonies, Lord Hillsborough, dispatched an order to all colonial governors to ignore Adams's letter, which he described as "seditious" and "of a most dangerous and factious tendency."[33] In a separate letter to the Massachusetts governor, Francis Bernard, Hillsborough demanded, in the name of the king, that "the resolution which gave birth to the circular letter" be immediately rescinded by the House of Representatives and that it "declare their disapprobation of that rash and hasty proceeding."[34] If the legislature so refused, proclaimed Hillsborough, then the king ordered Bernard to dissolve the house itself. In the words of one historian, "Indeed, from this moment the march of events tends straight towards the dissolution of the empire."[35]

On June 30, the Massachusetts House of Representatives met in private session and refused to rescind the circular letter by a vote of ninety-two to seventeen. In the first of nine days of debate leading up to the vote, the fiery James Otis exclaimed, "Lord Hillsborough knows that we will not rescind our acts . . . He should apply to parliament to rescind theirs. Let Britain rescind her measures, or the colonies are lost to her forever."[36] The following day, Governor Bernard duly dissolved the Massachusetts assembly.

Contrary to Hillsborough's order to the colonies to ignore Adams's circular letter, most were in complete accord with their Massachusetts neighbors. Town and county meetings expressed concert and solidarity, and soon, Committees of Correspondence sprang into effect across colonial America in an effort to open direct and speedy lines of communication among "the friends of liberty."[37]

In Boston, the "trumpeters of sedition" as Hillsborough called the publishers of the *Boston Gazette*, openly toasted the "Massachusetts Ninety-two" for their brave vote of refusal[38]—and chastised the cowardly seventeen.

And again, Paul Revere's talents were put to use.

Commissioned by fifteen of his fellow Sons of Liberty, Revere crafted a large silver punch bowl elaborately engraved with scrolls, wreaths, and symbolic gestures of patriotism and bearing the inscription:

> To the Memory of the glorious NINETY-TWO Members of the Honbl House of Representatives of the Massachusetts-Bay, who, undaunted by the insolent Menaces of Villains in Power, from a Strict Regard to Conscience and the LIBERTIES of their Constituents, on the 30th of June 1768, Voted NOT TO RESCIND.

The Liberty Bowl, as it would come to be known, would stand as a living tribute to the bravery and defiance of the "Glorious Ninety-Two."[39]

As warmly as Revere honored the "nay" voters of the House of Representatives, he aptly lambasted the seventeen "Rescinders." In an engraving entitled "A Warm Place—Hell," Revere depicted, in farcical caricature, the seventeen "scoundrels" who voted for rescission being prodded by the devil into the fiery jaws of hell. "Now I've got you, a fine haul by Jove," the devil exclaims. Above the terrified group flies an ominous demon with extended pitchfork urging, "Push on, Tim," referring to the Tory legislator, Timothy Ruggles.[40] Among the seventeen ridiculed votes to rescind appeared Dr. John Calef of Ipswich who, eleven years later, would witness many of the events of the doomed Penobscot Expedition and record his detailed observations in a daily journal.

As Revere finished the artwork for the plate, which by all accounts was a virtual replica of an earlier British engraving bearing the same name, one of his friends, Dr. Benjamin Church, came by the shop, observed the engraving, and suggested the following lyrical inscription, which Revere promptly added:

> On brave RESCINDERS! to yon yawning cell,
> SEVENTEEN such Miscreants there will startle Hell;
> There puny Villains damn'd for petty Sin,
> On such distinguish'd Scoundrels gaze and grin;
> The out-done DEVIL will resign his Sway,
> He never curst his MILLIONS in a day.[41]

Revere's print was sold and widely circulated amongst the town, galvanizing opinion and rousing an already angered public.

As the events set in motion by Adams's circular letter overtook the colonies, John Hancock's sloop *Liberty* arrived in Boston Harbor carrying an illegal shipment of wine from Madeira. Customs officials seized the vessel, and Boston erupted into riots. Great Britain had already been alarmed by "a long concerted and extensive plan of resistance" to the authority of the Crown,[42] and now, with the renewed violence in Boston, it had become clear that the only possible course to prevent open revolt and its spread throughout the colonies was the introduction of military force.[43] The order to General Gage, commander in chief of His Majesties forces in America, to "strengthen the hands of the Government in the Province of Massachusetts Bay"[44] went out on June 8, 1768.

On Governor Bernard's refusal to convene the Massachusetts legislature in the face of the pending emergency, a convention comprised of nearly all towns and settlements in Massachusetts was held at Faneuil Hall to consider the situation. The convention was called by an earlier Boston town meeting, which had resolved that "money could not be levied, nor a standing army be kept up in the province, but by their own consent."[45]

Though the convention was mindful to remain moderate in tone and respectful of the King throughout, the governor perceived the meeting as "an offence of a very high nature"[46] and urged the members to disband. Clothing itself in the spirit of law and avoiding any talk of treason or rebellion, the convention passed a series of grievances and adjourned on September 28 after six days of meetings. Within hours of the adjournment, the first two regiments of British troops arrived in Boston Harbor. Thus, according to historian Bernard Bailyn, "One of the classic stages in the process of destroying free constitutions of government had been reached."[47]

In the coming weeks the Royal forces in Boston swelled to menacing proportions. Revere would later memorialize the unwelcome arrival with a copperplate print showing the ships landing in the harbor. He described the peril of those uncertain days in Boston: ". . . the Ships of WAR, armed Schooners, Transports, &c., Came up the Harbour and Anchored round the TOWN: their Cannon loaded, a Spring on their Cables, as for a regular Siege. At noon on Saturday, October the 1st the fourteenth & twenty-ninth Regiments, a detachment from the 59th Regt and a Train of Artillery, with two pieces of Cannon, landed on the Long Wharf; there Formed and Marched with insolent Parade, Drums beating, Fifes playing and Colours flying, up KING STREET, Each soldier having received 16 rounds of Powder and Ball."[48]

The Sixty-fourth and Sixty-fifth Regiments soon joined the Fourteenth and Twenty-ninth, and eight men-of-war advanced upon the harbor, flags unfurled and guns positioned. With loaded muskets and fixed bayonets, the Redcoats marched through the streets of Boston to the Common and to Faneuil Hall, where they sought shelter and station. Under the Billeting Act, Colonel Dalrymple, the British commanding officer, demanded quarters and supplies, but would encounter few friends among the populace of Boston.

Though little formal resistance was offered by the people, they welcomed the troops with indignation and open bitterness. "They were often abused and insulted, scurrilous attacks upon them made in the newspapers, and frequent affrays between the soldiers and townsmen took place."[49] The citizens threw caustic barbs of "tyranny!" and "treason!" at the soldiers, and the divide between Tory and Whig became wider than ever.

For the next two years, a troubled peace would hold between the two factions, but this stalemate of resentment and mutual hostility would not last for long.

Revere had begun 1768 with the addition of his fifth child, Mary, born on March 19. (Another daughter by the name of Mary had died in 1765 at the age of one.) By then the family had changed their church affiliation from the Cockerel, whose pastor had become too aligned with the Loyalists, to the more liberal congregation of the West Church where, to the consternation of his father, Revere frequently had visited as a boy.[50]

Despite the arrival of British troops in Boston, Revere's Masonic activities strengthened during this period and, by the close of 1769, he held the lofty position of royal arch Mason of St. Andrew's Lodge. At about the same time, the Massachusetts Grand Lodge received its charter and appointed Dr. Joseph Warren as grand master and Revere as senior grand deacon. Revere's more clandestine activities within the Sons of Liberty also expanded, as did his alliances with the statesmen and leaders of the opposition movement. Though he missed little opportunity to propagandize against and profit from the British presence in Boston through inflammatory prints and publications, Revere curiously did not discriminate when it came to business interests. Even as provincial life bent and swayed under the weight of the British occupation, Revere maintained cordial relations with his Tory customers, several of whom would prove, in 1769, to be among his most important customers. At this time Revere also began to expand his professional interests into the practice of dentistry. Despite the dramatic geopolitical shifts that were occurring beneath his feet, his goldsmith business began to increase and, together with his foray into dentistry, he found a way to prosper financially. In early 1770 Revere purchased a two-story house in North Square, a short walk from his goldsmith shop on Clark's Wharf.[51]

Even as Revere personally thrived, the fragile standoff in the Town of Boston continued. The presence of British soldiers continued to irk the citizenry, and petty quarrels began to escalate the tensions. "The troops greatly corrupt our morals and are in every sense an oppression," wrote a Boston minister. "May Heaven soon deliver us from this great evil!"[52]

Nonimportation, the colonial boycott of certain British goods, had taken hold throughout the region and, by 1770, had begun to affect British commerce. Economic pressures were mounting on the Crown, and the Sons of Liberty sought, as always, to unify the colonies in their resolve. This was not always possible. Bowing to financial and political pressures, several Boston merchants elected to ignore the popular sentiment and deal in some of the forbidden goods.

On February 22, 1770, a bitter confrontation between one such merchant, Theophilus Lillie, and a band of unruly boys exploded on Middle Street behind Revere's new home. When Lillie's neighbor, Ebenezer Richardson, a roundly hated British informant, came upon the scene, chaos turned to violence. After briefly coming to Lillie's defense, Richardson fled to his home with the crowd in hot pursuit. Finally, under a barrage of snowballs and invective, he "discharged a loaded Gun into the midst of the people"[53] and eleven-year-old Christopher Seider became the victim of a "barbarous murder."[54]

Four days later, Seider's funeral procession, led by five hundred children and followed by another thirteen hundred citizens, wound through the streets of Boston amid tolling bells and cries of bitter indignation. Little Christopher Seider had become "a *martyr* in the cause of liberty."[55]

In an emotionally charged trial viewed by "a vast Concourse of Rabble," Ebenezer Richardson was convicted of murder in a classic case of jury nullification, despite convincing evidence of self-defense. Hesitant to order his execution, the court sought and obtained a pardon from the Crown, and Richardson was ultimately released.[56]

Boston now simmered like a kettle on an open hearth. On the night of March 5, despite snow-covered streets and frigid temperatures, mobs of men and boys roved about Boston taunting and insulting British soldiers. Sharp altercations flared between troops and citizens on King Street, Draper Alley, and at Dock Square. Soldiers were reported to be carrying clubs and cutlasses, while mobs of unruly countrymen armed themselves with sticks and canes.[57]

Private Hugh White, a posted sentry at the Custom House, was confronted by a young apprentice seeking satisfaction for services from another officer thought to be nearby. The altercation ended with White striking the man with the butt of his musket.

Shortly after nine o'clock, meetinghouse bells clanged a false alarm of fire, and a flood of townspeople poured into King Street to find only agitated soldiers and marauding gangs. A young man suddenly extended an accusatory finger at Private White and cried out, "There's the soldier who knocked me down!"

"Kill him! Knock him down!" joined other voices.[58]

As a barrage of snowballs pelted Private White, he nervously retreated up the steps of the Custom House and loaded his musket.

"The lobster is going to fire!" shouted a boy.

A bookseller, Henry Knox, warned the sentry, "If you fire you must die for it."[59]

White leveled his weapon and warned the rampaging crowd to stay back. He then shouted loudly to the main guard across the street for assistance, and moments later he was joined by seven soldiers who rushed upon the scene with bayonets fixed and muskets primed and loaded. An officer of the Twenty-ninth Regiment, Captain Thomas Preston, also arrived at the Custom House and took charge of his men.

The crowd goaded the soldiers to fire, hurling insults and striking them with sticks and snowballs. The air was thick with voices and confusion.

"Fire, fire if you dare!" a voice called out. "Why don't you fire?"

Though some in the melee would later testify that they heard the word "fire," it is unclear whether Captain Preston issued the order. History records, however, that on that evening of March 5, 1770, soldiers from the Twenty-ninth Regiment discharged their weapons upon the citizens of Boston, killing five and seriously wounding six others.

The "Horrid Massacre," as it would come to be known, bonded the colonies and shaped public opinion like no previous act of the British government had done. "On that night," John Adams later wrote, "the formation of American Independence was laid."[60]

The funeral procession for the slain was attended by as many as ten to twelve thousand citizens, who mournfully wormed their way from the site of the massacre through the streets of Boston to the Granary Burying Ground.[61] "So large an assemblage" had never been seen before in the town.[62]

After an inquiry ordered by Lieutenant Governor Thomas Hutchinson on the night of the shooting, Captain Preston and his men were arrested by the Suffolk County sheriffs pursuant to a warrant issued by Justices Richard Dana and John Tudor, and the following morning a committee of Whig leaders convened at Faneuil Hall and demanded that all British soldiers be removed from the town. Immediately, each side clamored to depose witnesses and to publicly issue their version of events in an effort to gain the informational high ground. Though it is unclear whether Paul Revere was present on King Street on the evening of the fifth, it is believed that he generated a detailed pen-and-ink plan of the massacre scene ostensibly for use at the legal proceedings ultimately brought against the soldiers.[63]

Revere's creative involvement did not stop with evidentiary diagrams. On March 26, as the political fallout from the killings began to crystallize, the *Boston Gazette* advertised Revere's copperplate engraving of the "Bloody Massacre," as he called it. An inflammatory—and generally inaccurate—depiction of the event, Revere's print shows a well-organized row of British soldiers firing in unison upon a helpless and peaceably assembled gathering of townspeople. Behind the Redcoats, Captain Preston stands with sword elevated, sternly commanding his men to shoot, and above him, one of Boston's buildings bears the sign "Butcher's Hall." The bewildered crowd recoils in fear, and several citizens are shown gruesomely bleeding on the street from head, neck, and chest wounds. Beneath the print, Revere placed, as usual, a tirade of provocative verse, which included doggerel such as:

> ... With murd'rous Rancour stretch their bloody Hands;
> Like fierce Barbarians grinning o'er their Pay.
> Approve the Carnage and enjoy the Day.[64]

The print, which Revere sold and willingly profited from, is perhaps his best-known work of copperplate engraving and has been reproduced innumerable times through the years. As one Revere biographer explained, however, "Revere is under grave suspicion of having in this instance appropriated the work of another."[65] On March 29, 1770, following the advertisement of the print in the *Gazette*, a Boston engraver by the name of Henry Pelham penned a scathing letter to Revere:

> SIR:
> When I heard that you was cutting a plate of the late Murder, I thought it impossible as I knew you was not capable of doing it unless you coppied it from mine and as I thought I had intrusted it in the hands of a person who had more regard to the dictates of Honour and Justice than to take the undue advantage you have done of the confidence and trust I reposed in you.
>
> But I find I was mistaken and after being at great Trouble and Expense of making a design, paying for paper, printing &c., find myself in the most ungenerous Manner deprived not only of any proposed Advantage but even of the expense I have been at as truly as if you had plundered me on the highway.
>
> If you are insensible of the Dishonour you have brought on yourself by this Act, the World will not be so. However, I leave you to reflect and consider of one of the most dishonourable Actions you could well be guilty of.
>
> H. Pelham.[66]

Revere's plate asserts only that it was "Engrav'd Printed & Sold by Paul Revere *Boston*" and gives no hint of attribution to another. Certainly eighteenth-century standards of provenance and derivation were fairly lenient, but it does appear that Pelham entrusted his depiction of the "late murder" to Revere, and that his trust was shamelessly violated.[67]

In April, Great Britain repealed the Townshend revenue measures with the exception of the duty on tea, and later in the year, Boston's merchants voted to terminate the nonimportation measures. Though trade and commerce slowly began to improve, Governor Hutchinson was ordered by the Crown to relinquish civil control of Castle Island to British authority, thereby essentially placing Massachusetts under martial law.[68] For the next several years, an unsteady truce was maintained, and Boston found a semblance of calm amid the underlying anguish of British oppression.

On the first anniversary of the massacre, memorials and tributes appeared throughout the town—none, however, surpassing the "very striking Exhibition"[69] prepared by Paul Revere. In the evening hours of March 5, his North Square dwelling was converted into a solemn monument adorned with creations and symbols depicting the events of the previous year. "The whole was so well executed," wrote the *Boston Gazette*, "that the Spectators, whole Number amounted to several Thousands, were struck with solemn Silence, and their Countenances were covered with a melancholy Gloom."[70]

At one chamber window of the house, Revere placed an illuminated depiction of Christopher Seider, mortally wounded and fighting for life while his friends helplessly look on. Nearby, an obelisk appeared bearing the face of Seider and the names of all five victims of the Horrid Massacre, and beneath were printed the lines:

Seider's pale Ghost fresh-bleeding stands,
And Vengeance for his Death demands.[71]

Through another window was seen a row of pitiless British soldiers firing into a crowd of citizens, several of which lay wounded and bleeding on the ground, and above, the words "FOUL PLAY" were boldly transcribed. And through the last window, a woman, representing America, sits on the stump of a tree and points accusingly at the unfolding tragic events. The "never-to-be-forgotten 5th of March 1770"[72] was soberly and stirringly memorialized by the Revere family.

The next several years marked a pause in the patriotic fervor that earlier had gripped the Town of Boston. Nonetheless, Whig leaders mustered the spirit of dissent with printed political invective and annual orations marking the anniversary of the Horrid Massacre. During this period of "superficial tranquility,"[73] Revere remained active in Masonic activities, local politics, and the North Caucus. He continued his interest and awareness in the cause of economic freedom, and he greatly strengthened his associations with leaders of the movement such as Joseph Warren, Thomas Young, and Samuel Adams.

In October of 1772, word arrived in Boston of a requirement that the governor and provincial judges receive their salaries from the Crown rather than from the people whom they served. Predictably, the Whig leaders of Boston strenuously objected to the measure and conducted a series of town meetings to formulate a response.

At the urging of Samuel Adams, a formal Committee of Correspondence was unanimously voted on in Boston to meet and circulate "the infringements and violations"[74] of Great Britain and the colonial responses thereto. Twenty-one men of stature, wealth, and education were chosen by town meeting vote to man the committee and to apprise the people in the most articulate and intellectual manner. Though not chosen as a member of Boston's Committee of Correspondence, Paul Revere would nonetheless soon be called on to play a central and vital role in its work.

By 1773 the Revere family had swelled to seven children. Elizabeth had been born in late 1770 and Isanna, two years later. Of the eight children she delivered, Sara Revere would nurture all beyond infancy, though Mary, the fourth child born to the couple, died in 1765 at the age of one. With the difficult birth of Isanna, however, Sara would soon become weak and fall sick. On May 3, 1773, she died at the age of thirty-seven. Paul Revere would find himself alone, tending to the needs of seven children, a goldsmith shop, and a fledgling nation that would soon require his services.

No doubt Revere's greatest distress in the days following Sara's death was the care of the infant Isanna, who was sickly and not thriving. Though Revere's mother and eldest daughter, fifteen-year-old Deborah, were a constant and supportive presence in the household, it became abundantly clear that a mother's touch would be required to bond the family and allow it to endure.

Whether through true love or simple expedience, Revere would quickly find the answer to his wishes. Rachel Walker, a twenty-seven-year-old plain but educated Bostonian, caught his eye one afternoon in the summer of 1773. Esther Forbes writes, "Probably it was the attraction of Paul himself that made Rachel go with him, but the story is that it was pity for poor Isanna that made her stay that evening, and soon return for good."[75] They were married on October 10, 1773.

Though Isanna would die just weeks before they wed, Paul and Rachel Revere would have eight more children of their own in the coming years and enjoy a long and happy union that would endure late into their lives.

As Revere personally toiled and then recovered in 1773, the movement toward colonial unity likewise faltered despite the proliferation of Committees of Correspondence. Political factions developed among the Whig party, and the rallying cry of "British tyranny" seemed to evaporate with the repeal of the Townshend Acts and the withdrawal of the nonimportation measures. Overall interest in the militant exploits of the Sons of Liberty also began to wane as lethargy and division within the ranks seemed to cast doubt on the movement.

Whatever rancor and disunity existed among the colonies in the early 1770s, however, quickly and unambiguously evaporated with the passage of the Tea Act of 1773 on May 10, 1773. In an effort to save the cash-starved East India Company, which maintained excessive stockpiles of tea in its warehouses along the Thames River, Parliament passed a measure, effectively giving the company a monopoly on all teas sold in the colonial market and allowing these exports to be accomplished duty-free. The result, of course, was the undercutting of all other sources of the product while ensuring that the only remaining measure of the Townshend Acts—a tax on tea—was complied with in full.[76]

The North Caucus expressed the unified sentiment of Boston and provincial America when on October 23, 1773, it voted, "That this body will oppose the vending of any tea, sent by the East India Company to any part of the Continent, with our lives and fortunes."[77] In an unequivocal stroke, Paul Revere and his fellow caucus members had drawn the line against the oppressive Tea Act.

The resistance effort, led by the North Caucus and implemented by the Boston town meeting and Committee of Correspondence, sprang into action. They passed resolutions aimed at preventing the sale and consumption of East India tea and sent circular letters to the towns and villages of Massachusetts to implore compliance. The resistance used strong-arm persuasion on the various appointed "tea consignees" to resign their positions; upon their failure to do so, they were to be branded "enemies of their country."[78] Rachel Revere dutifully informed her family, "Children, this is the last cup of tea you will get for a long while."[79]

On November 28 the British ship *Dartmouth* sailed into Boston Harbor carrying its cargo of one hundred and fourteen chests of East India Company tea. Immediately, the cry went forth in a handbill posted across the town:

> The hour of Destruction or manly Opposition to the Machinations of Tyranny, stares you in the Face; every Friend to this Country, to himself and to Posterity, is now called upon to meet at FANEUIL HALL, at Nine o'clock THIS DAY, (at which Time the Bells will ring), to make a united and successful Resistance to the last, worst, and most destructive Measure of Administration.[80]

The meeting at Faneuil Hall—a graceful, red-brick Georgian structure built in 1742 near Dock Square and never meant to host the largest public events—was so roundly attended by the citizens of Boston that the leaders were forced to relocate to the Old South Meeting House. As thousands looked on, a resolution was passed on the motion of Samuel Adams "that the tea should not be landed,"[81] and a round-the-clock guard of twenty-five men, including Paul Revere, was appointed to stand by the ship to ensure compliance with the decree.

Meanwhile, the *Eleanor* and the *Beaver*, both carrying a similar shipment of the "detested tea,"[82] arrived in Boston and were moored along-side the *Dartmouth* at Griffin's Wharf, where the appointed party stood guard. Frantic negotiations ensued with the ships' owners and the tea consignees for the return of the cargo to England, but on each occasion, they answered that it was beyond their collective power to send the tea back. As the tense standoff continued, time would quickly become of the essence; for according to the law, twenty days after arrival, the ships could be seized by British authorities for nonpayment of duties and their contents sold at auction.[83]

On December 11 the owner of the *Dartmouth*, a Nantucket Quaker by the name of Francis Rotch, again informed the Committee of Correspondence that it was out of his power to return the tea to England.

"The ship must go," came the response. "The people of Boston and the neighboring towns absolutely require and expect it."[84] To make matters worse, Governor Hutchinson was preventing passage of the ship in the absence of a permit that he refused to grant.

On December 16—the final day for the colonists to act—again permission to return the loaded *Dartmouth* to England was denied. As Rotch once again appealed to the governor for leave, the Old South Meeting House swelled with over seven thousand citizens from Boston and her surrounding towns. Josiah Quincy, Samuel Adams, Thomas Young, and others delivered impassioned discourses. "Who knows," queried one speaker, "how tea will mingle with salt water?"[85]

As dusk fell upon Boston, Rotch finally returned with word that Governor Hutchinson had once again refused to allow passage to the *Dartmouth* without first offloading its cargo. Instantly, the crowd of people leapt to their feet with excited shouts and cries. "A mob! A Mob!"[86] Samuel Adams slowly rose and was heard to say, "This meeting can do nothing more to save the country."[87]

At that moment, a group of about forty or fifty men wearing decorated blankets and other Mohawk garb appeared at the church doors and loudly shouted their "war whoop," which was enthusiastically returned by those in the gallery. "Depend upon it, they were no ordinary Mohawks," wrote John Adams.[88]

The horde made its way to Griffin's Wharf, where the three ships and their incendiary cargo lay. "[W]hooping like Indians . . . ," recorded the writer of the *Dartmouth* ship's journal, "[the party] came on board the ship; and after warning myself and the custom-house officer to get out of the way, they unlaid the hatches and went down the hold, where were eighty whole and thirty-four half chests of tea, which they hoisted upon deck, and cut the chests to pieces, and hove the tea all overboard, where it was damaged and lost."[89]

The "Tea Party," as it would come to be known, was carefully planned and orchestrated by a clandestine gathering of the North Caucus in a meeting room of the Green Dragon Tavern, and Paul Revere and his Masonic brothers are known to have been active participants in both its preparation and execution. The records of St. Andrew's Lodge, which typically met in another room at the Green Dragon Tavern, simply indicated that, as the action on Griffin's Wharf was planned, the lodge was adjourned "on account of few Brother's present."[90]

Shortly after the Tea Party, a ballad by an anonymous author could be heard at the taverns and waterfront shops of Boston:

Rally Mohawks! Bring out your axes,
And Tell King George we'll pay no taxes
On his foreign tea . . .

Our Warren's there and bold Revere
With hands to do, and words to cheer
For Liberty and laws;

Our Country's 'braves' and firm defenders
Shall ne'er be left by true North-Enders
Fighting Freedom's call!

Then rally boys, and hasten on
To meet our chiefs at the Green Dragon.[91]

Now Revere's role would change from propagandist engraver to envoy. As wooden fragments of battered tea chests washed up along the shores of Dorchester, Samuel Adams was busy transcribing a statement of the events of the previous evening for the Committee of Correspondence. Word of the destruction of the tea would have to be sent quickly to New York and Philadelphia. "The bearer," wrote Adams, "is chosen by the committee from a number of gentlemen, who volunteered to carry you this intelligence."[92]

With the scent of tea perhaps still lingering on his clothes and body, and fatigued by the tumultuous events of the previous night, Revere mounted his horse and journeyed south through the frigid air of the early winter. With Adams's communiqué tucked safely in his satchel, he moved with remarkable speed for two hundred miles through the well-traveled post roads leading to New York and arrived on the night of December 21.

Revere delivered the committee's message of "perfect jubilee"[93] and provided the Whig leaders of New York with a detailed description of the tea's destruction. Word of the event quickly circulated among the colonies and was accepted with satisfaction and support. Two days after Christmas, Revere arrived home in Boston bearing the news that New York's Governor Tryon had pledged that all tea ships bound for New York would be denied port. The next morning, "all the Boston bells were rung."[94]

The mood in Great Britain stood in stark contrast to that of the colonies. "The offence of the Americans . . . is flagitious. The Town of Boston ought to be knocked about their ears and destroyed," the prime minister of England, Lord North, proclaimed before Parliament.[95] While in America, John Adams described the event as "so bold, so daring, so firm, so intrepid and inflexible, [that] it must have so important Consequences, and so lasting, that I cant but consider it as an Epocha in History."[96]

The Crown's punitive response to Revere and his Tea Party began on March 31, 1774, with the passage of the Boston Port Bill, which essentially closed Boston Harbor to all further commerce until restitution was made to the East India Company for its losses in connection with the destruction of its tea. In the following days, Parliament sought to stymie the "tumultuous and riotous rabble"[97] of Boston by the enactment of various measures requiring that the Massachusetts legislature be appointed by the king, that town meetings be abolished, that superior court judges serve and be accountable only to the king, that juries be selected by sheriffs loyal to the Crown, that British soldiers and officials charged with capital offenses be tried only in England, and that British troops be freely quartered within the province. The "Intolerable Acts," as the legislation was called by the colonists, attempted to isolate the Town of Boston from the rest of America and divide the colonies with a wedge of coercion.[98]

On May 12, the Boston Committee of Correspondence resolved that "the impolicy, injustice, inhumanity, and cruelty of the act exceed all our power of expression"[99] and voted unanimously to recommend that the colonies unite in a resolution terminating all trade with Great Britain. Again, Revere was chosen as an envoy to deliver the resolution to New York and Philadelphia. "My worthy friend again revisits you," wrote Dr. Thomas Young to an acquaintance in New York. "No man of his rank and opportunities in life deserves better of the community. Steady, vigorous, sensible and persevering."[100]

As Revere began his journey, word arrived in Boston that General Gage was to immediately replace Thomas Hutchinson as governor of Massachusetts. Gage had been stationed in New York City for much of the decade as commander in chief of British forces in America, yet he kept a watchful eye on Boston. "America is a mere bully . . . ," he wrote in 1770, "and the Bostonians by far the greatest bullies."[101] Following the removal of his two infantry regiments from Boston after the Horrid Massacre, Gage had been angered and maintained that the Crown's actions would be viewed by the colonies as capitulation and would encourage further acts of insolence. He argued in letters to his superiors that the prevalence of democracy was the root of the problem in the colonies and that restrictions on settlement beyond the coastal areas would allow London to better contain the proliferation of rebellious acts. American faith, laws, customs, and institutions, posited Gage, were adverse to British rule and required reforms or abolishment. Once accomplished, he argued, America would become dependent upon the Crown and dependence would breed submission. Though Parliament initially did not agree with the harsh measures advocated by General Gage, the Boston Tea Party would quickly change that view. In June of 1773 he had returned home to London on leave, and when word of the Tea Party reached King George III in February 1774, Gage was instructed to return immediately to Boston and to compel the town's compliance with the Port Bill and all other measures of the Crown.[102]

By June 1, mere weeks after Gage's arrival, Boston Harbor was subjected to a blockade of armed and uncompromising British vessels, and Boston herself fell victim to military rule. Four British regiments and twenty-two cannon manned by three artillery units were placed on Boston Common, and the Welch Fusiliers, an infantry company of the Prince of Wales Division, encamped at Fort Hill. Several companies of the Sixty-fourth Regiment oversaw the powder and artillery stores of Castle Island, and British troops were stationed in nearby towns to protect the governor's residence and mandamus council, a body installed by Gage to replace the Massachusetts Assembly.[103]

Again New York and Philadelphia, and now Rhode Island and even the Tory stronghold of Connecticut, pledged their steadfast loyalty to Boston and communicated to Revere their willingness to stand shoulder-to-shoulder with their Massachusetts brethren. As a result of Revere's tireless embassies, "the continent, as one great commonwealth, made the cause of Boston its own."[104]

🕯 During the summer of 1774, Revere grew in political savvy and patriotic rank. He was appointed to a town committee; and when called upon to serve on a Suffolk County grand jury, he refused, along with twenty-one others, on the ground that the judges' salaries were paid by the Crown. And in June he issued his most provocative—almost scandalous—print engraving, again copied from a London cartoonist, of a helpless and bare-breasted woman representing America, held down by a series of British officials, one indignantly gawking beneath her robe, while another, the prime minister, forcibly pours a goblet full of tea down her throat. The obvious target of Revere's inflammatory dramatization was the Boston Port Bill, a copy of which conspicuously protrudes from the pocket of one of the assailants. The bill itself, demonized by Revere's inflammatory engraving, had the immediate effect of uniting and galvanizing the colonies against British acts of tyranny.

As the First Continental Congress convened in Philadelphia, Revere would maintain the integral bond between the remaining political leaders of Boston and the congressional delegates hungry for news. In September he journeyed to Philadelphia bearing a copy of the Suffolk Resolves, drawn up by Joseph Warren and enacted by a convention of Suffolk County delegates to reinforce Boston's opposition to the Intolerable Acts and to recommend the formation of a provincial congress. The body quickly endorsed the resolves and passed further resolutions condemning the acts of Parliament, which Revere duly brought back to Boston.[105]

As tensions grew in the colonies, Revere continued his envoy missions between Boston and the Continental Congress and, despite the growing sense of siege in his seaport home, remained optimistic and satisfied with his pivotal role in the revolutionary movement. He would write to his friend John Lamb, "We are in spirits, though in a garrison; the spirit of liberty was never higher than at present . . ."[106]

By early September, General Gage, with full understanding of the rebellious posture of Boston, began seizing powder and reinforcing his fortifications in and around the town. The Massachusetts legislature, having lacked the requisite legal recognition of the governor, soon reemerged as a newly formed provincial congress, named John Hancock as president, and reconvened in Concord.

Meanwhile in Boston, Revere joined a committee of nearly thirty men, mostly local mechanics, charged with "the purpose of watching the Movements of the British Soldiers, and gaining every intelligence of the movements of the Tories."[107] "For a time it was quiet," records Justin Winsor in *The Memorial History of Boston*. "[B]ut it was only the lull before the storm; and the hour of the American Revolution, which had been so long in coming, was near at hand."[108]

Chapter **3** *"Listen, My Children . . ."*

THERE WAS NO mistaking the intent of the maneuvers of His Majesty's troops in the early spring of 1775. Late on the night of Saturday, April 15, members of a clandestine committee of thirty Patriots, formed to monitor British movements in the Town of Boston, had word of the launch of transport boats and the stealthy dispatch of grenadiers and light infantry. General Thomas Gage, the installed royal governor of Massachusetts, had received orders from London to confiscate the military stores at Concord and to arrest those who "have committed themselves in acts of treason and rebellion."[1] In recent days the Patriots had received corroborative intelligence of a secret British operation through their network of spies, and they recognized the danger to their munitions and even to members of the Massachusetts Provincial Congress, John Hancock and Samuel Adams. "Nothing was wanting," wrote one contemporary historian, "but a spark to set the whole continent in a flame."[2]

The Provincial Congress had adjourned earlier that day, and Hancock and Adams were safely lodged at the home of Reverend Jonas Clark in Lexington. Of the menacing peril to his boarders, Reverend Clark later observed, "As both these gentlemen had been frequently and even *publicly* threatened, by the enemies of *this people*, both in *England* and *America*, with the *vengeance* of the *British Administration*:— And as Mr. Hancock in particular had been, more than once, *personally insulted*, by some officers of the troops, in Boston, it was not without some just grounds supposed, that under cover of darkness, *sudden arrest*, if not *assassination* might be attempted by these *instruments of tyranny!*"[3] Circumstances thus prevented the men from returning to Boston, and soon they would leave for Philadelphia as the representatives of Massachusetts at the Second Continental Congress. At the time, Hancock was in possession of a large trunk that contained "papers so treasonable they must not fall into the British hands."[4]

Tensions remained high in the Town of Boston, and by April of 1775 many of the Whig leaders were marked men and had elected to leave the area to avoid British reprisals. The Crown essentially had placed a bounty on the heads of both Hancock and Adams; yet Dr. Joseph Warren, "Chief" as he was known among his fellow agitators,[5] bravely remained in Boston as the leader of the town's Committee of Correspondence, recognizing the critical need to deliver news of British maneuvers to the men and also the gathering danger that loomed before them.

The thirty-four-year-old Warren was born in Roxbury, just south of Boston Neck, and at the age of fourteen, he began study at Harvard. He was recognized as a rambunctious yet gifted student who, while at college, developed an interest in the field of medicine. As a young doctor and with limited medical experience, Warren served with a group of other physicians during the smallpox outbreak in 1764, administering inoculations and providing care to many citizens of Boston including John Adams. As a close ally of Samuel Adams, Warren developed an interest in the political affairs of the town and by 1772 had distinguished himself as a trusted leader of the North Caucus, a clandestine political society formed to steer policy and choose candidates for office. It was here and through the meetings of St. Andrews Lodge, of which he would become grand master, that Warren developed his close political affiliations — as well as a deep confidence in and friendship with the artisan and Patriot Paul Revere.[6]

On the evening of April 15, Warren sent for Revere, known to Boston as a reliable foot soldier for the American cause, and dispatched him to warn and advise Hancock and Adams in advance of the provocative British march.

Early the next day, Revere crossed the Charles River most probably in a small boat that had been hidden beneath a Boston wharf,[7] and then he traveled to Lexington without fanfare or molestation to warn Hancock and Adams that General Gage's troops may soon move. Word traveled to

Concord, and soon cannon and stores of munitions were stowed about the countryside—and old men and farm boys stood at the ready to defend their homes and their liberties.

After delivering the news to Hancock and Adams and meeting with other Whigs in the surrounding towns, Revere made for Boston through Charlestown, aware that the tightening grip of British aggression would make travel and the dissemination of alarm in the coming days difficult if not impossible. Revere knew that the Regulars would begin their march at any time, and he worried that he or some other courier would be captured and prevented from alerting the region when they were. A contingency plan would be needed.

In Charlestown, Revere met with Colonel William Conant, a trusted member of the Sons of Liberty and a respected military officer. He informed Conant of his concerns about getting word out of Boston of the coming British excursion. Across the river in the distance, Revere eyed the familiar North Church spire rising above the clamoring streets and wharves of Boston, and he knew that the sight was visible at a good distance. In 1775 it was the tallest structure in Boston. Then and there the men agreed "that if the British went out by Water, we would shew two Lanthorns in the North Church Steeple; and if by Land, one, as a Signal; for we were apprehensive it would be difficult to Cross the Charles River, or git over Boston Neck."[8] In years hence, Revere's scheme would be etched in history.

The fact of the coming British expedition was obvious to all as a result of the clandestine efforts of the Boston mechanics, yet the actual target and timing remained a mystery. General Gage was jealously circumspect with the details of the operation and observed complete secrecy in its planning. Though he believed his aims were safely guarded, word began to circulate quietly through the town.

On the afternoon of April 18, a young stable hand at Province House, where General Gage now maintained his headquarters, was, according to most histories, informed of a muffled conversation among Regulars preparing their horses for travel, in which one was overheard to boast of, "hell to pay tomorrow."[9] The boy dashed through the dusty streets of Boston to the North Square dwelling of Paul Revere, where he informed the goldsmith of what he had heard. Revere already had been told similar news on two separate occasions that morning; indeed, the unmistakable readiness in the British garrisons and throughout the harbor informed the buzzing community as a whole that the Regulars would soon march.

At Province House, Gage began to implement his plan in what he still believed was a shroud of absolute secrecy. Through a network of spies, Gage earlier had learned of munitions stores and powder magazines kept by the Rebels in Concord. That March he had been advised by two British scouts of an acceptable northerly route from Boston through Lexington and Menotomy (present-day Arlington) that afforded his troops open spaces in which to maneuver with relative safety from ambush. Gage had appointed Colonel Francis Smith as commander of the expedition with orders to "seize and destroy all Artillery, Ammunition, Provisions, Tents, Small Arms, and all Military stores whatever" in Concord.[10]

Though he did expect some light resistance from local Rebels along the route, Gage believed that the raid could be swiftly accomplished with minimal risk. He informed London that "if a respectable force is seen in the field, the most obnoxious of the leaders seized, and a pardon proclaimed for all others, Government will come off victorious."[11] The actual details, location, and timing of the final plan, however, were revealed only to his most trusted subordinate, Lord Hugh Percy, who was to command a British relief column for the mission—and to Gage's American-born wife, Margaret Kemble Gage.

On the morning of April 18, after learning for the first time that the artillery stores of Concord would be the target of the British campaign and being warned by the general of the need to observe absolute silence on the topic, Lord Percy, on his way back to his quarters, overheard a group of Bostonians on the Common clamoring among themselves. Upon inquiry, the men informed him that the Regulars had begun their march— "but will miss their aim." Percy probed the men as to what "aim" they spoke of. "Why, the cannon at Concord," they responded.[12]

Dumbstruck, Percy hurried back to General Gage and informed him that the secrecy of his plan had been violated. Gage immediately feared that his wife—the only other person who was aware of the details—had, perhaps, betrayed him.

Joseph Warren was acutely aware of the British movements in and around Boston, and he knew that the awaited excursion was afoot. He had maintained contact with an informant—someone very close to top British command—who now provided him with confirmation that, indeed, the Regulars would march that evening, and their design was, in fact, to "seize Samuel Adams and John Hancock, who were known to be at Lexington, and burn the stores at Concord."[13] Warren never divulged the true identity of his informant, but shortly after the British expedition to Concord, Margaret Kemble Gage was unceremoniously returned to Britain by her husband aboard the ship *Charming Nancy*.[14]

With news of the British objective now whirling about Boston, Gage realized that he must take immediate measures to prevent the further dissemination of his plan. On that morning of April 18, he sent a hand-picked patrol of officers and sergeants, laughably masquerading as a casual social jaunt, to points of access throughout the town and on the roads leading to Concord and Lexington. The stated purpose of this mounted company was to intercept all messengers and envoys, thus thwarting the transmission of news to Concord. In realty, the odd presence of the soldiers in full military attire (as opposed to the usual informal garb worn by British troops during periods of nonengagement), with weapons clumsily concealed beneath their cloaks, and in the late hours of the day, set off an alarm throughout the nervously vigilant countryside. And in an even more provocative display, the British warship *Somerset* ominously sailed into the ferry way between Boston and Charlestown to prevent the crossing of any vessel carrying intelligence to the countryside.

Sometime after nine o'clock on the evening of April 18, Doctor Warren sent an urgent communiqué to Paul Revere directing him to Warren's house. The British were, this night, congregating on the lower Common, boarding their river transports, and launching their mission to Concord. Warren charged Revere to "immediately Set off for Lexington, where Messrs. Hancock & Adams were and acquaint them of the Movement" and to warn them of their imminent danger.[15]

Warren, aware of the risk and difficulty of Revere's mission, had already dispatched another rider, William Dawes, to Lexington via a different route over Boston Neck. Dawes, a cobbler and ardent Whig, was relatively unfamiliar to British sentries, and it was hoped that his innocent almost "half-witted" looks would allay any suspicions of his journey.[16]

Revere bade farewell to Doctor Warren, aware that it might be for the last time. Though the two men came from separate social and cultural spheres, they were Masonic brothers and intimate friends, united in spirit and purpose. Two months hence Warren would die at the Battle of Bunker Hill, and his friend would solemnly name his fourth son, Joseph Warren Revere, after the fallen hero. On this evening, however, Revere's thoughts were soberly focused on the task ahead of him and the dangers facing his countrymen. He left Warren's house and quietly disappeared into the night.

Earlier in the day, Revere had called upon a friend, twenty-three-year-old Robert Newman, to assist him with his plan of signals at the North Church. Newman was the sexton at the church, and though he had no liking for the job, he held the keys to the building and was known to be steadfast and reliable in character. Newman was willing to assist Revere with his "lanthorns," yet danger lurked; his mother's house, which sat across the street from the church, was used as a boardinghouse that at the time quartered several British officers.

As William Dawes made his way through Boston Neck toward Roxbury, Revere rushed to the Newman house on Salem Street. It was after ten o'clock, and Robert Newman nimbly slipped out of an upper-story window to the ground below, wishing to avoid the scrutiny of the officers who were congregated on the lower floor. He joined an acquaintance, Captain John Pulling, a vestryman of the North Church and friend of Paul Revere, who earlier had agreed to assist Newman in the task. Shortly after, Revere emerged from the darkness, greeted the men, and hurriedly instructed them to hang two lanterns in the north-facing window of the church steeple. The Regulars would begin their journey by water.

As Paul Revere dashed home to prepare for his trek, Robert Newman ascended the dark wooden steps of the North Church. He passed the chamber that housed the oldest chime of bells in America—the great bells that Paul Revere himself once tolled as a child—and, guided only by the faint glow of the rising moon, he scaled his way to the uppermost window of the tower. Braced against the timbers of the bell tower, he looked north toward Charlestown aware that, in the distance, Colonal Conant and his fellow Whigs were peering back, searching through the night sky for Paul Revere's signal. Newman sparked each of the candles within the two square lamps and watched as the flames leaped to attention. For no more than a moment he draped the glowing vessels from the window opening, and in that moment, the men across the river understood its mean and sprang into action.[17]

Dodging congregations of British soldiers and officers making their way to the Common, Paul Revere arrived home and prepared for his night's journey. He was forty years old. His eyes were dark and bold, and on this night, his rather casual expressions were sternly focused. He was of "indifferent height,"[18] stocky in build, and his clothes were small and outdated. His face was round and his hands were rough; they were the hands of an artisan who toiled daily in the tasks of his trade.

His wife, Rachel, perhaps was apprehensive of her husband's designated mission, but she assisted him, as did the oldest of his seven children, in retrieving his heavy riding boots and frock coat for the trip. In his haste, Revere forgot to secure his boot spurs and left without them. For generations hence, Revere's descendants would insist that later, upon realizing that he had left his spurs behind, he affixed a note to his dog's collar and sent him home. Within a short while, the dog returned—spurs in tow.[19]

Beneath a wharf on the shores of north Boston was hidden Paul Revere's small rowboat, which now served as a rendezvous point for Revere and two friends. Joshua Bentley and Thomas Richardson were both familiar with the tides and currents of the Charles River and had agreed to ferry Revere across the open water to the shores of Charlestown for his journey beyond.

As the men pushed off from the rocky beach, they suddenly realized that they had no cloth or glove with which to muffle the sound of the oars from the crew of the lurking man-of-war *Somerset*. One of Revere's helpers had a young female acquaintance who lived nearby. Legend recalls, "One of the two stopped before a certain house at the North End of the town, and made a peculiar signal. An upper window was softly raised, and a hurried colloquy took place in whispers, at the end of which something white fell noiselessly to the ground. It proved to be the woolen undergarment, still warm from contact with the person of the little rebel."[20]

The ferryboats of Boston were required to moor alongside the port of the *Somerset* after nine o'clock, and the British permitted no further water passage after that hour. Watchmen aboard the ship peered intently over the harbor and river mouth searching for movement and clandestine messengers. Quietly, Revere and his escorts rowed through the still water, wide and east of the hulking ship and finally beyond. "It was then young flood . . . ," Revere later wrote. "[T]he ship was winding, & the moon was Rising."[21]

The wharf at Charlestown Battery seemed to emerge from the darkness suddenly, yet it was a welcome sight for Revere and his boatmen. Revere bounded to the shore and headed for town, where Colonel Conant and several other militiamen were waiting. On meeting, the men informed Revere that they had seen his signal from the North Church spire but knew little else of the British movements. "I told them what was Acting, and went to git me a Horse," Revere would record.[22]

The men of Charlestown knew in advance that Revere would require an able horse to complete his mission. They earlier had arranged with John Larkin, a wealthy merchant and church deacon, for the use of his father's best animal—a mare, according to family histories, named "Brown Beauty."[23] Of the animal, Esther Forbes poetically mused: "It would be slender and nervous in the Yankee manner, small by modern standards, surefooted, tireless. Now for the remainder of the night Revere's success, perhaps his life and the lives of others, would depend upon this horse."[24]

Revere himself later wrote simply, "I set off upon a very good horse."[25]

As the men bade him farewell, Richard Devens, a fellow member of the Committee of Safety, cautioned Revere to watch out for General

Gage's advance guard, who had been sent along the access roads to prevent the passage of couriers carrying news of the coming British army. Devens himself had traveled the road earlier that evening and had encountered "ten British officers, all well mounted, & armed, going up the Road."[26]

By about eleven o'clock the air was "pleasant," according to Revere, and the moon was shining brightly.[27] He galloped north past Charlestown Neck toward the thinly inhabited moors and salt marshes of the Common. He noted with morbid interest the ghastly remains of the runaway slave "Mark," who had been executed twenty years earlier for the murder of his master and hung in chains as a hideous forewarning to any other slave contemplating similar acts of disloyalty.[28] He wondered, perhaps, of his own punishment should he be captured by the king's soldiers.

Just beyond Charlestown Common on a narrow in the road to Cambridge, Revere approached two soldiers on horseback beneath the moonlit shade of a tree. He was close enough to discern that they were British officers, and he nervously eyed their holsters and ornamental cockades. Instantly, the men divided; one broke toward Revere and the other galloped up the road to head off an escape. "One tried to git a head of Me," wrote Revere years later, "& the other to take me."[29]

With a heave of the reins Revere pulled his animal about and darted "upon a full gallop for Mistick Road."[30] For about three hundred yards a dramatic chase ensued; then in a desperate attempt to overtake Deacon Larkin's bold mare, the officer galloped beyond the road but quickly fell upon a clay pit. The remaining soldier quickly gave up the chase, and Revere continued back toward Charlestown Neck to the east and pushed for the Medford Road. Abandoning his earlier intended route toward Cambridge, he followed the Mystic River north and crossed into Medford at a flat timber bridge. There he awakened the captain of the local Minutemen, Isaac Hall, a distiller by trade, and then rode north to Cambridge and Menotomy, proclaiming the clarion call to arms that would one day propel him to enduring fame. "I alarmed almost every House, till I got to Lexington," Revere later recalled.[31]

At midnight the Jonas Clark house in Lexington was quiet. Inside, asleep, were the Clark family and their guests, Samuel Adams and John Hancock, as well as Hancock's fiancée, Dorothy Quincy, and his Aunt Lydia. The Clarks and Hancocks were cousins, and when the party had first arrived eleven days earlier, they thought the parsonage was appropriately removed from the dangers that lurked in Boston. Now, on hearing the news that a small patrol of the king's troops was "out upon some evil design," a guard of ten to twelve local militiamen was assembled to protect the house from harassment or attack.[32]

Suddenly the quiet of the night was broken as Paul Revere burst from the darkness and galloped upon the Clark house. The guardsmen tensed and hailed Revere as he loudly demanded admittance. Sergeant William Munroe, head of the protective company, did not recognize the visitor or his business and refused to let him pass. Sternly, Munroe insisted that the family had retired for the night and had requested "that they might not be disturbed by any noise about the house."[33]

"Noise!" shouted Revere. "You'll have noise enough before long. The regulars are coming out."[34] With that, Revere brushed past the sergeant and rapped solidly upon the door. Awakened by the commotion, Jonas Clark opened the bedroom window above and demanded the identity and business of the boisterous visitor.

"I wish to see Mr. Hancock!" shouted Revere.

Observing the lateness of the hour, Clark, "with his usual deliberation," resisted and inquired further of the man's errand, when John Hancock, who had peered through a first-story window, cried out with relief, "Come in, Revere; we are not afraid of *you*."[35]

The men hastened their greetings in the downstairs parlor, and Revere breathlessly reported that their problem went well beyond a small patrol of Redcoats harassing travelers on the road to Concord. He informed the gathering that, indeed, a full brigade of about twelve hundred to fifteen hundred Regulars had embarked in water transports from Boston and was now marching north from Cambridge.[36] "It was shrewdly suspected," continued Revere, "that [the troops] were ordered to seize and destroy the stores, belonging to the colony, then deposited at Concord."[37]

Hancock, dressed, no doubt, in a fine silk nightdress and slippers,[38] demanded to join his brethren and to take up arms against the British, but instead was quickly persuaded to move the families north to the town of Woburn for better security. "If I had my musket, I would never turn my back upon these troops," Hancock lamented.[39]

"That is not our business," Samuel Adams responded. "[W]e belong to the cabinet."[40]

As the Clark and Hancock families rushed about in preparation to leave the house, Revere inquired about William Dawes, the second courier sent by Joseph Warren, but was informed that he had not been heard from. Since Dawes had departed before Revere, it was immediately feared that he had been captured by the British patrols; however, half an hour later, Dawes arrived at the Clark house unharmed and corroborated the news that the Regulars were on the march.

The men refreshed themselves and then once again mounted their saddles. The village of Concord had received word several days earlier that it might be the target of the British march, and thus much of its munitions already had been hidden away. Revere and Dawes nonetheless decided to make their way to Concord with the news that the hour was at hand.

On April 18, a young and promising physician, Doctor Samuel Prescott, was keeping late hours courting his fiancée, Lydia Mulliken, in Lexington. As the British troops silently amassed at Phipps Farm on the Cambridge shore, Prescott was traveling back to his Concord dwelling, when he came upon Revere and Dawes charging through the night. Revere informed the doctor of their mission and alerted him to the British advance scouts that were patrolling the roads. Noting the high probability of capture, Revere declared that "we had better alarm all the Inhabitants till we [get] to Concord."[41]

Prescott enthusiastically volunteered to assist the men in their call of alarm, adding that he was well known in the area and that his participation would surely add credibility to their mission. Years later, Revere recalled young Prescott as a "high Son of Liberty."[42]

The men briskly made their way up the Great Road between Lexington and Concord pausing at each farm and homestead to arouse the inhabitants and urge that they likewise spread the alarm. About halfway between the two towns, as Dawes and Prescott approached a farmhouse in the village of Lincoln, Revere, who was riding about two hundred yards ahead, suddenly saw two figures in the moonlight. Assuming that he had stumbled upon an unfriendly patrol, he immediately gestured to his companions, thinking, perhaps, that they could overcome the two. Instantly, however, he found himself surrounded by four mounted British soldiers, angry and armed with pistols and swords.

"God Damn you! Stop!" shouted one of the men to Revere. "If you go an Inch farther you are a dead man."[43]

Prescott, seeing the commotion, galloped toward the men with the butt end of his horsewhip turned forward ready for attack, but he was unable to break through the line of mounted soldiers. The soldiers stopped him, and at pistol point, he and Revere were corralled into a nearby pasture and informed that if they didn't comply as ordered, "[the Regulars] would blow our brains out."[44]

With the British soldiers both in front of and behind them on horseback, Prescott spied an opening as they left the road and signaled to Revere to "put on!" Instantly, each rider spurred his horse and broke in opposite directions. The doctor, knowing the terrain well, jumped his nimble animal over a stone wall and sprinted hard through the darkness for Concord. Revere headed to the right, toward a forest at the bottom of the pasture, with the idea of leaving his horse and disappearing into the woods by foot. As he reached the tree line, however, six more British officers appeared on horseback and, with pistols pressed firmly against his chest, ordered Revere to surrender. The men seized his reins and, with little alternative, Revere somberly dismounted and conceded his capture.

As Revere and Prescott struggled with the British patrol, William Dawes made his own bid for escape. He shouted, "Haloo boys, I've got two of 'em," in a fruitless effort to divert the soldiers and then bolted down the road to a nearby farmhouse.[45] In the chaos of the moment, Dawes fell from his horse and watched helplessly as the animal disap-

peared into the night. He stumbled back to Lexington on foot, frightened and exhausted.[46]

It was past one o'clock in the morning before General Gage's force
finally was amassed on Lechmere Point, a quiet shore to the south of
Cambridge occupied by a single farmhouse. The logistics of the transport across the river had been poorly managed, and the men were forced
to mire in the cold swamps and tidal marshes surrounding their landing point. Many of the transports had run aground in the shallows of
the river, and the men were forced to walk through the icy water to the
shores. Soaked and chilled to the bone, about eight hundred British
grenadiers, light infantry, and marines finally began their trek to the
Charlestown and West Cambridge Road toward Menotomy and beyond.
"No martial sounds enlived their . . . march; it was silent, stealthy, inglori-
ous," said one historian.[47]

Meanwhile, in a pasture adjacent to the Great Road in the town of
Lincoln, several of the British patrol circled around Paul Revere in a
menacing formation, taunting and abusing him with their horses and
swords. One of the officers—"much of a Gentleman," according to Revere—told him not to be afraid, that his soldiers would not harm him.
Revere indignantly replied that the men would "miss their aim" if they
made any such attempt.[48]

The officer then began questioning his prisoner. Was he an express?
From where had he come? What time had he left?—and Revere answered every question honestly and unafraid.

"Sir, may I crave your name?" the officer asked.

"Revere."

"*Paul* Revere?"

"Yes." Revere was a well-known messenger of Rebel news and proc-
lamations among the various colonies, and his name, familiar to the soldiers, evoked further anger among them. The "gentleman" officer again
reassured his prisoner that he would not be harmed and insisted that
the men were only on a mission to apprehend deserters in the area. Revere scoffed at the notion and stated that he had, in fact, alarmed the

entire countryside of the coming British excursion. "I should have 500 men [here] soon," he warned.

The officer peered suspiciously at his captive and, apparently alarmed by the claim of coming reinforcements, galloped down the road to alert the remaining patrol. Moments later, the entire band rushed back led by their commander, Major Edward Mitchell. Greatly agitated, Mitchell placed his pistol to Revere's head and informed him that he intended to ask some questions and that if he did not receive truthful answers "he would blow [Revere's] brains out." "I esteemed myself a Man of truth," Revere later recorded. "[H]e had stopped me on the high way, & made me a prisoner, I knew not by what right; I would tell him the truth; I was not afraid."

The questions were similar to what had already been asked, and Revere answered them plainly, but the officers were now clearly worried about the prospect of Rebel patrols. They searched Revere for arms and ordered him, and several other prisoners that had been taken through the night, to mount their horses. "We are now going toward your friends," Major Mitchell hissed. "[I]f you attempt to run, or we are insulted, we will blow your Brains out." Revere impassively told him to do as he pleased.

The soldiers formed a menacing circle around their prisoners and positioned Revere in front, without reins, to prevent any thought of escape. They rode briskly toward Lexington and abusively harassed Revere as they traveled. One officer informed Revere that he was "in a damned critical situation."

About half a mile from Lexington Green, the grassy triangular center of town, the men were startled by the sound of a musket shot in the distance. Major Mitchell turned to Revere and angrily demanded an explanation. Revere inflamed the major's already heightened sensibilities by insisting that it was a signal to "alarm the country"—and, in fact, it may have been.

Sensing a volatile situation, the officers hastily convened and determined that they must quicken their pace. They ordered their several prisoners—except Revere—to dismount. The prisoners' horses were driven away into the darkness, and the men were freed on foot. Revere requested that he likewise be set free, but the major refused.

Several moments later, the men heard a full barrage of musket fire coming from the direction of the Lexington Meetinghouse at the southeastern corner of the Green, and the officers became greatly alarmed. Soon the Lexington town bells began to toll, and it was clear to all that General Gage's plan of secrecy had failed. The widespread British belief that the Rebels "are but a mere mob, without order or discipline,"[49] had been shattered as the men of Lexington gathered themselves for battle.

Major Mitchell was now determined to warn the approaching British army of the lurking danger of Rebel resistance. He asked Revere the distance to Cambridge and what the appropriate route would be. He then turned to one of his men and inquired if his horse, smaller than the rest, was fatigued. Hearing that it was, Mitchell ordered Revere to dismount and turn his horse over to the soldier. The men then quickly rushed back toward Cambridge, leaving Revere and the other prisoners alone and disoriented on the muddy road.

The alarm that Paul Revere had set into motion now spread throughout the countryside. His journey had covered nearly thirteen miles, and by the early morning hours of April 19, as he toiled in British captivity, many other riders picked up the mantle and warned the colony of the Redcoat march.[50]

By two o'clock in the morning, the local militia, under the command of Captain John Parker, began to assemble on Lexington Green. "Capt. Parker ordered the roll to be called, and every man to charge his gun with powder and ball."[51] A series of inconsistent reports flowed into the town, and upon one rider's insistence that the British were, in fact, *not* marching, Parker dismissed the gathered militia but ordered them to be "within call of the drum."[52]

With spurs and bulky riding boots making travel by foot difficult at best, Paul Revere hobbled through the darkness back toward the Clark house just to the north of the Lexington Green. He crossed several pastures and a Lexington burial ground, and sometime after three o'clock in the morning, he arrived at the parsonage, dismayed to find the house in a state of confusion with Hancock and Adams still arguing among themselves about what action to take. Elizabeth Clark, Reverend Clark's twelve-year-old daughter, later recalled the sight of, "Aunt Hancock and Dolly Quincy, with their cloaks and bonnets on, Aunt crying and wringing her hands and helping mother dress the children, Dolly going round with Father to hide money, watches and anything down to the potatoes and up in the garrett."[53] And Dorothy Quincy, Hancock's fiancée, later recorded, "Mr. H. was all night cleaning his gun and sword, and putting his accoutrements in order."[54]

Amid this chaotic scene, Revere informed the group of his detainment by the British patrol and warned them not to further delay their departure. After much haranguing, Hancock was persuaded that his service to the country as a statesman was of greater value than that of soldier, and as the first faint light of dawn appeared, Revere and John Lowell, Hancock's clerk, escorted Adams and Hancock north toward Woburn.

Meanwhile, the British expedition moved briskly and silently toward Lexington. As Revere dealt with the turmoil at the Clark house, Major Edward Mitchell, who earlier held his pistol to Paul Revere's head, now galloped with his men toward the body of advancing British troops. On arrival he breathlessly revealed that the entire countryside had already received warning of their mission and that his men earlier had captured the well-known emissary Paul Revere, who informed them of some five hundred Rebel soldiers waiting at Lexington. Colonel Smith immediately sent a request for reinforcements to General Gage, and he dispatched six companies of light infantry—about 250 men—under the command of Major John Pitcairn as an advance force to capture the bridges of Concord.

After journeying with his wards for about two miles, Revere was confident that they were safely on their way, and he and John Lowell stepped off the coach and bid Hancock and Adams farewell. Resting for a short while, the men made haste back to Lexington "to enquire the news."[55]

As Major Pitcairn rushed forward in advance of the main army, he successfully apprehended nearly every Rebel scout on the road. The Lexington militia was, accordingly, unaware that Pitcairn's six companies were closing fast upon them. Finally, with the advancing British troops less than two miles from the Green, definitive word came of their approach; and at about five o'clock in the morning, Captain Parker ordered "the drum to beat, alarm to be fired, and Sergeant William Munroe [the same Munroe who had earlier protected Hancock and Adams] to form his company in two ranks a few rods north of the meeting-house."[56] No more than seventy militiamen were arrayed on the Green.

As they approached Lexington, John Lowell informed Revere that Hancock had left a trunk filled with extremely important—and incriminating—documents pertaining to the provincial government and the Rebel cause in the attic of Buckman's Tavern, adjacent to the meeting-house on Lexington Green. The men agreed that the trunk was of sufficient importance to keep it from British eyes. "Mr. Lowell & myself went towards the Tavern, when we met a Man on a full gallop, who told us the Troops were coming up the Rocks," Revere later wrote.[57]

The two men dashed across Lexington Green to Buckman's Tavern and climbed to an upper floor where the trunk rested. As they contemplated how best to remove the heavy chest, Revere glanced out the chamber window into the pale flush of dawn and saw "the orderly scarlet ranks of marching grenadiers . . ."[58] approaching in the distance.

As he approached the Green with his men, Major Pitcairn heard the rallying cadence of the Lexington drums and correctly regarded it as a provocative call to arms. He ordered his Regulars to halt their march, prime and load their muskets, and then charge at the "double-quick" toward the Green.[59]

Meanwhile, Revere and Lowell painstakingly lowered the heavy trunk down the stairs of Buckman's Tavern and awkwardly made their way across Lexington Green, where Captain Parker's anxious militiamen stood at the ready. As the two men passed seemingly without notice through the lines of grim-faced brothers, cousins, fathers, and sons, Revere heard Captain Parker sternly instruct his heavily outnumbered men, "Let the troops pass by, and don't molest them, with out [they] being first."[60]

As the Regulars approached, a British officer, most probably Pitcairn, galloped forward with pistol in hand, and reportedly demanded, "Ye villains, ye Rebels, disperse; Damn you, disperse!"[61] Captain Parker ordered his men to withdraw, and in doing so a rush of confusion ensued.

Paul Revere made his way across Lexington Green, laboring hard with Hancock's trunk, when he heard the report of a gun firing. He turned back and saw a pall of gray smoke in front of the Regulars. "[T]hey immediately gave a great shout, ran a few paces, and then the whole fired," he would record.[62] A Bostonian later wrote to a friend, "The shots at Lexington alarmed the country so, that it seemed as if men came down from the clouds."[63]

Paul Revere hurried away, doggedly lugging Hancock's trunk into the nearby woods. He continued this task "with that simple absorption in what was to be done at the moment which characterizes the whole man. Embattled farmers might stand and shots fired that would be heard round the world," wrote Ester Forbes.

"He gave them one glance and went on with his job."[64]

Chapter 4   *Seeds of Discontent*

As THE WARY and tattered British regiments reeled east from Concord and Lexington, an alarmed and agitated countryside watched their every step and laid ambush from stone walls, trees, and fences. "The 'promenade' to Concord had been a ghastly failure," wrote Esther Forbes. "Gage had lost one in nine of the number he had sent out."[1]

With the first shots of the American Revolution, the Whig leaders of Boston fled to the surrounding towns and villages, while Tories and British Loyalists poured into Boston in droves and faithfully submitted to the authority of General Gage. Immediately following his return from Lexington, Revere met with Joseph Warren at the Jonathan Hastings House in Cambridge. Warren was then serving as president of the Committee of Safety, an organization that launched and coordinated the military and propaganda response to British aggressions. Warren engaged Revere "to do the out of doors business"[2] for the committee and prudently avoid the Town of Boston and the watchful eyes of British officials. He initially stayed in Charlestown and sent for Rachel and the children to join him, with the exception of his fifteen-year-old son, Paul Jr., who would stay and look after the family house. "It is now in your power to be serviceable to me, your mother and yourself," Revere wrote to the boy.[3]

Aware that most of his time would now be devoted to service of country, Revere's role as messenger for the Committee of Safety would become as much a commercial enterprise as it was a display of patriotism. As early as December 1773, following the Boston Tea Party, Revere was asked to courier messages throughout Massachusetts and beyond, and he promptly began submitting bills of five shillings per day for services rendered to the colony. Though no evidence exists that he ever charged a fee for his ride to Lexington on the night of April 18–19, he did submit bills for all future official trips. If the committee was going to call on him to neglect his prosperous business in favor of public service, Revere would insist that he be paid for it. Interestingly, Revere's daily rate was deemed excessive by the committee and promptly reduced to four shillings.[4]

With the authorities in Boston under General Gage heated and unfriendly to Whig leaders, the Massachusetts Provincial Congress reconvened at the meetinghouse at the corner of Common and Mill Streets (now Mount Auburn Street) in nearby Watertown, which for a period of time served as the capital of the Patriot effort in the colony. Here Dr. Warren worked tirelessly to coordinate the government in Massachusetts and to raise an army to defend it, while Hancock and both Adams served as Massachusetts delegates to the First Continental Congress, convened at Carpenter's Hall in Philadelphia in September, as a first response to the Intolerable Acts.

Warren constantly called on his friend Revere, and others, to summon legislative meetings and to deliver messages to Congress, but it was during this period that Revere served the colony and his country in another equally important way. With little financial means to pay for a growing local and federal army, both Massachusetts and the Continental Congress in Philadelphia commissioned him to engrave plates for the printing of notes. Practically worthless on its face, this "paste-board currency of the rebels,"[5] as the British called it because of the absurd thickness of the paper, was seen as an absolute necessity in a time of a dwindling public treasury. Again, however, an audit committee of the Provincial Congress questioned Revere's bill for services rendered and subsequently reduced it as excessive. "[T]he Committee of the House ordered the paper to be made & did not agree for the price," he wrote.[6]

While General Gage solidified his defenses in Boston with the arrest of known and remaining Whig activists, the confiscation of weapons, and the limitation of travel out of the town except via a "pass," Revere watched with mounting resentment as the Provincial Congress of Massachusetts pondered the selection of officers to lead the revolutionary forces and to oversee an eventual attack on the occupying army in Boston. Two veterans of the Seven Years' War, Richard Gridley and William Burbeck, both tested and able artillerymen, were appointed as chief engineers of a newly raised artillery regiment and, along with the members of the Provincial Congress, were charged with the task of selecting military officers for the defense of the American continent. Though Revere had served with Gridley during the Crown Point expedition of 1756, and though Gridley and Burbeck were both fellow Masonic brothers, neither man chose Revere to serve in the vaunted position of army officer.

Despite Revere's indispensable service to Massachusetts and the country at large, with a growing sense of personal frustration he would find himself consistently bypassed for the prominent and coveted role of an officer in the Continental Army, even as friends and acquaintances received such appointments. His dissatisfaction about the perceived snub was unmistakable. "I did expect . . . to have been in the Continental Army," he wrote to his friend John Lamb in April of 1777.[7] Samuel Adams would later chide Revere for his display of ambition: "We are contending, not for Glory, but for Liberty Safety & Happiness of our country," Adams wrote.[8]

During this period Revere would be described by historians as conscientious, intelligent, and resourceful.[9] He was an active member of the Sons of Liberty and had courageously participated in nearly every critical phase in the lead-up to the American Revolution; yet despite this proven record of loyal patriotism, members of the Massachusetts Provincial Congress and the Continental Congress viewed him, perhaps, as lacking in the attributes required of a Continental officer. At the time, the process of making military appointments was often fraught with politics and nepotism, and Revere had not attained the level of education, wealth, and the status of a "gentleman" deemed necessary for positions of military leadership by General Washington and others in command.[10] His military service in the Seven Years' War was unremarkable; and though he had exhibited courage and agility as a mounted courier spreading word of the Crown's tyranny, there is no record of Revere reaching for a musket at Lexington to oppose the coming Redcoats as others had, nor of him heeding the call to arms on June 16, 1775, on Breeds Hill, where his friend Dr. Warren heroically would lose his life. "Paul Revere was a good many things," wrote Forbes, "but not a soldier."[11]

Had he burned with an eager desire to fight for the independence of his country, Revere could easily have volunteered in any number of local regiments that were raised around Boston in the spring and summer of 1775.[12] There is no indication that he did so. He may have learned through his limited military experience just enough to realize that life as an enlisted foot soldier was not for him. His eyes were, nonetheless, fixed on the prospect of a high-status post as an officer in the Continental Army.

An earlier rift with William Burbeck also may have alienated Revere from his Masonic brother and possibly blocked an appointment in Gridley's prestigious artillery company.

In 1764 the two men were involved in a complicated set of transactions centered on the purchase of the Green Dragon Tavern by St. Andrew's Lodge for its use as a Masonic meeting place. The title was taken in Burbeck's name on behalf of St. Andrew's, and he agreed to advance all costs and expenses of the lodge for a ten-year period, after which time he would reconvey the property and be reimbursed for his expenditures.[13] At some point during his ownership, however, Burbeck apparently felt insecure in his investment, and he unilaterally seized possession of the St. Andrew's charter and held it at Castle Island, where he served at the time as keeper of the ordnance. Burbeck may have taken his action less for his own personal benefit than as a tool to shield the lodge from the zealous political leanings of Paul Revere, who he feared would seek the partition of St. Andrew's from its parent, the Grand Lodge of Scotland, as the percolating revolution came to life.[14] Whatever the cause, Burbeck still refused to relinquish the document even after he was repaid the monies due to him.

Revere became the point man in the lodge's quest for its charter and repeatedly warned his fellow Mason of the consequences of continued defiance. Finally, on May 13, 1773, Burbeck was suspended from the lodge until such time as he could provide satisfactory reasons for detention of the charter. None were given, and it would be forty years before the charter was finally returned to the lodge.[15] The rift between Revere and

Burbeck, however, would stifle Revere's military career and, in coming years, impact his reputation throughout Boston.

Despite the influence of John Adams, Samuel Adams, and James Warren in matters of military appointments, there appears to have been little they could do for Paul Revere. Even as several of his contemporaries received (and sometimes turned down) commissions in the federal army, General Washington and the Continental Congress had many other capable names from which to choose, and the ambitious Revere simply did not carry the military clout and political weight required for serious consideration. Though he was unquestionably "a person in good Circumstances . . . [having] many friends at Boston and other places on the Continent,"[16] as his cousin John Rivoire observed in 1775, Revere would be "obliged to be contented" with local service to the Town of Boston and the Colony of Massachusetts during the Revolution, leaving the enviable Continental Army commissions to his friends and acquaintances.[17]

On April 10, 1776, Revere finally received a commission as a major with the Massachusetts State's Train, a local militia regiment consisting of ten companies formed for the defense of Boston and its harbor. His assumptions about the lack of prestige of the local militias, however, were quickly validated. Though he would swiftly rise to the position of lieutenant colonel—a rank he would hold for the duration of the war and a title he would use for the rest of his life—Revere soon would find himself stationed with the train of artillery, amid the familiar isolation of Castle Island. The post was a far cry from the vaunted status of an officer in the Continental Army.

Working under the command of Colonel Thomas Crafts Jr., with whom he had served as an ardent member of the Sons of Liberty, Revere adjusted to his diminished role in the service to his country. He drilled his troops as a forward defense of Boston in the event of attack, and he duly showed the colors and fired salutes to passing ships of war. He endlessly marched and exercised his men and, on occasion, readied the fort to receive prisoners. He presided over numerous courts-martial for deserters and others engaged in such egregious offenses as drunkenness and playing cards on the Sabbath,[18] yet he humanely issued pardons as often as he doled out the punishment of "Lashes on . . . [the] Naked Back with a Cat of Nine Tails."[19] Revere maintained a tidy and disciplined regiment with officers, gunners, and matrosses (artillery soldiers who assisted the gunners) dressed clean and powdered, and on July 4, 1777, the first anniversary of the signing of the Declaration of Independence, he fired the island cannon and prepared his men for a parade to Fort Hill in a "Grand Salute."[20] In short, life at Castle Island proved repetitive and uneventful. The ennui of the tedious routine and lack of military engagement ultimately would make it difficult for Revere to maintain order and make his duties as company officer frustrating and often confrontational.

With General Howe's army vanquished from Boston and the focus of British operations turned south to New York and Rhode Island, the interest and dedication of Revere's men continued to wane. The laurels of war seemed to pass Revere's company by, and boredom and discouragement permeated its ranks. "Non Commissioned Officers and Matrosses have almost lost every Idea of Military Subordination and Discipline, and . . . many of them Totally Neglect their Duty and make the miserable Plea of Forgetfulness there [*sic*] Excuse,"[21] complained Colonel Crafts.

❦ By June of 1777 General John Burgoyne had led the British army south from Canada seizing Fort Ticonderoga in pursuit of his plan to split off New England from the rest of the colonies. As the summer progressed, Burgoyne began to meet heavy colonial resistance; and on August 16 General John Stark and his militia unit of some two thousand men from New Hampshire, Massachusetts, and Vermont routed one of Burgoyne's detachments near Bennington, taking nearly seven hundred prisoners. The victory was absolute and its significance to colonial forces overwhelming. The "steam roller"[22] Burgoyne had, at last, been stalled. To Paul Revere and his men, however, the American triumph finally would provide an opportunity to assume a more useful role—minor as it may have been—outside of Castle Island.

On August 27, "five Drums & five fifes, one Hundred & twenty Sergeants, Corporals, Bombardiers, Gunners & Matrosses,"[23] all under the command of Lieutenant Colonel Paul Revere, were ordered to march for Worcester to take custody of the British prisoners who had been captured in the Battle of Bennington. At the commencement of the expedition, Revere admonished his men, "As Strict Discipline, and Good Order is the life & Soul of a Soldier, the Lieutenant Colonel expects that there will be the best Order observed on the March . . ."[24] Despite the fanfare of Revere's orders, the greatest challenge that he faced on the mission still appeared to be containing the overly exuberant conduct of his men, who were only too happy to escape the monotony of daily life at Castle Island.

Once arrived in Worcester, Revere and his men quartered at the county courthouse and, four days later, took possession of Burgoyne's captured troops, comprised of mostly Hessians, and escorted them back to Boston without incident.

The following month, Colonel Thomas Crafts issued orders to Revere and his artillery regiment to take part in what would be the first futile attempt to dislodge the British from Newport, Rhode Island. With the British occupying New York and parts of Rhode Island, there was a continual danger of attack on Boston from the south, and this effort to dislodge the enemy was welcome news to Massachusetts — and perhaps even more welcome to Revere and his men, who yearned for an opportunity to engage the enemy.

On September 27, the artillery regiment began its trek to Newport and by the first few days of October was stationed about four miles from the enemy readying itself for battle. General Joseph Spencer, chosen by Washington to command the mission, faltered when violent weather and a change in British defenses delayed the attack. As the morale of the troops began to wane in the coming days, Spencer abandoned the attempt. The "secret expedition,"[25] as Colonel Crafts described the mission of his artillery regiment in Newport, encountered no enemy hostilities and returned safely to Boston without a serious conflict or casualty.[26] On November 3, however, ignoring the futility of the effort, Crafts issued compliments to Revere and his men for "their extraordinary Military & Soldier-like behavior on the Rhode . . ."[27]

With the Revolutionary War being waged seemingly in his absence, Revere felt sadly removed from the march of the new nation. The Continental Army fought at Trenton, Brandywine, Germantown, and Stillwater, and General Washington at first floundered and then regrouped at Valley Forge. The momentous American victory at Saratoga in October of 1777, and the resulting surrender of General Burgoyne, would seal the alliance with France, and soon Boston would be protected by new French fortifications at Hull, relegating Castle Island to near obsolete status.[28] Revere eventually would be appointed full commander of Castle Island and, from time to time, Hull, Long Island, and Governor's Island, with responsibility for an ever-discontented company of men.[29]

Nearly a year after the first failed attempt to dispossess the British of their positions at Newport, George Washington once again turned his attention to the island stronghold. General John Sullivan, joined by an armada of French warships, attacked the enemy in a joint naval and land assault that would mark America's initial act of military cooperation with France in the Revolutionary War. The call would go forth throughout New England to man the campaign at Newport, and Revere's artillery regiment once again would return south to assist in the battle. "You have heard this Island is the Garden of America," he wrote to his wife Rachel. "[B]ut those British savages have so abused and destroyed the Trees . . . that it does not look like the same Island."[30]

Initial optimism over the siege of Newport was high. Sergeant Major William Russell of Revere's regiment wrote, "We have almost surrounded the Enemy by Land, and the French by Water . . . In a few days by the Blessing of God we shall be in Newport and Masters of it."[31] On August 12, however, a gale brewed over the Atlantic—"the most severe N. East Storm I ever knew,"[32] wrote Revere—frustrating the plans and maneuvers on both sides of the conflict. The French fleet would retreat to Boston, and the second Newport campaign would end in confusion and failure, again with little opportunity for Revere or his men to confront and engage the enemy.

By the winter of 1778–79, British operations had turned to the southern states in an effort to create new bases from which the rebellion in the north could be quelled. With the surrender of Burgoyne the previous year, the situation in and around New York had deteriorated into a standoff of surgical raids and petty attacks, which were carried out by both sides to little advantage.

In Boston, circumstances for Revere and his men continued to be uneventful and difficult. They were short on provisions and blankets, and pay was sporadic. Poor conditions and lack of meaningful activity often led to petty squabbles and desertions, and Revere petitioned the Massachusetts Council for assistance. The previous summer Thomas Harrison, a soldier in an adjoining regiment, had been found guilty of "the Agravated Crime of Desertion" and was sentenced to be shot to death. Even as the roar of musket fire signaling Harrison's execution echoed through Castle Island, General William Heath, in charge of the Continental Army in Massachusetts, admonished all the local militia units to "learn from this example" that such a crime "will not escape a punishment Adequate to the Infamy of the Offence . . ."[33]

As the tension and tedium among the men at Castle Island steadily increased, Revere began to intensify his grip of authority on the garrison. Despite the harsh treatment of regimental deserters, the lure of Continental service and the lucrative bounty of privateering proved too much of a temptation for many of his men.

In March of 1779, fifteen of the train's enlistees boarded, without authorization, the frigates *Providence* and *Boston* moored in the harbor. The ships' commanders had actively recruited from the ranks of the Castle Island artillery regiment, and Revere had been justifiably angered by their brazen enticement of his men. Upon the failure of the captains to relinquish his men on demand, Revere sent a dispatch to the Massachusetts Council prudently seeking legal assistance. "I lay these matters before Your Honors, hoping something may be done . . . ," he wrote. "For it is in vain for us to Recruit men, if the Marine Officers may take them from us."[34] Immediately, the Council ordered the return of the deserters to Castle Island and instructed Revere to prevent the passage of the ships until the men were duly surrendered.

In the coming days, the tensions escalated, and the *Providence* finally approached the island. Revere, shouting through a bullhorn, ordered his men to alight the ship. When only ten of the fifteen acquiesced, and after a heated exchange between Revere and the ship's officers, Revere ordered the Castle Island cannon to fire upon the *Providence*. The remaining five men quickly rowed ashore, but the event served only to anger the regiment and heighten already tense feelings toward the commander. It was now clearly understood that Paul Revere was a man who would not hesitate to fire even on American ships in the interest of preserving order and decorum.[35]

🐛 By early 1779, the Castle Island artillery regiment had become neglected and relatively depleted. With provisions scarce and pay sporadic, the lure of Continental service and the profits of privateering led to rampant desertions, and soon the Massachusetts House ordered a reduction of the regiment to three companies. With the resulting diminished need for regimental officers, several of the commanders, including Captain William Todd, Captain Winthrop Gray, Lieutenant John Marston, and even Colonel Thomas Crafts himself, all of whom served with Revere in the state militia, offered their resignations by petition to the Council. Revere, however, refused to join in the petition. Though perhaps meant as an admirable assumption of patriotic duty in the face of a restructured force, his rivals viewed his unwillingness to relinquish control, while others had, as a sign of selfish ambition.[36]

The malevolent feelings of some militia commanders toward Revere after the reduction of the artillery unit would quickly result in an angry rejoinder. William Todd and Winthrop Gray, both infuriated over Revere's unwillingness to relinquish his command as they had, called on General Artemas Ward, who was serving at the time on the executive council of the Massachusetts General Court. Todd and Gray bitterly complained about Revere; and then, in a private room of the legislative chamber, Todd informed Ward that Revere on occasion had drawn rations at Castle Island for thirty more men than were present and posted in the regiment and that the charges could be easily proven. The implication, of course, was that Revere had appropriated these rations for his own use and profit.

Several days later, Revere was served with an order to appear before the Council to answer to a petition signed by Todd, Gray, and others that formalized their allegations. "I appeared at the appointed time and they never produced a single article against me," Revere bitterly recalled. "Ever since they have done everything in their power to hurt me, by insinuations: Though none of them ever charged me to my face."[37]

Those charges would not be long in coming.

Chapter 5 New Ireland

HE WOULD LIVE to the age of 101 and become the oldest living New England veteran of the American Revolution. Seventy-five years after the event, however, William Hutchings still recalled the British landing on Majabigwaduce as if it were yesterday. The disquieting sight of His Majesty's fleet silently advancing through the vast inlets of Penobscot Bay had been seared into his memory like a childhood trauma. Hutchings, a mere teenage boy in 1779, had lived in the coastal Maine village of Majabigwaduce nearly his entire life and had been fishing with his uncle on the morning of June 16 when the approaching spectacle came into sight. "There comes the devils," the old man sneered.[1]

Five square-rigged ships of war escorting an equal number of naval transports manned by 650 of the king's troops cast anchor off Dyce's Head, a steep and heavily wooded elevation on the western shores of Majabigwaduce, and a small party of advance scouts rowed through a heavy rain and choppy seas to the rocky beach below. Hutchings watched with puzzlement as the unopposed team made their surreptitious approach. "They seemed as frightened as a flock of sheep, and kept looking around them as if they expected to be fired on by an enemy hid behind the trees," recalled Hutchings.[2] For the next three days the British would reconnoiter the area for the ideal site on which to construct their coastal fortress.

The British plan to establish an eastward post in the Province of Maine found its roots with an eccentric Loyalist carpenter from Massachusetts by the name of John Nutting. A land speculator and shrewd political mover in circles of the British government, Nutting laid claim to various territories east of the Penobscot River and, "with a fine mixture of self-interest and loyalty,"[3] steadily petitioned those in power to secure his titles and maximize his profits with the occupying British force.[4] Nutting, along with John Calef, a Boston-area physician and leading Tory with similar interests in the Penobscot Bay region, whom Paul Revere had unflatteringly depicted with a calf's head in his engraving *A Warm Place—Hell*, counseled and curried favor with the office of the secretary of state for colonial affairs. Soon, both men and their cause found a friendly ear with William Knox, undersecretary to Lord George Germain.

Though Germain initially was cool to the plan, Knox gently apprised the diplomat of the compelling reasons for a British presence on the coast of Maine. The ongoing problem of New England privateers that had pirated British shipping for years could finally be curtailed, argued Knox, and the abundant timber of Maine, the lifeblood of Yankee shipbuilders, could finally be denied to the Rebels.[5] A protective force much closer than the existing base at Halifax would help to defend the Bay of Fundy, Nova Scotia, and southern Canada from Rebel attack; and a reinforcement of the existing blockade of New England, Knox posited, would create the foundation for a burgeoning new province to which a growing stream of Loyalist refugees would flock in search of a peaceful new homeland. The envisaged provincial settlement was to be named "New Ireland," in a nod, perhaps, to William Knox's own nationality.[6]

Several possible locations, including Falmouth, Great Deer Island, and Townsend, initially were considered for the post,[7] but with the "Yankee shrewdness and eloquence"[8] of Nutting and Calef, the geologic and strategic benefits of the lands surrounding Penobscot Bay were quickly identified and the choice was made clear.

On September 2, 1778, Lord Germain dispatched Nutting with a message to General Henry Clinton, the British commander in chief for North America: "Provision to be made for loyalists by erecting a province between the Penobscot and St. Croix rivers. Post to be taken in Penobscot River."[9]

 "Glad to hear Nova Scotia is still tranquil," began Henry Clinton in a "most secret" communiqué to Brigadier General Francis McLean in early 1779.[10] Original dispatches regarding the contemplated post at Penobscot had been destroyed reluctantly by John Nutting when his transport ship, the *Harriet*, was intercepted by an American brigantine in the fall of 1778, and plans for the campaign were, consequently, slow to evolve. Now, as details of the strategy began to take shape, Clinton informed General McLean, who was then the military governor at Halifax, of his coming role as commander in the nascent operation. "Erect a fort on Penobscot River . . . prepare materials for a respectable work capable of containing 3 or 400 men," directed Clinton.[11]

A sixty-two-year-old bachelor of Scottish decent, McLean had dedicated nearly his entire life to military service. Early on he had served in the Netherlands in a Scottish regiment commanded by his father and quickly gained a reputation for valor and battlefield prowess. In 1747, during the War of the Austrian Succession, he was present at the bitter two-month siege of Bergen-op-Zoom, which ended in a fierce storm of French grenadiers who besieged the city and overcame the Dutch and their allies. McLean's regiment, clothed in woolen kilts and red mosaic knee socks, fought valiantly to repel the French onslaught; but as the city fell and most of the Scots retreated, the young lieutenant and his cousin were taken prisoner and brought to the feet of the victorious French general, Lowendahl. "Gentlemen, consider yourself on parole," the general bellowed with a wide grin. "If all had conducted themselves as you and your brave corps have done, I should not now be master of Bergen-op-Zoom."[12]

Upon his return to Scotland, McLean was promoted to the rank of captain and took command of the Forty-second Royal Highlanders Regiment, also known as the Black Watch.[13] He was gravely wounded at the invasion of Guadeloupe during the Seven Years' War, and after his recovery, was appointed governor of the island of Marie-Galante. During the attack on Belle Isle off the coast of France, his right arm was severely injured by enemy fire, and he was taken prisoner. Upon his ultimate release and return to England in a prisoner exchange, McLean once again would rise in reputation and military stature, gaining a promotion in

rank to lieutenant colonel. After assisting the Portuguese to repel an attack of the French and Spanish in 1762, he was selected as commander of
Almeida, an outpost on the borderlands of Spain, and ultimately served
in the local government of Lisbon. Throughout his demonstrative career,
McLean fought bravely in no less than nineteen military engagements on
multiple continents and would gain the reputation as an agile, yet good-
natured warrior with a potent understanding of political structures and
administrative control.[14]

In 1778 McLean again returned to Great Britain, and as a result of his
well-respected governmental service, he promptly was appointed to the
role of governor of Nova Scotia in an effort to manage a growing tide
of fleeing Loyalists.[15] When news of the coming post along the Penobscot River reached General McLean, he met it with a degree of pensive
ambivalence. "He might have an enormous success at Penobscot," wrote
historian Charles Bracelen Flood. "On the other hand, a man of his vast
experience had only to look at the map, to see that he was going to set
up an isolated post where he might be captured, along with every man
of his force."[16]

McLean's landing off the shores of Majabigwaduce as witnessed by
young William Hutchings was followed by a flurry of activity between
seafaring vessels and land in the days to come. A flotilla of rowboats
ferried soldiers and supplies to the rocky beaches, and temporary en-
campments on the northeast ridge slowly took shape. The harbor of
Penobscot Bay itself was "spacious & capable of containing all the Navy
of the World," wrote one marine officer.[17]

Majabigwaduce, the site of present-day Castine, variously known
since the seventeenth century as Pentagoet, Penobscot, and the Bagaduce Peninsula,[18] consisted of a small jut of land connected to a larger
peninsula by a narrow marshy isthmus that, like Boston Neck, often
would flood during high tides and rainy periods, converting the angular
"hump of granite-sprinkled lava"[19] into an island. Majabigwaduce extended into the bay at the mouth of the Penobscot and Majabigwaduce
Rivers and rose steeply on the west in a precipitous cliff of earth and
trees that then sloped off an additional three hundred feet to a thickly

wooded and level highland. The north and southeast rises of Majabigwaduce were gradual compared to the west; and on the southern inclines of
the peninsula, farms and paddocks of various settlers dotted the slopes
toward the shore. The topographic features of this seaward outcrop of
land offered sweeping and tactical vantages of the bay below and the
vital protective cover of natural barriers.[20] McLean ordered his fort to
be constructed on the summit of Majabigwaduce, a slog of more than a
quarter mile from the closest harbor shore.[21]

As part of his noble (if not infamous) service to the Crown, John
Nutting wangled employment "as overseer of the carpenters who are to
rebuild the Fort at Penobscot."[22] The original fort constructed by the
French had been abandoned in ruins around 1680 and had been the last
incarnation of defense in a long and bloody string of battles for the possession of Majabigwaduce. McLean's engineers decided to disregard the
silhouette of the ancient fort and elected to construct an entirely new
redoubt in a nearby location.

From the start, the British faced great difficulty in establishing their
Majabigwaduce post. The entire peninsula was heavily wooded, and the
area designated for the intended fort required clearing and preparation
before construction could begin. The engineering stores, artillery, and
provisions for the troops had to be manually rolled up the steep inclines
to the plateau above, and a solid defense of the works had to be maintained at all times against the possibility of Rebel attack.[23] The original
plans for the fort laid out by the British engineers proved defective in design, and John Nutting, as master carpenter, was forced to alter the plans.
It would be July 2 before the actual lines of the garrison were staked and
construction could begin.[24]

The adversity and laborious hardships endured by McLean's men in
the landing on Majabigwaduce and their preparation of the site for construction immediately placed them in a position of disadvantage. As one
British officer lamented, "Let any one conversant in Matters of this Nature, reflect what a work it was for 700 men, And he will also readily
allow, that in the Course of it they could not possibly, whether from
fatigue, or in point of Necessary Preparation be in Condition of repell-
ing any powerful attack."[25]

McLean's military force, charged with the task of establishing the fort at Majabigwaduce and then holding it, was composed primarily of soldiers from two separate units. Four hundred and fifty were kilted Scotsmen drawn from the Seventy-fourth Regiment of Foot, "The Argyll Highlanders," organized by John Campbell of Barbreck, whose clan of twenty-three cousins—all named Campbell—manned the unit's officer corps. Another two hundred men were taken from the Eighty-second Regiment of Foot, "The Hamilton Regiment," a division from the Scottish lowland raised by the Duke of Hamilton. And finally, a company of fifty English engineers and artillerymen rounded out McLean's body of manpower.[26]

As valuable to McLean as his serviceable military force was, his prized asset on Majabigwaduce was, perhaps, his naval commander, Captain Henry Mowat. Being an "utter stranger" to the shores of Maine,[27] McLean would rely heavily on a detailed set of maps and charts compiled for the British Admiralty by the renowned cartographer J.F.W. Des Barres and on Captain Mowat's extensive experience in the area to plot strategy and to gain an understanding of the populace. "[M]y ideas are chiefly founded on his intelligence and knowledge of the country," McLean wrote to General Clinton.[28] To the people of Maine, however, Mowat was spoken of only with "detestable memory."[29]

The forty-five-year-old Mowat, also born in Scotland, joined the Royal Navy in 1752. His journeys around the New England coast began prior to the Revolution as a maritime sentry aboard the HMS *Canceaux*, thwarting foreign smugglers. In May of 1775, as hostilities with the colonies began to escalate into war, he was taken prisoner by a band of local militia in Falmouth, Maine. After a strenuous split of opinion among the citizens of the town, most of whom had not yet felt the zeal of rebellion, he was released on a solemn promise to return the following morning—a promise Mowat failed to keep. Several months later, the vigorous and spirited commander revisited Falmouth with a heart of vengeance and a flotilla of small British cruisers, which he menacingly anchored in the harbor. His hair powdered white and his distinctive blue naval coat visible on the *Canceaux*'s deck, Mowat gave the population several days' advance notice—and then commenced a bombardment of cannon fire that destroyed nearly two-thirds of the town. This "unwarranted and savage piece of vandalism upon an inoffensive people"[30] would result in the unbridled hatred of Captain Mowat by the citizens of Maine for generations to come.[31] General McLean, however, would view Mowat as an indispensable asset in his possession and defense of Majabigwaduce.

Almost from the moment of the British landing, McLean worried that the naval contingent deployed for the mission had left Halifax precariously unprotected. Sporadic yet reliable reports of eight or nine Rebel ships lurking in the waters of the North Atlantic further anguished the general, and by June 25 he was left with no choice but to allow several of his most able warships, the frigate HMS *Blonde*, the brig *Hope*, and the armed schooner *Arbuthnot*, each of which had provided escort to McLean's troops on the journey to Majabigwaduce, to depart for "other objects of the King's Service . . ."[32]

Remaining for the protection of McLean's vulnerable outpost on Penobscot Bay were Captain Mowat aboard the *Albany* and two other sloops of war under his command, the *North* and the *Nautilus*. Of his hapless commissioned vessel, Mowat would later reflect, "[I]f the *Albany* had happened to lead the Expedition . . . the whole must have been intercepted . . . & carried to Boston for a mere Novice might have conceived at once She was not fit to conduct it safely."[33] Indeed, McLean would lament to General Clinton, "I cannot help deploring that the Ship . . . [Mowat] commands is of so small force and so very bad as often to prevent his good intentions taking place."[34] The "wretched *Albany*," as Mowat referred to her, was outfitted with only sixteen guns, each capable of firing no more than a six-pound iron ball[35]—a force insufficient to provide adequate protection to the harbor even in conjunction with the twenty guns of the *North* and the eighteen of the *Nautilus*.[36] The fear of a Rebel attack on the fortification at Majabigwaduce was present from the start of the mission. McLean was aware that, until the garrison could be completed, his site was exposed—as were his meager naval resources in the harbor. Artillery batteries were immediately placed upon Dyce's Head in defense of the fort and along the southern shore to protect the *Albany* and Captain Mowat's other sloops of war. In addition, the contingent erected a position at the mouth of the harbor on Cross Island to the south—often called Banks' Island and soon to be renamed Nautilus Island—as well as one along the swamps on the narrow isthmus leading to the mainland.

Despite McLean's seemingly formidable defenses, however, it became immediately apparent that his reserves of artillery were insufficient for the defense of the outpost, and he petitioned General Clinton for an increase in his supply.[37] Likewise, Captain Mowat, absolutely aware of the limitations of his meager nautical force, strenuously informed Clinton of the vital necessity of a robust naval component and expressed his dismay that the primary warship designated for the protection of Majabigwaduce, with its small size and poor armament, was "the worst calculated of any vessel in the King's service . . ."[38]

As governor and administrator of populations in various locales, General McLean readily understood that his mission in Penobscot Bay could not be achieved without a robust political outreach. Naval and artillery needs aside, it was absolutely necessary that the local inhabitants of the area be contacted and coaxed into allegiance to the Crown. McLean had been dismayed to learn that many of the residents had been led to believe that British troops were accustomed to plunder and abuse in their areas of operation,[39] and he set about "to remove that prejudice as early as possible."[40]

Shortly after his arrival at Majabigwaduce, McLean disseminated a "Proclamation" among the people pledging protection and freedom from molestation for all who shall "return to that state of good order and government to which the whole must in the end submit, and . . . within eight days . . . take the oaths of allegiance and fidelity to his Majesty."[41] As a further incentive beyond safety and security, McLean promised to all inhabitants of the Province of Maine who had, according to the common practice, informally settled upon and cultivated lands without actual legal authority or title, that they "shall receive gratuitous grants from his Majesty" forever quieting title to these lands to themselves and their heirs.[42] Finally, with a firm understanding of the hardships caused by the blockade of New England during the war[43] and of the provincial notion that "his Majesty's sea and land forces willingly add to their sufferings," McLean extended to all inhabitants who "behave themselves in a peaceable, orderly manner" (even if they hadn't actually sworn allegiance to the Crown) permission to fish in the open waters free from harassment and with full British protection.[44] As McLean's invitation circulated among the farmers, fishermen, and families of Majabigwaduce, its draftsman waited with anxious determination for whispers of popular reception.

Notwithstanding McLean's munificent outreach, the British landing in Penobscot Bay had clearly filled the local inhabitants with a sense of foreboding and consternation.[45] The British embargo, however, had taken its toll on the people, and arms and provisions were a scarce commodity. On receipt of McLean's proclamation, the local militia leaders conferred and decided to send a party to "treat" with the general. Upon receiving assurances that the people would not be disturbed if they would "mind their business, and be peaceable,"[46] it was quickly determined that organized popular opposition to the British force would be futile and unwarranted.

In the coming days, 651 inhabitants of the towns surrounding Penobscot Bay poured into the appointed areas and swore allegiance—or at a minimum, neutrality—to the Crown.[47] Aboard the *Albany*, Captain Mowat had forwarded a dispatch to Colonel Jonathan Buck, the commander of the "the king's deluded Subjects," of the Fifth Regiment, Lincoln County Militia, and less delicately demanded a complete muster roll of the soldiers under his command.[48] Anxiously compliant, Buck immediately forwarded a list of his men to the British command, boarded his sloop *Hannah*, and fled the area.[49]

Reverend John Murray, "a burning light"[50] to the people of coastal Maine in the days of the Revolution, had been a persistent advocate for his flock and a frequent petitioner to the General Court of Massachusetts for a departure from the enduring pattern of neglect imparted to the "Eastern Country" by the legislative body in the colony. Destitute of equipment, provisions, and bread, the inhabitants of the region had suffered greatly and, despite the urgings of local leaders and townspeople, Massachusetts had been either unwilling or unable to offer any tangible relief from their plight. On June 18, 1779, however, Reverend Murray took quill to paper and notified Boston of "credible intelligence . . . of a Fleet of British Ships of war . . . in Penobscot bay."[51] Men had begun to fortify the area of Majabigwaduce, he claimed, and the local inhabitants had been obliged to submit to British authority and to assist in the construction of the bulwark. "The various clamours of the most alarming representations from divers part of the country & sometimes from the whole being treated with neglect by the Legislature, of the State," he chided, "do not in the least deter me from assuring myself, that, on the *present* crisis the Honorable Council will not overlook the extremity to which we are likely now to be reduced . . ."[52]

Now, thought Murray, they must respond.

McLean was in a race against time. He was confident that the extensive Rebel navy on the east coast surely would respond to his landing and that a fight for Majabigwaduce inevitably would ensue. Mindful of his limited naval defenses and exposed position on the heights, he accelerated work on the fort and impressed the local citizens into laborious industry. Some willing, others not, the people of eastern Maine toiled in a single-minded effort for His Majesty the King. "I helped to haul the first log into the south bastion," recalled William Hutchings years after the event. "It was on the Sunday before the Americans arrived, and was the only Sunday on which I had to work in my life."[53]

Chapter 6 Captivate, Kill, or Destroy

THE COMMANDER OF Castle Island was accustomed to spending evenings in the comfort of his home in the North End of Boston, away from the dreary harbor outpost that housed the Massachusetts Artillery Train. To the consternation of some, he would often be rowed ashore by his men at the end of the day in the Castle barge or whatever small vessel was available and spend time with his family and among the town's people. One historian described him as "a military commuter who slept with his wife."[1] Paul and Rachel Revere would, in fact, have three more children during the period of 1776 to 1780.

When Revere finally received orders on June 26, 1779, to hold himself and his men in readiness for a planned attack on the enemy at Penobscot Bay, it was surely with a sense of ambivalence that he prepared himself for the hardships to come. Though it would be difficult to leave the comforting arms of his wife and family for the uncertainties of battle, his wholehearted loathing for the oppression that had led his comrades to war nearly overwhelmed him. He had confessed to Rachel while in Newport with his regiment the previous year, ". . . were I at home I should want to be here."[2] Finally, Revere mused, it was his turn to partake in the glories of war that had been, to that point, so unjustly denied him.

Reverend Murray's castigation of the Massachusetts Council was but one of many notifications and pleas for assistance that would follow the British landing on Bagaduce Peninsula. Though Colonel Buck had fled the area like so many others who refused to swear allegiance to the Crown, he did travel south to Pownalborough to notify his regional commander, General Charles Cushing, of the size and scope of McLean's force and its intended purpose. On June 19, 1779, Cushing forwarded the first official notice of the landing to the council. "Col. Buck is here . . . to inform your Honors of the arrival of the Enemy at Penobscot . . . ," he wrote. "If the General Court should think proper to send a suitable force of shipping which with other assistance by Land—It is thought they might easily be dislodged."[3]

Several days before Paul Revere and others would receive their embarkation orders, a committee of both houses of the Massachusetts General Court, appointed by Speaker John Hancock, grimly considered the British presence on the shores of Maine. Despite their traditional posture of indifference toward the territory, it was evident that unambiguous and determined action was now required. The committee, instantly realizing the threat posed to the region by the eastward stronghold, directed that all ships of war in Boston Harbor and its surrounding ports, including any private armed vessels in those ports, be prepared for a "cruize against [the] enemy . . ."[4] Aware that the British were laboring day and night to construct their garrison, and fearing the arrival of reinforcements to aid in their defense, the committee set a date for the launch of the American expedition of just six days' time.[5]

Hancock's committee sent urgent dispatches to the counties surrounding Penobscot Bay urging "spirited exertions" by land and sea to assist in the dislodging of the enemy from the Maine coast, and new conscription efforts for Continental service were suspended to allow the manning of regiments for the undertaking.[6] Though the inhabitants of many eastern counties lacked food, provisions, and armaments, they beseeched the government to intervene against the enemy, and they pledged whatever troops they could raise in the effort. They also informed the committee of British overtures to the Penobscot and Norridgawalk Indian tribes and pleaded for measures of friendship to be extended to those tribes. The specter of a foreign army enlisting Indians in a war against the colonists was too fresh in the minds of many to be borne lightly. The members of the council seated at Boston and led by its president, Jeremiah Powell, took careful note of every appeal and petition that arrived; and though it fully expected provincial militia units to cooperate with the provision of manpower for the coming expedition, it was clear that the primary contribution of officers, supplies, and finances would fall upon the Town of Boston.

As preparations for the Penobscot Expedition got under way, members of the council and the people of Boston at large brimmed with the confidence of ultimate victory, and all thoughts of a petition for assistance to the Continental Congress evaporated. "Such was their zeal and confidence of success," wrote army surgeon James Thacher in his military journal, "that . . . the General Court neither consulted any experienced military character, nor desired the assistance of any continental troops on this important enterprise; thus taking on themselves the undivided responsibility, and reserving for their own heads, all the laurels to be derived from the anticipated conquest."[7] Indeed, neither General Horatio Gates, the adjutant-general of the Continental Army, nor George Washington himself, was consulted until well after preparations for the mission were under way.[8]

Despite the council's reluctance to seek congressional assistance or troops for the expedition, the question regarding warships was an entirely different matter. In 1779 the Massachusetts navy consisted of only three armed vessels, the brigs *Tyrannicide*, *Active*, and *Hazard*, each equipped with fourteen guns.[9] The overwhelming show of naval force that would be required to remove the British from Bagaduce Peninsula would, accordingly, have to be supplied by other sources.

As word of the enemy's landing arrived at the Massachusetts statehouse, three serving Continental ships of war, the thirty-two gun frigate, *Warren*, the twelve-gun sloop, *Providence*, and the twelve-gun brig, *Diligent*, were moored in Boston Harbor.[10] The council quickly informed the Continental Navy Board stationed in Boston of the emerging plans to dislodge the British from Maine and, in an effort to generate a "Superior Naval Force," petitioned the board for use of its three vessels on the expedition.[11] On the same day, the board readily agreed to the request, assuring the council "that no exertions of Ours shall be wanting on this Occasion."[12] The flagship *Warren* would lead the expedition to Maine.

As Boston worked with the navy board to prepare its Continental ships for battle, officers of the Massachusetts Board of War, charged by the council with the responsibility of acquiring the private and state naval force for the expedition, adroitly canvassed the harbors of Massachusetts and New Hampshire and implored the holders of all available armed vessels to contribute their ships to the Penobscot Expedition. In the coastal village of Newburyport, Massachusetts, the owners of four private vessels—the twenty-gun warship *Vengeance*, the twenty-four-gun warship *Monmouth*, the sixteen-gun warship *Sky Rocket*, and the fourteen-gun brig *Pallas*—willingly offered their vessels for use in the expedition on the promise of the state to incur the cost of manning, equipping, and insuring the ships against loss.[13] In Boston the Board of War "engaged" the twenty-gun ship *Charming Sally* and the six-gun sloop *Charming Polly* "upon the same Conditions as have been offered by the General Court for the Penobscot Expedition."[14] And in Salem, a committee of the council conferred with owners of the armed ships *Hector*, *Hunter*, and *Black Prince*, and under the threat of forced seizure, successfully "endeavored to impress upon their Minds the Importance of these Vessels being engaged . . ."[15]

Where gentle persuasion failed to achieve the desired result, the council did not hesitate to exert its legislative power to impress naval assets into service. On July 2 it ordered the sheriffs of Suffolk County to impress the armed ship *General Putnam*, then moored at Boston Harbor with its compliment of twenty guns, "for a Two Months Cruize" to Maine,[16] and in New Hampshire, Governor Meshech Weare seized the twenty-two gun privateer *Hampden* and offered her to the Massachusetts Council to oppose the British at Majabigwaduce.

By the first week of July, the council and the Massachusetts Board of War had amassed an imposing armada of twenty Continental, state, and privately owned warships that had been either donated or impressed from the coastal ports of Massachusetts and New Hampshire, together with a compliment of twenty-one unarmed transports, comprised mostly of sloops and schooners.[17] Equipped with a total of 324 guns of various scale,[18] the State of Massachusetts Bay had assembled "the strongest and finest naval force" of the Revolution.[19]

With the issue of naval equipment firmly resolved, the problem quickly became one of manpower. Few incentives existed for a Rebel soldier or sailor to enlist for service on a state or Continental vessel, when a position on a privately owned ship could offer an inviting share in the "plunders" of war well in excess of any government-paid wage.

Privateering, as it was known, flourished along the shores of New England during the Revolution and was aimed not at military or naval victory, but at pirating the valuable freight of wealthy merchant ships. "It was easy to slip into almost any [bay or harbor] with a prize, by men familiar with every inlet; and it was equally easy, also . . . to spring out upon their unsuspecting prey," wrote one historian.[20] These "little wasps,"[21] as they came to be known, shared in the profits generated by their efforts and operated with the sole purpose of personal gain, with little thought of service to country. Though the private vessels employed for use in the Penobscot Expedition were to sail under the color and authority of the Massachusetts government, their owners and crews would be entitled to retain the fruits of any plunder and profit derived on the mission; and though bound by public duty to fulfill official orders, these men remained driven by speculation.

For those unwilling to undergo the personal risk of boarding the private vessels bound for Maine on the Penobscot Expedition, other opportunities for speculative profit still existed. Widespread confidence in the coming mission prompted the formation of private syndicates, whose investors purchased shares in private armed vessels with the hope of taking part in the gains to be derived through the labors of the captain and crew. Public auctions of captured and plundered goods—cannons in particular—would be advertised in Boston newspapers; and after the payment of expenses, the gains would be divided in proportion to the investments made.[22] Private opportunities thus would cloud the ultimate objective of the Penobscot Expedition and place the state in a disadvantaged position in the manning of its public vessels.

Time was becoming a critical factor to the council, and it was now clear that its six-day target for the commencement of the expedition would not be met. The *Warren* alone required a crew of nearly one hundred men, and sluggish recruitment severely hampered the process. With the meager wages of the state and Continental navies competing against the financial opportunities presented by twelve private vessels, enlistment on the government ships came to a standstill. In a classic "carrot and stick" proposition, on July 3 the council issued two resolutions designed to solve its conscription problem. First, it relinquished all public right to the expected spoils of the expedition, reserving such claim to any crew members who victoriously captured such prizes,[23] and failing that measure, it simultaneously authorized the sheriffs of each county to "seize & impress any able-bodied Seamen, or Mariner to serve on board any of the Vessels . . . employed in the proposed expedition to Penobscot."[24] With these measures in place—together with the posting of armed guards at the docks and ferries of Boston Harbor to prevent the escape of sailors—an additional sixty men were cajoled into service on state and Continental ships, thus completing their need.[25]

Recruitment efforts for the undertaking within the regional militia units were not going much better. In Maine, some men concealed themselves to avoid conscription, while others joined under force or threat. Major Jeremiah Hill, adjutant-general of the Maine Militia, wrote of the call to arms: "[S]ome sent Boys, old Men, and Invalids . . . [T]hey were soldiers whether they could carry a Gun, walk a mile without crutches, or only Compos Mentis sufficient to keep themselves out of Fire & Water."[26]

Colonel John Brewer of Penobscot, who was part of the initial delegation sent by the local inhabitants to treat with General McLean, had been provided a full view of the British encampment and later recommended to the Massachusetts Council that at least three thousand men be sent to dispossess the enemy from Majabigwaduce.[27] With the relentless tug of Continental enlistment and lucrative privateers swallowing up the available pool of soldiers, it would be a challenge for the state to raise half that number.

🎗 The captain of the frigate *Warren* sullenly trudged upon the ship's deck and peered across her bow to the maddening commerce and activity of Boston Harbor beyond. He watched with mounting resentment as privateers with pirated wealth came and went, always anxious to avoid the watchful eyes of the county sheriffs who patrolled the docks in search of sailors attempting to evade naval impressment. The captain would be glad when the Massachusetts embargo on commercial shipping went into effect, as a further measure to encourage seaman to join the coming expedition. He had spent a portion of his capable yet undistinguished naval career as a privateer himself, and he had assumed command of several Continental vessels during the Revolution, yet Boston and her busy trade seemed to irk him.[28]

A native of Connecticut and a son to a prominent and wealthy New London family, Dudley Saltonstall had been appointed as an officer of the Continental Navy, less for his seamanship than at the urging of his brother-in-law, Silas Deane, a member of the Continental Congress. Thickly set and of modest height, the forty-two-year-old Saltonstall was a dour and obstinate presence among his men. A fellow captain described him as "a Sensible indefatigable Morose Man,"[29] and the renowned John Paul Jones, who served with Saltonstall on HMS *Alfred*, would comment that he "behaved toward inferiours indiscriminately as tho' they were of a lower species . . . [H]e was a sleepy gentleman — ill-natured and narrow-minded."[30]

As Jeremiah Powell and the members of the Massachusetts Council teamed with Speaker of the House John Hancock and Board of War member Samuel Adams, who had returned to Boston after recently chairing the Marine Committee in Congress, to work through the process of manning the Penobscot Expedition, local military officers began receiving appointments for the prominent and critical leadership roles of the mission. The Continental Navy had graciously consented to the use of its three warships stationed at Boston, but it was made abundantly clear that the intractable captain of the *Warren* was to be included in the compact — Massachusetts could not have the Continental fleet without its commander.[31] In the opening days of July 1779, Dudley Saltonstall received a dispatch from the council chamber appointing him as commodore of all armed vessels for the expedition to Penobscot. "We wish you a Prosperous Cruise & sincerely pray that all your Exertions in the Cause of your Country may be attended with a Divine Blessing," the order observed.[32]

Perhaps in recognition of Saltonstall's prickly disposition, the council opted to divide authority for the mission between two leaders, asking each to "promote the Greatest Harmony, peace and concord . . ." among the infantry and sea divisions.[33]

To the post of commander for American land forces, the council turned to one of its own. Solomon Lovell was a longtime representative for the Town of Weymouth in the Massachusetts General Court and had been active in state and local politics for most of his adult life. A successful agriculturalist by trade, Lovell also had served under Richard Gridley during the ill-fated Crown Point expedition in the Seven Years' War, where he first made the acquaintance of Paul Revere.

While carrying on his promising political career, Lovell steadily rose through the ranks of the Massachusetts State Militia, and in 1777 he was elected by the council to the venerated post of brigadier general for Suffolk County. He served creditably in the Newport campaign in the summer of 1778 and later stood in command of one thousand militiamen in defense of Boston.[34] Yet, for all the admiration from his political contemporaries in the General Court and the lofty positions of command granted to him, the forty-seven-year-old Lovell was largely untested in the ways of actual warfare. The man whom the Council had chosen to conduct the perilous ground assault against General McLean and his Scottish regiments at Majabigwaduce was, in truth, a gentleman farmer and a career politician.[35]

As one of Lovell's men would soon lament, "Our general was said to be a very good sort of man, but these good sort of men seldom make good generals."[36]

"Captivate Kill or destroy" the enemy, came the council's clear and unequivocal order to both Saltonstall and Lovell.[37]

Through the first days of July 1779, Boston hummed with activity in preparation for the coming expedition. Vast supplies of food and munitions were gathered, and the impressment of seamen and militiamen continued in Massachusetts and throughout the coastal counties of Maine. Though Adjutant-General Hill had reported widespread problems in recruitment around Cumberland County, and continued difficulties in the manning of Boston's warships led to alarming delays in the start of the mission, one dispatch from William Frost in Falmouth, Maine, boasted, "We can't but flatter ourselves, that from the Active Zeal & Spirited Exertion of our worthy Brethren in the Eastern part of the

State, the Army will be rais'd & in such force as may effectually crush this daring attempt of the presumptuous foe, & render [Majabigwaduce] as brilliant in the annals of the United States as Saratoga or Charlestown."[38]

On June 26, the council issued orders to Lieutenant Colonel Paul Revere to hold himself and one hundred matrosses under his authority in readiness to embark for Maine on the Penobscot Expedition. The council's demand for peace and harmony among the forces would be immediately tested, however, when Revere, the appointed commander of the artillery for the expedition, learned with dismay that Captain William Todd, his vexing nemesis from Castle Island, had been named by General Lovell as one of his brigade majors for the operation. Outraged by the appointment, Revere sent an emissary of officers from his regiment to Boston to meet with Lovell in an attempt to dissuade him from including the captain on the mission. One of the general's underlings assured the men that Todd would, in fact, be omitted, and they returned to Castle Island to inform their commander of the good news. Shortly thereafter, General Lovell engaged William Todd as he had always intended.

Revere was incensed. At once, he crossed the harbor and personally called on the general at his makeshift headquarters in the state house, informing him of how "very inimical to the Corps of Artillery"[39] was William Todd. "He would do everything in his power to hurt them,"[40] Revere insisted. Despite this haranguing, however, Lovell persisted in his decision, refusing to involve himself in the personal quarrels of his men. Revere's response was one of derisory pettiness: "I represented to the General how disagreeable [Todd] was to me, and my Officers, and that I should never speak to him but in the line of my duty."[41] It was surely a harbinger of a systemic and pervasive problem of leadership that would plague General Lovell throughout the coming weeks.

"The expedition is a matter of much speculation here . . . ," wrote Seth Loring, secretary of the Massachusetts Board of War, to his superior, General Heath. "I imagine it will not be so easily accomplished as many of our sanguine citizens suppose."[42]

Chapter 7 The Penobscot Expedition

GENERAL FRANCIS McLean, commander of His Majesty's forces at Majabigwaduce, extended his telescope and gazed wearily over the open bay searching for enemy masts on the horizon and any sign of an attacking force from the south. Mounting rumors of troop movements in and around Boston Harbor had raised British concerns that an expedition was being prepared; yet, with the war being fought on multiple fronts, the object of that expedition was uncertain and the threat seemed almost remote. "I do not see any reason to apprehend an immediate attack on us," he wrote to Henry Clinton on June 26, "but we are threatened ."[1] Long-term defense of Fort George, as the British works on Majabigwaduce had been christened, would require a much greater presence of ships, men, and guns, warned McLean.

To Captain Mowat, commander of HMS *Albany*, the Rebel threat was of much greater imminence. His infamous encounters with the people of New England, and his understanding of what a British post in Maine would mean to them, led him to the inescapable conclusion that an attack undoubtedly would come quickly.

In Boston, preparations for the expedition were indeed taking on a frenetic pace. Apprehensive that the Royal Navy would reinforce its position at Majabigwaduce with additional warships from New York or Halifax before an American attack could be organized, the council advised its officers to proceed with the utmost urgency. Despite the absolute requirement of swift action, however, incessant problems hampered the mission from the start, and delays frustrated the undertaking. Far short of the three thousand men recommended by Colonel Brewer after surveying the menacing British force, the council issued orders for only fifteen hundred militia and an additional one hundred from Paul Revere's train of artillery[2]—and the militia commanders in the several counties surrounding and including Majabigwaduce had difficulty in meeting even that quota.

On July 7 the Navy Board complained that it saw "no probability" of its ships departing by the following Friday as had been hoped. "Men Enter but slowly," William Vernon Jr., president of the board, wrote to the council, "especially American Seamen which are most wanted & must be had before the *Warren* can go to Sea . . ."[3] And by July 14, the evident frustration of the navy erupted into caustic anger: "So much time has been taken in preparing for this Expedition that we doubt the Success of it," the board informed the Continental Congress sitting in Philadelphia. "The Enemy must be Stupid indeed if they do not reinforce . . . that [post] with some additional ships."[4]

A flurry of orders had been delivered with dispatch to the captains of each vessel bound for Majabigwaduce, and by Thursday, July 15, the fleet finally appeared ready to sail. Stormy weather and contrary winds, however, delayed the departure of the fleet, which had been directed to gather in Nantasket Harbor just south of Boston and then navigate north to a rendezvous point with the Maine militia in Townsend, present-day Boothbay Harbor.

In the early morning hours of July 19, the greatest flotilla of the Revolutionary War finally assembled in the harbor amid warm southwesterly breezes and cloudless skies and prepared to set sail for Maine. "We are well Manned; in good Health & high spirits . . . and are in readiness for Sea," wrote the captain of the privateer *General Putnam*.[5]

The sight of the fully armed and rigged warships, proudly bearing names of rebellion and uprising such as *Tyrannicide, Diligent, Hazard*, and *Defiance*, brought cheers and applause from the onlookers who had gathered at the shore. "[A] flotilla . . . more beautiful had never floated in the eastern waters," wrote Maine historian William Williamson.[6]

As the *Warren* at last weighed anchor and Commodore Saltonstall began escorting the procession toward Nantucket Light and the open sea, an order inexplicably was issued for the fleet to heave to and hold its position. All of the captains clamored for explanation and impatiently strode upon their decks while marines and sailors looked on with bewilderment and annoyance, wondering what was delaying their departure. Gradually, the source of the holdup became obvious to all.

Despite clear and incontrovertible orders from the Council Chamber on July 8 and July 12 to embark with the troops to Penobscot "without a moments delay,"[7] Lieutenant Colonel Paul Revere, commander of the Massachusetts Train of Artillery for the Penobscot Expedition, was nowhere to be found—and the fleet could not depart without him.

The night before, Revere had taken the Castle barge back to Boston to spend the evening in the arms of his wife and, apparently, could not arise early enough to join his men back aboard the ordnance brig *Samuel*, which had taken position with the rest of the fleet off Nantasket. Now, as the brig tacked back and forth at the mouth of the harbor anxiously awaiting its artillery commander, tensions began to escalate and anger welled. At about 8:00 A.M., the barge emerged from the shoals of Hull and into Nantasket Harbor, where Revere and several of his officers who also had spent the night in Boston finally climbed aboard the *Samuel* with a train of personal baggage in tow. The fleet was on its way, but the lateness of the hour and the cause of the fleet's delay were noted by all.

By July 19 believable intelligence of the coming Rebel attack had reached General McLean, and work on Fort George abruptly shifted from the deliberate construction of bastions and quarters to the frenzied erection of stalwart defenses. As the scope of the crisis revealed itself, additional "volunteers" from the region were called in to assist in the work, who labored day and night to construct gun batteries, remove trees from the front of the fort, and raise an abatis, a barrier of trees and branches erected as a defense against attack. Though advancing in years, McLean, according to John Calef, displayed "the utmost vigilance and activity, giving every where the necessary directions, visiting incessantly ... the different parts of the works, and thus by his example animating his men to proceed, regardless of fatigue, with vigour and alacrity in their operations."

In spite of the general's best efforts and the arduous labors of the local inhabitants, however, Fort George remained little more than a jumble of earthworks and logs as Rebel forces sailed up the coast of New England. Square in shape, with bastions on each corner and a blockhouse set upon the center for quarters, the redoubt extended about two hundred feet in length; and its walls, in most sections, reached only to a man's waist.[8] Understanding the stark limitations of his land and naval forces and expecting an overwhelming armada of American military power, General McLean resignedly had constructed Fort George "to make but the pretense of resistance, expecting to be captured at once."[9]

Two days after its inauspicious send-off from Nantasket Harbor, the Rebel fleet emerged from the Atlantic fog and sailed into the seaside village of Townsend, Maine, roughly seventy-five miles south of Majabigwaduce, for the purpose of joining the Maine militiamen and five ships of the fleet that had begun the journey from points north of Boston. Here, General Lovell took up headquarters at the home of Reverend John Murray, who had been one of the first to notify Boston of the British trespass on Maine soil, and found himself "very agreeably and sociably treated by the worthy Clergyman."[10]

Less agreeable to Lovell, however, was the state of his army. The bulk of his fighting force, the men of the Maine Militia, had arrived in Townsend to rendezvous with the warships and transports for the daylong journey north to Majabigwaduce. On viewing his assembled and paraded troops, however, the general found only 873 men—a number well short of the quota ordered by the Massachusetts Council. Jeremiah Hill, adjutant-general of the Maine Militia, who was present during Lovell's inspection, noted that the men were "very poorly equipped . . . [and] unacquainted with any military Maneuver."[11] Paul Revere observed that a full third of the available troops were "boys and old men."[12] Lovell ordered the brigadiers of each militia unit to supplement the numbers with additional men as soon as they were able and to send them along in transports or on foot to meet the remainder of the army at Penobscot Bay.

While in Townsend, a chief of the Norridgawalk Indians brought the welcome news to Lovell that British overtures to members of the tribe had failed and that his men would be friendly to the American cause at

Majabigwaduce. Cheered by this news and enjoying the hospitality of Reverend Murray's family, Lovell lingered in Townsend with his armada idly anchored in the harbor. Thomas Philbrook, aboard the Continental sloop *Providence*, was mystified by the delay. "Here we wasted several more days," he wrote, "seemingly, for no other purpose, but to give the enemy sufficient time to prepare for us."[13]

On the evening of June 22, the first of many councils of war between General Lovell, Commodore Saltonstall, the army field officers, and the captains of the armed vessels was held at Townsend. "It was an epitome of the whole campaign," recorded Paul Revere. "There was nothing proposed, and of consequence nothing done. It was more like a meeting in the Coffee House, then a council of war. There was no President appointed, nor any minutes taken; after disputing about nothing [for] two hours it was broke up."[14]

Eighty-one years later, as America teetered on the brink of civil war, Henry Wadsworth Longfellow would immortalize Paul Revere with a poem entitled "Paul Revere's Ride." In a stroke of incalculable irony, Longfellow's maternal grandfather, Peleg Wadsworth, the appointed second in command to General Lovell on the Penobscot Expedition and at thirty-one years of age the youngest brigadier general in the Massachusetts Militia, was present at the council of war at Townsend and now contemplated leading Lieutenant Colonel Paul Revere and others into battle.

A Harvard-educated schoolteacher, Wadsworth worked as an aide to General Artemas Ward and in 1778 was appointed adjutant-general of the Massachusetts Militia. He was widely recognized as a man of courage, intelligence, and ability.[15] William Hutchings, who would encounter many of the officers on both sides of the Penobscot Expedition, would later write, "I did not like the appearance of Lovell very well, but Wadsworth was a beautiful man."[16]

The Massachusetts Council had heard rumblings of a possible British fleet sailing from England, Halifax, or New York to support McLean's men at Majabigwaduce. Alarmed by these rumors and mindful of the need for swift and decisive action in the mission, Artemas Ward and Samuel Adams forwarded an urgent dispatch to General Lovell on July 23: "It is the Expression of the Council that you . . . will push your Operations with all possible Vigor and dispatch and accomplish the business of the Expedition before any reinforcement can get to the Enemy at Penobscot."[17]

On July 24 the American flotilla finally sailed north from Townsend toward Penobscot Bay. Sightings of sporadic smoke columns at various points along the shore informed Lovell and his officers that furtive intelligence of their approach was being delivered to the British virtually as it occurred. Indeed, firm confirmation of the coming attack already had been received at Majabigwaduce through an elaborate spy network even as Lovell and his men tarried in the home of Reverend Murray. Dr. Calef noted in his journal on July 23, "All doubt of an attack from the Enemy is now vanished."[18]

In preparation for the coming attack, a team of British sailors, who previously had been ferried ashore for added manpower in the construction of Fort George, were now returned to their ships and readied for battle. Captain Mowat, understanding the strategic importance of Majabigwaduce Harbor to the protection of the British garrison on the ground above, arrayed the *Albany, North*, and *Nautilus* in a battle line across the mouth of the waterfront in the narrows between the peninsula and Nautilus Island to the south. Behind, and out of the line of fire, he arranged his three transports, which were prepared to further impede any advancing enemy ship with designs of entering the harbor beyond.

On the afternoon of Sunday, July 25, the American fleet sailed grandly into Penobscot Bay, mainsails buffeting against a mounting west wind, and came to anchor in the waters off the cliffs of Dyce's Head on the west side of the peninsula—well clear of the harbor and Captain Mowat's naval arrangement. From the *Samuel*, Paul Revere raised his telescope and searched the heavily wooded crest. "I could plainly see with my glass, the enemy had begun a Fort, on one of the Heights," he would record in his journal.[19]

Though manned only by a force of 1,157 militia, marines, and artillerymen, and 41 Penobscot Indians who had joined the fleet the previous night, the British manning the heights of Majabigwaduce were convinced by the sheer number of warships and transports that no less than 3,000 men had arrived to attack them.[20] Colonel John Brewer of the local militia had been waiting for the expected arrival of the Rebel forces and searched daily for their appearance. Traveling down the Penobscot River on July 25, he and his companion peered beyond the bay and then stopped, eyes transfixed on what they knew to be the approaching American fleet. "[I] got little sleep for joy at what we had seen, and what we expected would take place" wrote Brewer.[21]

On the previous evening as the fleet lay anchored nine miles south of Fort George, Commodore Saltonstall had ordered the *Hazard* and *Tyrannicide* to sail ahead and gather intelligence of the British works on Majabigwaduce. Landing off of Fox Island, Lieutenant William Downe and twelve of his marines quietly rowed ashore and questioned some of the residents, who openly informed the men that the British defenses were feeble at best and that their fort could be "a very easy conquest."[22]

Buttressed by this news, Solomon Lovell, aboard the transport *Charming Sally*, immediately began drawing plans and circulating orders for an initial landing of 350 men on the shores of Majabigwaduce. He instructed that upon their arrival the flat-bottomed transport boats should be held in readiness for a sequenced landing of troops and artillery in multiple waves, and in a flourish of confidence, he boldly implored his men "to add new Lustre to the Fame of the Massachusetts Militia"[23] through their coming actions.

When Captain Philip Brown of the *Diligent* audaciously suggested to Commodore Saltonstall, however, that the British defenses could easily be taken and that never was there a better opportunity to attack, the commodore bristled and scolded that "it would be the height of madness"[24] to attempt to take Majabigwaduce Harbor without further reconnaissance.

It was the first hint of a simmering discord between the stalwart leaders of the Penobscot Expedition, and one that would profoundly impact every aspect of the ill-fated venture.

By the late afternoon of July 25, as the full might of the American fleet lay anchored in Penobscot Bay, the Rebel forces, led by General Wadsworth, attempted their landing on Majabigwaduce. Despite his reluctance to enter the harbor and directly engage the British warships, Saltonstall formed several of his vessels into divisions to cover the assault and, from a distance, turned broadside and fired his guns at Captain Mowat's alignment of ships. Dr. Calef witnessed the "very brisk cannonade" and recorded in his journal, "The King's ships suffered only in their rigging. The fire of the [Rebel warships] was random and irregular, and their maneuvers . . . bespoke confusion."[25]

As Saltonstall cautiously engaged the British ships at the mouth of the harbor, General Lovell's men began boarding the longboats and rowing through choppy seas toward the heights about a half mile north of Dyce's Head. The chosen landing area was heavily wooded terrain, and howling winds now hampered the transport effort, making a swift and coordinated approach increasingly difficult. As preparations for the landing progressed, the New England weather began to worsen, and Lovell's apprehension over the movement of his men intensified. While his first division began disembarking the transports, Lovell realized that delays in transporting successive waves would leave his landed troops in danger of being overrun by the enemy, and he immediately sent out the signal to abandon the attack.

Amid the turmoil and confusion, a volley of enemy musket fire erupted from the cliffs above, hastening the retreat. Paul Revere, who was ordered to ready the artillery and stores for landing, witnessed the debacle from the ordnance brig and later wrote, "[A]s soon as they got near the shore, which was covered with a thick wood, the enemy fire upon them . . . they are ordered to return, we loose one Indian."[26]

From Fort George and the woods overlooking the beach, chants of three cheers were heard from jubilant Scottish soldiers.

By sunrise of the following morning, as the weather at Majabigwaduce improved, Colonel John Brewer arrived at the American fleet and was granted a meeting with General Lovell and Commodore Saltonstall aboard the *Charming Sally*. Brewer advised the men that he had personally viewed the British garrison and its surrounding defenses, and he provided detailed descriptions of each to the officers. Similar to William Downe and his team of advance scouts two days earlier, Brewer advised the men that the fort was only partially completed and that the gun batteries and artillery positions were rather limited. He then turned to the commodore and excitedly suggested that, with such meager defenses to breach, a vigorous naval attack on the British ships and batteries combined with an assault on the fort by land could result in a speedy victory.[27]

Lovell brimmed with excitement at the news, yet Saltonstall balked. "He hove up his long chin," recalled Brewer years later, "and said 'You seem to be damn knowing about the matter! I am not going to risk my shipping in that damned hole!'"[28]

Saltonstall's apprehensions were not entirely without merit. Though the Rebel forces clearly held a superiority of naval power and armaments, the position of Mowat's warships aligned in a broadside blockade at the mouth of the harbor, adjacent and to the east of Bagaduce Peninsula, combined with the strategic placement of British artillery batteries on the high ground with guns aimed toward the waters below, made a cruise into the harbor with its fluctuating tides a perilous undertaking with precious little opportunity for escape. Without any real assurance that a confrontation with Mowat's three sloops of war would result in the surrender of Fort George, Saltonstall appeared unwilling to risk his men or the flagship of the expedition in the precarious endeavor.

To allay Saltonstall's concerns about the risks of entering Majabigwaduce Harbor, it was agreed at a council of war held aboard the *Warren* that the British gun battery placed on Nautilus Island adjacent to Mowat's line of ships would first be attacked and captured by the marines. On the late afternoon of Monday, July 26, a contingent of three hundred Massachusetts and Continental marines led by Captain John Welch, a well-respected young officer who had several years earlier been captured and held in a British prison only to stage a daring underground escape,[29] rowed ashore past the rocky shallows to Nautilus Island under cover of three armed vessels and a militia division led by General Wadsworth. Despite Saltonstall's inexplicable decision to call off his ships as the attack progressed, and the drowning of one of Wadsworth's officers and two privates, the twenty or so Redcoats manning the battery realized that they were vastly outnumbered and fled into the woods with little armed resistance. The marines took possession of Nautilus Island and its cache of four cannons, and the British flag that had flown upon its summit was proudly delivered to General Lovell.

Immediately upon the capture of the island, Lovell sent orders to Paul Revere to fortify the post with additional cannon and munitions and to construct a breastwork on the island's strategic heights.[30] A potent battery of artillery aimed on Captain Mowat's ships finally could clear the way for the commodore to take Majabigwaduce Harbor—and for the land forces to attack Fort George. Timing was critical, and hands from every regiment were called to assist in the undertaking.

Upon receipt of his orders from the general, however, Revere wavered. The commissary of ordnance heard him indignantly complaining that the general could not possibly have meant *him* to go on the mission— that clearly some mistake had been made. Revere then ordered the Castle barge to carry him to Lovell's headquarters, where he personally questioned the general regarding the explicit meaning of his orders. On his return, Revere directed another officer not belonging to the artillery train to carry out the questioned order.[31]

All through the night, about three hundred Rebel soldiers labored with the marines on Nautilus Island, and by dawn they had erected a respectable artillery stronghold. The simple earthwork, containing four four-pound artillery pieces abandoned by the British during the attack, was improved and repaired, and in the hours to follow, the Rebels transported and placed into position a brass field piece, a howitzer, and one twelve-pound and two eighteen-pound cannons. During the fortification, however, the men were dismayed to find that the all-important ammunition supplied by Revere for the guns, so laboriously hauled into place, was inexplicably the wrong size. Revere also had failed to supply cannon wadding from the ordnance brig, a critical piece of equipment used to separate gunpowder from the round shot. After Captain Lawrence Furlong, one of the officers at work on the Nautilus Island battery, "applied several times to Colonel Revere, but could not get Shot that were suitable,"[32] he went directly to the commodore for assistance. Finally, the gunner aboard the *Warren* begrudgingly supplied ninety rounds of shot for the twelve- and eighteen-pound guns from the ship's own stores but refused to provide the wadding. "I told him it was Colonel Revere's business to supply himself," the gunner would later grumble.[33]

With the island guns finally in place and the flag of the Continental Marines hoisted proudly on a towering spruce, Captain Mowat was left with no alternative but to move his sloops and transports to a position farther up the river, leaving the mouth of the harbor undefended.

Receiving little sign that Saltonstall intended to act even against a greatly outnumbered and outgunned foe, the men were growing weary of their cantankerous commodore. Later in the morning as a barrage of cannon fire from Nautilus Island rained down on the *Albany, North,* and *Nautilus,* the officers of the Massachusetts Navy and the operators of the private vessels anchored in Penobscot Bay, frustrated by inaction, circulated and signed a petition to Saltonstall warning of the dangers of delay and imploring him to act. "[O]ur enemies are daily Fortifying and Strengthening themselves, & are stimulated so to do being in daily Expectation of a Reinforcement . . . ," they wrote. "We don't mean to Advise, or Censure Your past conduct, But intend only to express our desire . . . to go Immediately into the Harbour, & attack the Enemys Ships."[34] The men delivered their missive and impatiently awaited orders.

But still Saltonstall refused to press the attack.

It had become clear to General Lovell and many of his officers that if the council's order to "Captivate Kill or destroy" the enemy was to be accomplished, it would have to be initiated by the Rebel land forces. With Mowat's ships no longer guarding the mouth of the harbor, the main objective of the expedition—the taking of Fort George—could now be attempted.

On the afternoon of June 27, a council of war was held on the *Warren* among the various commanders, officers, and sea captains, and they arrived at a deliberative consensus for the mode and timing of a direct assault on the British garrison. At the meeting, General Lovell estimated his fighting force from the Maine and Massachusetts militias to be 850 men. Since the purpose of the strike would be to devastate the enemy with an overwhelming ground attack, Commodore Saltonstall agreed to contribute 227 of his green-coated marines from the various warships, while Lieutenant Colonel Revere committed an additional 80 men from the artillery train to be armed with muskets rather than cannon to augment the infantry numbers. They agreed that the attack would begin at 12:00 midnight.[35]

The schedule proved exceedingly optimistic. The previous night's work on Nautilus Island had left many of the men sleepless and weary. The marines had labored arduously to take possession of the site and to create the artillery battery that now guarded the harbor, but the success of a crushing land assault as agreed on by the council of war would, no doubt, depend on a rested and able soldiery.

As midnight approached and the preparation of the longboats and whalers for the transport of the men to the beaches of Majabigwaduce began, the operation was immediately beset with complexity and delay. Through the night a gloomy fog had blanketed the bay, making visibility and the movement of men difficult; and as the excursion began, a shortage of landing boats led to confusion and uncertainty among the fatigued troops. The simple logistics of lowering more than one thousand men from transports and warships into waiting rowboats and quietly shuttling them ashore would prove time-consuming and arduous.

Finally, at about 3:00 A.M., as the soldiers were still being ferried out of the fog toward the western shores of Majabigwaduce, Commodore Saltonstall gave the order to the captains of the *Tyrannicide*, the *Hunter*, and the *Sky Rocket* to open fire on the wooded heights housing the British troops above.

Instantly, the ghostly silence of the predawn murk was shattered by the explosive charge of iron cannonballs, chainshot, and grapeshot ripping through the forest canopy and slamming into the men and armament of the high ground. Under cover of the naval barrage, Solomon Lovell, Peleg Wadsworth, and Paul Revere rallied their anxious men and prepared them for the battle to come. "Our troops were entirely undisciplined," recalled Peleg Wadsworth years later. "[H]owever they were generally brave & spirited Men."[36]

Just before sunrise the sailors aboard the commodore's fleet of warships hailed the departing army with three cheers, and Peleg Wadsworth led the initial wave of soldiers into the early morning light of Majabigwaduce.

🎐 "We landed on a very rocky beach, and ascended a bank 300 feet high, covered with as thick a wood as ever grew," Paul Revere wrote. "It was so steep that no man could git up without taking hold of the bushes . . ."[37] The marines—led by Captain John Welch, who had daringly spearheaded the raid against Nautilus Island the previous afternoon, now accompanied by a contingent of Colonel Samuel McCobb's Lincoln County, Maine, militiamen—charged up the steep inclines to the right, north of Dyce's Head, and immediately came under heavy musketry from the enemy above. Struggling against the perilous terrain and withering fire, the men steadily advanced among a throng of wounded and dying comrades.

To the left, General Wadsworth, also with a division of the Maine Militia, faced similar travails as he and his men fought their way up the impossible incline toward the fortified enemy beyond. "There was now a stream of fire over our heads from the Fleet & a shower of Musketry in our faces from the Top of the Cliff. We soon found the Cliff insurmountable even without Opponents," wrote Wadsworth.[38] Yet the bloodied and battered men stumbled forward.

On the beachhead a marine fifer by the name of Israel Trask, all of fourteen years old, crouched behind a granite boulder and watched as the harried troops raced past. He had been employed on privateering vessels since he was ten and had embarked upon the Penobscot Expedition aboard the *Black Prince*. Nothing, however, prepared him for the horrors he now beheld. Nervously, Trask chirped a rallying tune on his fife and mustered as much bravery as his frightful circumstances could permit. When Captain John Hinkley of Colonel McCobb's Lincoln County militia regiment rose upon the boulder to exhort his troops, only to be shot dead on the spot by British musket fire, it was said that Trask "did not lose a note of the tune he was playing . . ."[39]

At the center of the attack, keeping up a steady fire in an effort to divert the enemy's attention from the beleaguered marine and infantry regiments on their flanks, was the remaining portion of McCobb's Maine militiamen, who labored against the cliff face and fought their way toward the slopes beyond.

From the moment the Rebel forces left the boats and began their ascent of the cliffs, they found themselves overwhelmed by enemy fire; and though they greatly outnumbered the British at the top of the crest, the steepness of the terrain and the constant stream of musketry from above made the attack chaotic and difficult. It was "a most gallant assault," historian Nathan Goold proclaimed to a gathering of the Maine Historical Society in 1898, "without order or discipline, each man dependent on his personal courage, against a most destructive fire, which they were in no position to return."[40]

To the rear of the attack, with the greater part of the fighting force far ahead, General Lovell assembled his militia regiment and, with Paul Revere and the men of the Massachusetts Artillery Train following close behind as a corps de reserve, began their assent of the heights. "I landed agreeable to Orders, after forming on the beach," Revere would write in his journal. "I see the General, who orders me to follow him with my men; we ascend the Steep; then formed and marched near the edge of the Wood next the Enemy . . ."[41]

At the crest of the western inclines of Majabigwaduce north of Dyce's Head, a small contingent of untested Scottish Highlanders formed an advance line across the ridge in the morning fog and watched with mounting alarm as a muster of Rebel soldiers gathered on the beach and began their assent. The unnerving barrage of cannon fire from the armada in the bay had shattered the relative calm of the night and sent shockwaves of fear through many in the British regiment. General McLean had been uncertain from where the Rebel attack would come, but he thought the unfriendly terrain to the west of the peninsula would be a sufficient deterrent to allow the concentration of his limited forces in other more vulnerable areas. Now, as the marines scrambled through the heavy brush along the rise north of Dyce's Head, McLean rued his posting of only eighty men in that location with just another seventy on the plateau above near Fort George.

As General Wadsworth's army emerged from the foggy beachhead and began its grueling ascent of the wooded cliffs, the soldiers of the Seventy-fourth Foot Regiment let off a volley of musket fire toward the pitching enemy and then, recognizing the great superiority of the coming throng, faltered and began to fall back in disorderly retreat.

An eighteen-year-old British lieutenant named John Moore, in charge of twenty soldiers on the left flank of the British picket, rose in defiance and valiantly implored his men to stand and fight. "Will the Hamilton men leave me?" he shouted. "Come back, and behave like soldiers!"[42] In years to come Lieutenant General Sir John Moore would revolutionize the training methods of British soldiers and, on his death in 1809 in the Spanish War, be immortalized by Charles Wolfe's sonnet, "The Burial of Sir John Moore after Corunna"; but now, in his first taste of battle, Moore bravely rallied his men on the cliffs of Majabigwaduce and poured relentless fire into the American marines below.

With excruciating determination and among a storm of musketry from Lieutenant Moore's men, the marines thrashed their way through the steep terrain to the more gentle slopes above and there, joined by the militia regiments to the left, bore down upon the small group of Highlanders and pinioned the unit, killing six.

Having been informed of the ferocious battle at the heights and the uncertain fate of Lieutenant Moore, General McLean ordered a fresh company to the front in an effort to stem the ongoing assault. Now, as reinforcements arrived upon the firestorm surrounding Moore's company, it was clear that a covered retreat through the woods to the relative safety of Fort George was all that could be safely and quickly accomplished.

Far below, in the bombarded and broken forest, word came to General Lovell of the stirring victory of his ground forces. "The General commanded a halt; we had not halted a great while, when he received accounts, they had got possession of the Heights," Revere impassively recorded in his journal.[43]

In a period of less than twenty minutes, Peleg Wadsworth and his tattered band of marines and militia had gallantly taken Dyce's Head and were now in plain sight of Fort George beyond. It appeared that the objective of the grand Penobscot Expedition was at hand and that the British evacuation of Majabigwaduce was all but assured. "I was in no position to defend myself," General McLean would say. "I only meant to give them one or two guns, so as not to be called a coward, and then [would] have struck my colors, which I stood for some time to do, as I did not wish to throw away the lives of my men for nothing."[44] Of McLean's resignation, William Hutchings would write, "He stood with the pennant halyards in his own hands all ready to strike the colors himself. He said he had been in nineteen battles without getting beaten, but he expected he should be beaten in the twentieth one."[45]

As Francis McLean gathered his defenses and waited in reconciled gloom for the tempest of Rebel infantry that he was sure would storm through the woods at any moment toward his beleaguered earthworks, an exhausted and disorganized American force stumbled about the upper slopes of Majabigwaduce merely two hundred yards from Fort George, unsure of what to do next. Many of the men fully expected the order to fix bayonets and ready themselves for attack at a moment's notice. Though tired and weakened from the perilous scale up the cliffs, the men understood that only a jumbled and unfinished redoubt within musket shot of their current site stood between them and absolute victory. It seemed a matter of military common sense that the men would form again and press the attack.

Upon finally reaching his victorious army at the top of the exhausting incline, however, General Lovell's guarded instincts prevailed. Satisfied with the achievements of the morning, he promptly ordered the army's current position to be fortified in defense of a possible counterattack. Rather than advancing his men to Fort George and to victory, Solomon Lovell was digging in.

Thomas Philbrook, who ascended the heights in the second wave of attack behind the marines, watched with growing disdain as the general began hurrying about the site supervising the construction of huts and roads, seemingly without a further thought of assault, while the British continued to fortify their garrison. "In three or four days the militia were comfortably housed as if we had come to spend the summer with our English neighbors," he later wrote.[46]

Upon returning to the shore later that afternoon, the general peered upward toward the heights that his men had so boldly conquered and absorbed himself in a moment of self-congratulatory adulation. "I don't think such a landing has been made since Wolfe,"[47] he would write in his journal in reference to James Wolfe's daring ascent of the cliffs along the St. Lawrence River in the Battle of Quebec in 1759.

Estimates of the number of Americans killed or wounded in the Rebel assault on the highlands of Majabigwaduce varied from fourteen to one hundred;[48] but all parties agreed that among all the dead, perhaps the most grieved was Captain John Welch, who fell from a musket ball fired from one of Lieutenant Moore's rallied troops on the cliffs above Penobscot Bay.

Paul Revere understood the lost opportunity and initiative in failing to carry the attack to Fort George. "In my opinion this was the only time in which we might have subdued the enemy had there been a plan laid; for the ships to have attacked the enemy's ships, and we to have marched on to the fort and stormed it . . ." he later wrote to his friend General William Heath. "[T]hey not knowing our strength, and we being flushed with victory, I have no doubt they would have lain down their arms . . ." And in a wistful flourish, he added: "Had we finally have come off victorious, this would have been called, the bravest action since the war commenced . . ."[49]

Meanwhile, as Solomon Lovell swelled with contentment over the achievements of his army at Majabigwaduce, and Paul Revere lamented opportunities lost, British naval forces in New York were stirring. "I received this morning certain intelligence that an armament sailed from Boston . . . to attack his Majesty's new settlement in Penobscot River," wrote Admiral Sir George Collier to the secretary of the Admiralty.

"I intend putting to sea at daylight tomorrow."[50]

Chapter 8 "What's Become of Colonel Revere?"

BEYOND THE PRECIPICE of Dyce's Head on the upper, gentler slopes leading to the wooded plateau into which Fort George had been carved, a battery of three British cannon ominously enhanced Captain Mowat's presence in Majabigwaduce Harbor. Manned only by a small group of Redcoats during the American assault of the heights, however, the post had been eagerly abandoned when a throng of Rebel marines with fixed bayonets stormed the nest and drove its defenders to the sea.

With the British redoubt now in Rebel hands, the call immediately went out to Lieutenant Colonel Revere to supply the necessary ramrods, cartridges, and sponges in an effort to repair and equip the guns and to turn them against the enemy. A battery of cannon so close to the British garrison would prove extremely useful in threatening its defenses—as well as the morale of the men who controlled it. As he done earlier, however, Revere balked at the request, citing the need to conserve his supplies should they be needed later in the conflict.[1] Again the call went out to the gunnery officer aboard the *Warren* to provide the necessary equipment. "The person applying said he had applied on board the Ordnance Brig . . . but had not been supplied by Colonel Revere," griped the gunnery officer, who begrudgingly supplied the battery from the ship's own stock[2]—but soon a hearty contempt began to grow among the soldiers and sailors against the commander of the Massachusetts Artillery Train.

With the obstacle of the British redoubt safely removed, Commodore Saltonstall cautiously edged four of his warships to the mouth of Majabigwaduce Harbor and, at 10:00 A.M., turned the thirty-two-gun *Warren* broadside and opened fire on Mowat's ships. The winds were

light, according to the logs of the *Albany* and *Nautilus*, and clearly Saltonstall feared venturing too deeply into the harbor with no ready means of
escape[3] from what he had called "that damned hole."

Buttressed by the "brisk and well directed fire" from the newly installed cannons on Nautilus Island,[4] Saltonstall cruised the *Warren* back
and forth across the entrance of the harbor and directed his cannonade of the enemy ships. Despite the formidable display of Rebel fire-
power from multiple positions, the attack proved relatively ineffective,
and Mowat's three sloops of war stood their ground and unleashed their
broadside fire on the flagship *Warren*, the primary target of the British
volleys. For half an hour the battle at sea raged, when finally the commodore decided he'd had enough. The Loyalist John Calef, who watched
the battle unfold from the heights, recorded, "The *Warren* suffered con-
siderably; her mainmast shot through in two places, the gammoning of
her bowsprit cut to pieces, and her fore-stay shot away. Their confusion
appeared to be great . . ."[5]

Despite Mowat's clear victory, the newly installed guns on Nautilus
Island continued the barrage of the British ships, forcing them to retreat
further up the harbor even as the injured *Warren* limped away. For two
days, the beleaguered warship lay motionless at the foot of Dyce's Head
while her damage was repaired. Saltonstall's natural timidity, however,
was only heightened. "The prospect of succeeding appears at present
very dubious . . ." wrote a sailor in the journals of the Continental ship
Hunter.[6]

Meanwhile, on the high ground of Majabigwaduce, General Lovell's
siege had begun. In rejecting the suggestion of an all-out assault on the
garrison, he concluded that his men would be unable to overrun the fortified British, and instead he began digging in. "I cannot but regret that
You have put the Event on such an Issue; Since I think the Enemy yet
might probably be reduced without ever directly Storming their Cita-
del," Lovell wrote to the commodore on August 6. "We often effect that
by degrees which cannot be done at once."[7]

Preparations for defensive entrenchments were quickly organized,
and Lovell ordered the cutting of cart paths for the movement of men
and artillery. On first word that the Marines had taken the heights, Lovell

immediately commanded Paul Revere to return to shore and retrieve a fieldpiece from the ordnance brig for use on the front.

On arriving back at the beachhead, Revere caught the eye of Thomas J. Carnes, captain of the Massachusetts Marines, aboard the privateer *Putnam*. Carnes earlier had led his men up the cliffs and, in the confusion of battle, was apparently separated from his company. He knew that Revere, as commander of the artillery, had been ordered to ascend the cliffs as a reserve corps; yet now, he could not recall seeing the lieutenant colonel until well after the heights had been taken.[8]

In 1775 Carnes had been an officer in Richard Gridley's Massachusetts Artillery Regiment;[9] and thus, he had practical experience with the workings of Revolutionary War cannon and the units that handled them. He well knew that supervision by officers of the artillery corps was an absolute necessity for the transport and placement of guns. He had also, no doubt, been informed earlier by William Todd of Todd's dubious assessment of the character of the Castle Island commander.

Now Carnes watched with interest as Revere ordered his artillery captain, Perez Cushing, to retrieve the needed fieldpiece from the *Samuel* and have it drawn to the siege above. On delivery of this order, according to Carnes and others, Paul Revere, apparently contented with his work for the morning, ferried himself to a nearby transport and ate a hot breakfast while Cushing's men painstakingly began hauling the fieldpiece on shore and up the heights of Majabigwaduce.[10]

Carnes would later write of the incident, "Mr. Revere, when ordered on shore with artillery, excused himself."[11]

☙ Intent on further enhancing his fortification of the heights, General Lovell surmised that the howitzer and fieldpiece currently on Nautilus Island could be put to better use bearing down upon Fort George. When Revere finally arrived back on shore, Lovell ordered him to retrieve these guns and have them carried to the lines, together with two additional eighteen-pound and one twelve-pound brass cannon with supplies and munitions from the ordnance brig. The undertaking would prove to be daunting.

Nearly two hundred seamen from the various warships were called to the task and, for almost three full days, strove in the humid and mosquito-filled air against gravity and the sheer weight of metal. The massiveness of the guns—at nearly five thousand pounds each—against the rocky and uneven incline made their transport close to impossible. Though most of Revere's artillerymen joined in the effort, some of the sailors resented being called from their assigned duties to perform what they viewed as the work of others. The task of transporting cannon, they charged, should have been left to the regiment that operated it. As for the artillery commander himself, there was apparently little need to concern himself with the endeavor. "[T]he Captains of the Fleet [were] obliged to get his Cannon on Shore, and hall them into the Batteries," Thomas Carnes would complain of Paul Revere. "[H]e hardly ever was there to see or to give any orders about them . . ."[12]

Apparently unaware of McLean's precarious situation at the British garrison beyond the clearing, General Lovell was concerned solely with the fortification of his own position against attack. With the capture of the heights he insisted that all able-bodied men stay on post and actively work on its defense. Indeed, the explicit orders of the afternoon stated, "The General positively commands that no man be permitted to leave the Lines without a permission from him."[13] Despite these unequivocal orders, however, Lieutenant Colonel Revere was, according to many on the Penobscot Expedition, nowhere to be found.

While the men continued the punishing task of hauling the guns to the front lines, Revere apparently had surveyed the shore and located an easier site on which to land his cannon. He informed the general, and soon carpenters, sailors, and officers were hard at work clearing Revere's path to the new Rebel battery. Notwithstanding this gesture of industry, Revere was widely observed leaving his men and returning to the transports at regular intervals for meals and to attend to menial tasks such as sawing fuses and culling shot. William Todd, Revere's longtime nemesis, would later observe, "[P]lainly . . . this man was very fond of being out of the way."[14]

On the first evening after the assault on Dyce's Head, and for several thereafter, as the marines and militiamen erected tents along the shore and upon the heights, Paul Revere and a portion of his regiment stole away to the transports and comfortably slept in their hammocks aboard ship. "For several days . . . he could not be found, and more especially the Night the Battery was erected at the edge of the wood, General Wadsworth asked after him Several times, and Could not find him."[15] Finally, out of frustration, Wadsworth employed Captain Cushing to cut out embrasures on the newly constructed breastworks—a task that the young general had intended for Revere and his men.

Lovell also was becoming increasingly frustrated by the absence of his artillery commander. On several occasions he had sent William Todd to the encampment of the train with orders to have Revere attend at the General's marquee. "I never found him there more than once," stated Todd. "General Lovell said that he was surprised at Colonel Revere's inattention to his duty . . ."[16] Gilbert Speakman, the commissary of ordnance, witnessed the general's dismay at Revere's conduct and later recounted, "The General . . . wondered . . . [why Revere] kept himself out of the way, and [turning] to me said 'do you know, Captain Speakman, what's become of Colonel Revere?"[17]

🎗 On the evening of July 28, General Lovell proudly forwarded a dispatch to the Massachusetts Council informing its members of his brave conquest of the heights and of his hope to soon capture the entire British army on Majabigwaduce.[18] At the same time, Lovell issued a proclamation to the people of the region that mocked and derided the "profane oath" of allegiance to the Crown compelled by General McLean several weeks earlier and sternly directed those who had sworn such loyalty to appear at his marquee within forty-eight hours ready to stand with the Rebel cause or otherwise to be "considered as traitors."[19]

Time, however, was not on the general's side. Though his proclamation would prompt many in the area to report to the Rebel camp, the men were, for the most part, untrained and undisciplined; and the overall morale of the American camp began to deteriorate. With every day that passed, more of his men skulked away into the Maine woods, and a restless frustration began to suffuse the navy. One captain of a privateer openly scorned that "he had Rather all the Penobscot Expedition would go to hell, then he should Loose the Benefit of his Cruse."[20]

John Singleton Copley's circa 1768 portrait of the artisan Paul Revere.
John Singleton Copley, American, 1738–1815. *Paul Revere*, 1768. Oil on canvas,
89.22 × 72.39 cm (35 ⅛ × 28 ½ in.). Museum of Fine Arts, Boston.
Gift of Joseph W. Revere, William B. Revere, and Edward H. R. Revere, 30.781.
Photograph © 2014 Museum of Fine Arts, Boston.

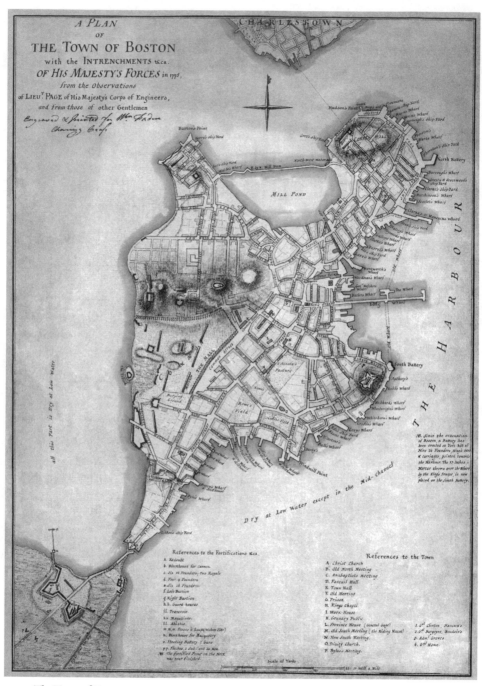

The Town of Boston, 1775.
Library of Congress, Geography and Map Division.

"On brave RESCINDERS!" Revere's farcical rebuke of the seventeen "scoundrels"
of the Massachusetts House of Representatives who voted for rescission of Samuel
Adams's Circular Letter on June 30, 1768.
Courtesy of the American Antiquarian Society.

London: Published as the Act directs July 1st, 1775 by J.S.

Reproduced from the original Print preserved in the John

London: Republished May 1911 by Henry Stevens, Son & Stiles. Map &
over against the South West Corner of the British

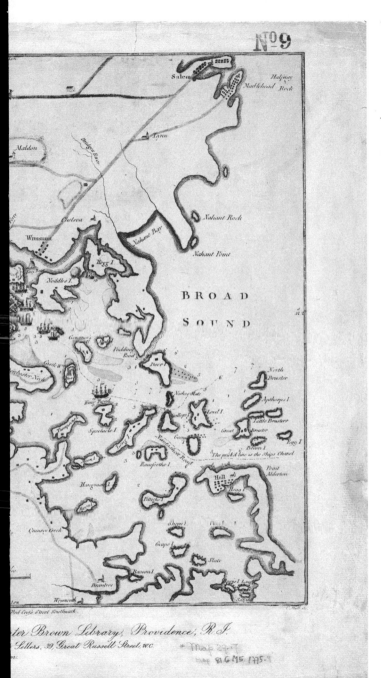

A plan of Boston, its harbor islands, and the surrounding towns, prepared by J. De Costa, taken from a British survey and showing the position of troops in and around Lexington on April 19, 1775. Library of Congress, Geography and Map Division.

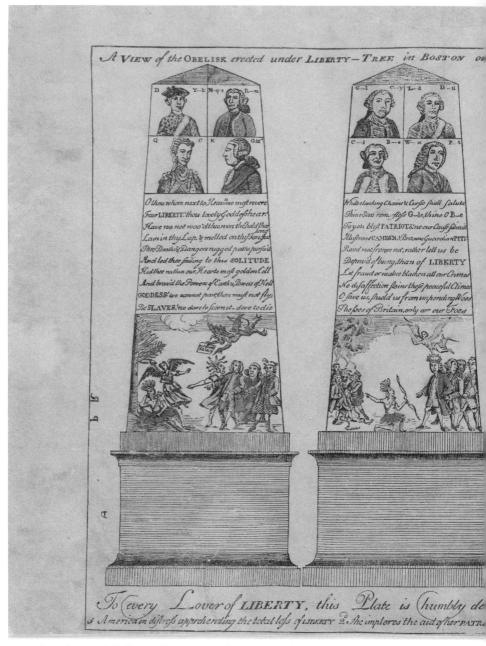

Revere's rendering of the "magnificent Pyramid" erected on the Boston Common in May of 1766 to celebrate the repeal of the Stamp Act. Across the bottom of the print, Revere inscribed, "To every Lover of LIBERTY *this Plate is humbly dedicated by her true born* SONS *in Boston, New England." Courtesy of the American Antiquarian Society.*

Rejoicings for the Repeal of the ——— Stamp-Act   1766

PaulRevere Sculp

Revere's inflammatory — and generally inaccurate — copperplate engraving of the "Bloody Massacre." The print helped to galvanize colonial opinion against British occupation of Boston, but Revere would be accused of misappropriating the artwork of Boston engraver Henry Pelham. Courtesy of the American Antiquarian Society.

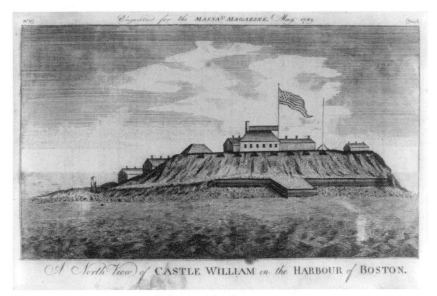

A *North View* of CASTLE WILLIAM *in the* HARBOUR *of* BOSTON.

A view of Castle Island, where Revere was stationed for much of the Revolutionary War. Library of Congress Prints and Photographs Division

Rendering by Charles H. Waterhouse of the assault on the heights of Majabigwaduce by American troops on July 28, 1779. The original of this work, which hung at the United States Pentagon, was destroyed in the attacks of 9/11. Courtesy of the Art Collection, National Museum of the Marine Corps, Triangle, Virginia.

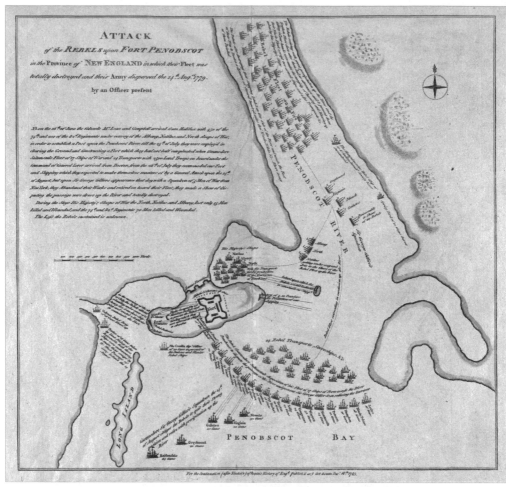

A map drawn in 1785 by an anonymous British "Officer Present" depicting the naval attack on Majabigwaduce and the subsequent Rebel retreat. Though meticulous in its detail, the map incorrectly positions the Penobscot River to the east of the peninsula, while its actual geographic location is to the west. Map image from the Richard H. Brown Collection courtesy of the Norman B. Leventhal Map Center at the Boston Public Library.

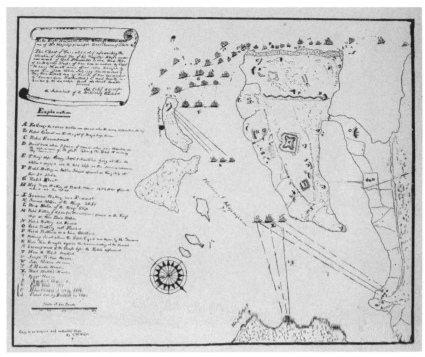

Chart of naval positions and battery placements at and surrounding Majabigwaduce in July 1779, drawn by John Calef for Lord George Germain, secretary of state for the Colonies. From George Augustus Wheeler, *Castine Past and Present: The Ancient Settlement of Pentagöet and the Modern Town* (Boston: Rockwell and Churchill Press, 1896), 75.

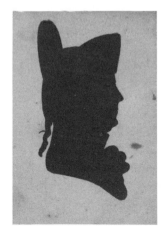

Silhouette of General Peleg Wadsworth, second in command of land forces on the Penobscot Expedition. Wadsworth, the man whose grandson would one day immortalize the name of Paul Revere, promised Revere's immediate arrest for refusing orders on the retreat from Majabigwaduce. Courtesy of the National Park Service, Longfellow House– Washington's Headquarters National Historic Site.

Dominic Serres's Destruction of the American Fleet at Penobscot Bay, 14 August 1779. Original housed in the collection of the National Maritime Museum, Greenwich, London.

Admiral Sir George Collier, circa 1795. On the first appearance of Collier's fleet approaching Majabigwaduce on August 13, 1779, the American forces abandoned their positions and began their ill-fated retreat up the Penobscot River. Original housed in the collection of the National Maritime Museum, Greenwich, London.

Sir George Collier's Victory in Penobscot Bay, 1779, *depicting the pursuit of the American naval force on the Penobscot River.* © Mystic Seaport: The Museum of America and the Sea, no. 1961.711.

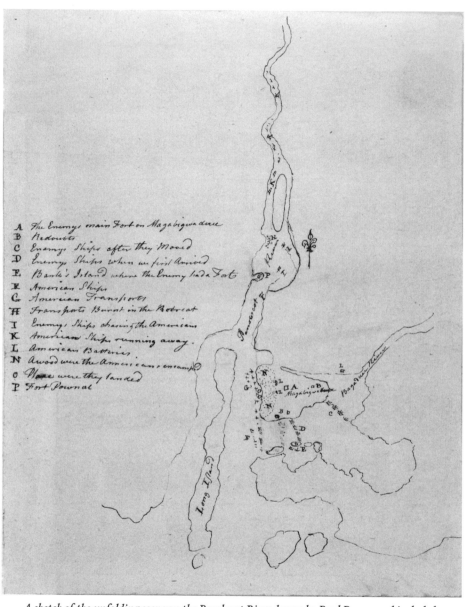

A *The Enemys main Fort on Magabigwaduce*
B *Redoubts*
C *Enemys Ships after they Moved*
D *Enemys Ships when we first Arrived*
E *Banks's Island where the Enemy had a Fort*
F *American Ships*
G *American Transports*
H *Transports Burnt in the Retreat*
I *Enemys Ships chasing the Americans*
K *American Ships running away.*
L *American Batteries*
N *A wood were the Americans encamped*
O *Were were they landed*
P *Fort Pownal*

A sketch of the unfolding scene on the Penobscot River drawn by Paul Revere and included with his letter to William Heath of October 24, 1779. Note his map key entry "K," "American ships running away." Courtesy of the Massachusetts Historical Society.

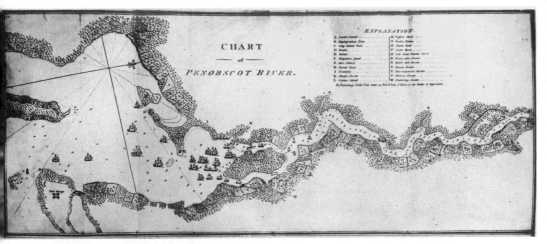

A chart of the Penobscot River drawn by John Calef, depicting the Rebel retreat from Majabigwaduce. From Calef, "The Journal of the Siege of Penobscot," 1910.

Faneuil Hall, "that guild of temple traders and aldermen, butchers and clerks, hucksters and civic magistrates . . . ," was donated to the Town of Boston in 1742 by Peter Faneuil and became the focal point of commerce and politics in colonial Boston. From September 22 through October 1, 1779, it was the site of the inquiry into the failure of the Penobscot Expedition. Library of Congress Prints and Photographs Division.

Portrait of Artemas Ward, painted in 1795 by Raphaelle Peale. Ward served as chairman of the committee of inquiry into the failure of the Penobscot Expedition and wrote prior to the hearing, "Lieut.-Col. Paul Revere is now under an arrest for disobedience of orders, and unsoldierlike behavior tending to cowardice, etc. As soon as the siege was raised, he made the best of his way to Boston, leaving his men to get along as they could (as it's said) . . ." Courtesy of the President and Fellows of Harvard College.

The September 6, 1779, order of the Massachusetts Council to Paul Revere to "Resign the Command of Castle Island" and to "repair to his dwelling house in Boston," pending inquiry into the charges filed against him by Thomas Carnes. Massachusetts Archives, vol. 175, p. 545. Courtesy of the Massachusetts Archives. Photo by Carolyn McPherson.

State of
Mass.ᵗˢ Bay } Council Chamber Boston; April 13ᵗʰ 1780.

Ordered That there be & hereby is appointed a General Court Martial, in Consequence of a Resolve of the General Court dated March 1 & 4th for the Tryal of Lieut. Col.ᵒ Paul Revere of the Corps of Artillery belonging to this State, touching his Behaviour as an Officer when, retreating from Majorbigwaduce as particularly set forth in the & Repᵗ of a Committee of the General Court appointed to examine into the Conduct of the Officers of the Train & Militia Officers employed on the Expedition to Penobscot, dated November 18ᵗʰ 1779 and Court Martial to sit on Tuesday the Eighteenth day of April curᵗ nine oClock A.M. at the County Court House in Boston —

Colonel Edward Procter President.

Cap.ᵗˢ Elias Parkman   Cap.ᵗˢ John Stutson
      Caleb Champney   John Newell
      David Bell   Carson Belcher
      Levi Jennings   Israel Loring
      John Kneeland   Joshua Farrington
      John Gill   Joseph Pratt   } Members

William Tudor Esq.ᵒ
Judge Advocate

And Colonel Edward Procter is hereby directed to Summon the several Members abovementioned to attend at time and place, and for the purpose aforesaid, and in case any of the before mentioned Members

On April 13, 1780, after a string of petitions and appeals, the Massachusetts Council finally ordered the appointment of a "General Court Martial for the Tryal of Lieutenant Colonel Paul Revere . . ." The president of the tribunal, Colonel Edward Proctor, refused, however, to convene the hearing "for reasons best known to himself."

Members thro' sickness, or any other substantial
Occasions shall not be able to attend, the said Tryal
the said Col.º Procter is further directed to
Summon other Captains from the Neighbouring
Militia Regiment, forthwith to attend said
Tryal as Members in their room. And to Summon
the said Lieut. Col.º Paul Revere to attend upon his
Defence at time and place aforesaid, by serving
him immediately on Receipt hereof, with a Copy
of this Order and the Charge against him herewith
inclosed. —————— And the said Court Martial are
hereby directed to Summon such Witnesses as
may be necessary to Examine, in the Course of
the said Tryal, and when they shall have finished
said Tryal to return a Copy of their Proceedings
and Judgement to the Council of this State
with their reasonable Account of Attendance
for Allowance and Payment.

~~True Copy~~ Attest
John Avery D.S. r

Profile of Paul Revere, from the drawing of Charles Balthazar Julien Fevret de Saint-Memin, circa 1800. Library of Congress Prints and Photographs Division.

Gilbert Stuart's oil painting of Paul Revere, circa 1813. Gilbert Stuart, American, 1755–1828. *Paul Revere,* 1813. Oil on panel, 71.75 × 57.15 cm (28 ¼ × 22 ½ in.). Museum of Fine Arts, Boston. Gift of Joseph W. Revere, William B. Revere, and Edward H. R. Revere, 30.782. Photograph © 2014 Museum of Fine Arts, Boston.

At a council of war held on July 29 aboard the crippled *Warren* among Commodore Saltonstall and the captains of the American warships, it was decided that entrance into the harbor to confront Captain Mowat was out of the question without further bombardment of British land positions by General Lovell.[21] Exploiting the already risk-averse attitude of his privateers and employing his relentless cynicism on the remaining captains, Saltonstall continued his timid disinclination to force the issue at sea while insisting upon decisive action on land.

But General Lovell had problems of his own. From the moment of his landing at Majabigwaduce, his army had exhibited what he called "loose and disorderly inattentive behavior,"[22] and he feared that, despite their recent gains, the men were not prepared to engage General McLean's troops in battle.

In an effort to regain some control over the expedition, General Lovell, in his field orders of July 30, adamantly reminded all soldiers and noncommissioned officers to remain on the lines unless otherwise directed by himself or General Wadsworth. He forbade the celebratory firing of muskets, and he reiterated that all directives from command be carefully communicated to the men by their adjuncts in order to avoid confusion or claimed ignorance of orders. And, in a direct and angry reproach of his artillery commander, Lovell ordered, for all to see, "that Colonel Revere and the Corps under his Command encamp with the Army in future on Shore, in order not only to strengthen the Lines but to manage the Cannon in our several Operations."[23]

To absolutely ensure that Revere received the order, Lovell had a "billet" personally delivered to him that had been drafted by William Todd expressing the general's dissatisfaction with Revere's absence from the lines and demanding his immediate attendance at the marquee. The missive was delivered late at night aboard the *Samuel* as Revere slept in the comfort of his quarters.[24]

Clearly annoyed by the intrusion, Revere expressed his surprise at the general's order but appeared before him as requested. Later, when he returned to the ship, the captain of the *Samuel* heard him make "a trifling matter of it"[25]—but by the following morning Paul Revere and the men of the Massachusetts Artillery Train rowed ashore with tents and camp supplies on their backs, and they remained on Bagaduce Peninsula for the duration of the expedition.

🎗 General McLean considered every day that the Rebel forces delayed their attack on Fort George to be "as good to him as another thousand men."[26] Day and night, his men and upward of one hundred inhabitants of the region labored to enhance the structure and strength of the garrison and to maintain its defensive capability. By the closing days of July, the chasm in the unfinished bastions had been filled with logs and debris, a functioning well had been dug with a ten-foot thick earthen fascine surrounding it, and artillery platforms had been laid and armed.[27] In a coordinated and systematic effort, McLean readied his fort for the Rebel onslaught that he was certain awaited him.

By the afternoon of July 29, three Rebel cannon and a howitzer finally had been dragged into place upon a newly constructed battery ahead of the former position on the heights and had begun a "warm and incessant" bombardment of Fort George.[28] Earlier in the day, Saltonstall had aligned his largest ships along the mouth of the harbor, and Captain Mowat, believing that an attack was imminent, had sunk all but one of his transports and sent the cannon and most of his crews to fortify the British land positions. At the same time, General McLean marshaled to the fort's own defenses six more artillery pieces from Half Moon battery at the south of the garrison overlooking the harbor.[29]

Now a fully defended Fort George exchanged a vicious nonstop cannonade with its enemy atop Majabigwaduce. For hours that would ultimately stretch into days, cannon shells and grapeshot ripped through the New England summer air and pummeled the positions of each fortified army on the heights, shattering nerves — and often flesh and bone. Within the British fort itself, alarmed Redcoats scurried to close breaches in the fortress walls caused by the occasional direct hit, and as the cannonade began, they quickly removed powder stockpiles from the framed storehouse to the safety of a ditch at the rear of the structure.

On the Rebel lines, the men of the Massachusetts Artillery worked tirelessly to arm and fire the howitzer and the twelve- and eighteen-pound guns trained squarely at their encamped enemy. The harrowing barrage continued at a constant and deafening pace, interrupted only by the peril of return fire. As the bombardment wore on, Paul Revere, the commanding officer of the artillery, was seen safely sheltered by a breast-work several hundred yards from the battery. Captain Carnes, an experienced artillaryman in his own right, later would note that Revere only seldom came out to direct his men or to provide training in the use of the equipment. "[I]f a good shot, he would say so, if a bad one he would say so, But never to give them any Instructions about the guns."[30] And on the rare occasion when Revere operated a fieldpiece himself, Carnes would note that Revere was astonishingly unskilled at the craft.[31]

Apparently General McLean shared Captain Carnes's opinion. Behind the walls of Fort George, McLean watched with dismay as his soldiers and officers, most of whom had never been the target of such a sustained blitz of cannon fire, sheltered their heads and cowered with fear upon every thunderous blast around them. Angrily, he shouted for his aides de-camp to open the fortress gates. With a look of disgust etched on his features, and with his full army curiously peering at him from behind the embrasures and the protective walls, McLean strode blithely out of Fort George toward the Rebel battery and into its line of fire. With shells streaking perilously above him, he smiled and turned to his aide, who himself was now trembling with fear. "You see," McLean crowed, "there is no danger from the fire of these wretched artillerymen."[32]

As he turned and slowly strode back toward the fort, the general knew that, win or lose, his men would now stand and fight.

With the Rebel position on the heights well established and with each side pummeling the other with artillery to a virtual stalemate, General Lovell again implored Saltonstall to proceed into Majabigwaduce Harbor and destroy the enemy ships. With 350 naval cannon at his disposal, Saltonstall outgunned Captain Mowat's three sloops of war nearly six to one,[33] yet he continued to shy away from his obligation to confront the enemy.

Making his utter disregard of duty all the more inexplicable, the commodore knew that time was of the essence. On the night of July 30, as Saltonstall lay resting in his cabin, Captain Philip Brown of the *Dili-*

gent informed him of an intercept of a British vessel carrying dispatches for General McLean. Though the dispatches themselves had been destroyed, a midshipman taken as prisoner confessed to Brown that transports from Halifax were already being boarded with reinforcements bound for Penobscot Bay. On reaching the *Warren* and delivering the sobering news, the commodore indifferently told Captain Brown that he "was fatigued & would examine [the prisoner] at another time."[34]

Earlier in the day, Saltonstall had received similarly distressing news from the Navy Board regarding a British fleet of reinforcements preparing to leave New York for Majabigwaduce. Still, when Lovell insisted that the Rebel ships enter the harbor and attack without delay, Saltonstall found yet another pretext to delay. Half Moon battery, a British position of three six-pound cannons to the south of Fort George, still threatened Rebel shipping in the harbor according to Saltonstall; and in a ploy of delay and obfuscation, he insisted that the small battery be removed before he would risk his warships in an attack. Though the American fleet easily could have destroyed what amounted to little more than an annoyance while sailing past, Lovell warily began drawing plans for another ground assault.[35]

On July 31 General Wadsworth led a force of three hundred marines, sailors, Indians, and militia through the early morning fog and at around 2:00 A.M. stormed the enemy battery overlooking the harbor. The startled Redcoats, numbering no more than fifty, rose and fired into the marauders with muskets and cannon, and soon the American sailors on the right faltered and ran. The marines under Captain Carnes, together with Colonel McCobb's militia unit, however, clashed viciously with their enemy in a hand-to-hand fracas that ended with the outnumbered British marines dashing for the safety of Fort George. The victory was short lived. By sunrise, as the Indians had completed taking the scalps and stripping the bodies of the enemy dead,[36] a swarm of fifty Scottish lowlanders poured down the slopes of Majabigwaduce and, though greatly outnumbered, drove the routed and confused Americans from the earthen redoubt.

In assessing the morning's events, Paul Revere, who had played no role in the assault, would write, "[W]e lost more men, killed, wounded, and prisoners than the place was worth; for when day light appeared they were obliged to leave it with all the cannon. We lost about 30."[37]

With the humiliating defeat of Lovell's men at Half Moon battery came a drenching rain and a dispirited morale.

With each passing hour clusters of soaked and doleful men disappeared into the Maine woods, and by the first few days of August, the American fighting force had fallen by almost 150 men.[38] As his already depleted army continued to deteriorate. General Lovell struggled with an inner turmoil. "I . . . conclude that my choice must be between the two parts of this alternative," he wrote to council president Jeremiah Powell, "either to continue a regular Siege with volunteer ships that cannot lie here long inactive; and a body of Militia where domestic affairs cannot admit of their being long from home; or risk the fate of a Storm [upon the fort]."[39] The only solution, mused the general, was the addition of in w and more disciplined troops into the equation. Later that afternoon he dispatched Reverend Murray to Denton aboard the row galley *Lincoln* with an urgent request for reinforcements.

Lovell also understood that British reinforcements were surely on their way, but he questioned the reliability of the reports coming into his camp daily. He could only wonder from where those reinforcements would come and what strength the force might be. Though it seemed out of his power to favorably conclude the mission that had been assigned to him, he was absolutely certain of one thing: time was running out.

A month earlier, George Washington had established his headquarters on the high ground above the Hudson River at West Point, New York. The single most strategic military site of the American colonies, according to Washington,[40] the commanding stronghold prevented the enemy from gaining free passage through the region and, accordingly, thwarted British intentions to isolate New England from the rest of the country.

On August 3, 1779, as the general of the Continental Army surveyed his daily correspondence at West Point, he felt compelled to quickly write the president of the Massachusetts Council. "I have Just received a Letter from Lord Stirling stationed in the Jerseys dated yesterday . . . by which it appears the Ships of War at New York have all put to sea," wrote Washington. "I thought it my duty to communicate this Intelligence that the Vessels employed in this expedition to Penobscot may be put upon their Guard, as it is probable enough these ships may be destined against them and if they should be surprised the consequences would be disagreeable."[41]

An increasingly frustrated Solomon Lovell now agreed, upon the grumblings of Commodore Saltonstall, to erect an artillery battery on the mainland north of Majabigwaduce overlooking the new position of Captain Mowat's three warships. On August 2, Paul Revere accompanied General Wadsworth to the area and, within a day, two cannon and a mobile fieldpiece were hauled into place and were firing across the inlet, present-day Hatch Cove, toward the British sloops. Despite the careful reconnoiter of the site, however, it quickly became obvious that the location of the battery was too far away to accurately strike its intended targets. On August 4, Lovell resignedly recorded in his journal, "[I]t's all that the Army can do & they have tried their best to destroy them." He concluded, "[T]he men are much fatigued being continually on some service or other, either Picket or throwing up works, and are beginning to sickly."[42]

As General Lovell grappled with an unpredictable enemy, a timorous commodore, and the deteriorating capacity of his own men, Paul Revere continued to cause him problems. A few days after the Rebel marines took the heights of Majabigwaduce, an envoy from Lovell's camp approached Revere and requested the use, on behalf of the general, of the Castle barge that had been towed up the coast by the *Samuel* with the rest of the fleet. Activity between land and shore had been brisk, and flatboats for the transport of men and equipment were in short supply. Lovell required the vessel, no doubt, for the movement of equipment to the front or for the delivery of munitions. Revere, however, turned Lovell's men away, tersely telling them that he had brought the barge for his own personal use and not the general's.[43] Lovell's requirements could be met elsewhere, he griped.

Revere's behavior at the councils of war also was being noted by the attending captains and officers. Within these councils, questions of risk and strategy were discussed and tactical decisions arrived at. Though not alone in his views and, indeed, often part of a unanimous decision, Revere consistently voted against further attack and often advocated termination of the siege. "It was always my sentiments," Revere wrote, "that if we could not Dislodge the Enemy in seven days, we ought to quit the ground . . ."[44] General Wadsworth later would suggest that Revere's "sentiments and opinions . . . 'where there was a division of voices' were always different from mine."[45] A less diplomatic William Todd assessed Revere's conduct at the various councils with the vitriolic fervor of an enemy. "[H]is absolute harangue . . . always overpowered those more mildly disposed," Todd would write. "His blustering rhetoric, which ever arose from his absolute arbitrary notions and false conceit of his superior genius was one of the causes of delay, and helped often to make the councils so unanimous as he says they used to be."[46]

Finally, on August 5, General Lovell forwarded a note to Dudley Saltonstall informing him that the army could accomplish nothing more without the destruction of the enemy ships. "I must therefore request an answer from you whether you will venture your Shipping up the River in order to demolish them or not," wrote Lovell.[47]

Aboard the *Warren*, Saltonstall regarded the general's request with rising ire and sneeringly convened a council of war among his various sea captains to debate the question. Though, as "a matter of indulgence," he endured the opinions of each man in the cabin, Saltonstall would be heard admitting that, in the end, it was solely his own opinion that would be followed[48] and thus "debate" was permitted in form only.

Immediately, the commodore began "preaching terror," arguing that even if the enemy's ships were destroyed it was no guarantee that the garrison itself would fall.[49] The risk to his own ships, he argued, was simply too great. A unilateral attack of the British sloops clearly was not an option to Saltonstall, and though several of the men vehemently argued in favor of it, he coaxed the majority to reject the motion. In begrudging acknowledgment of the imminent danger of British reinforcements, however, Saltonstall finally acquiesced, and the council so voted, to enter Majabigwaduce Harbor and attack Mowat's ships *if*, at the same time, Lovell stormed Fort George[50]—an act that all understood the general was incapable of properly effectuating with his current army.

Later that day, at another council of war called to consider the commodore's hopeless ultimatum, Generals Lovell and Wadsworth, Paul Revere, and others voted unanimously not to storm the British garrison—even if the enemy ships were to be attacked.[51] Recognizing the perils of a continuing deadlock, Lovell sent an envoy to the *Warren* to confer on the question, but the commodore, ever antagonistic, refused to discuss the matter with anyone other than the general himself at a grand council of war.

On August 7, the generals with their field officers together with the commodore and his sea captains convened aboard the *Hazard* and, for four straight hours, badgered one another, essentially agreeing upon nothing. While the sounds of McLean's fortifications echoed through the woods of Majabigwaduce, General Lovell detailed the declining state of his army and reiterated that it was in no condition to advance on the enemy fort. Saltonstall, for his part, indicated that rampant desertions and unease among the impressed seamen made a naval attack likewise problematic. Exploring the possibility of an attack upon the rear of the fort, Lovell suggested that, perhaps, four hundred men could take and hold the position. Paul Revere immediately answered that there weren't enough men to accomplish such a mission, and he repeatedly argued against making such an attempt, notwithstanding Lovell's belief that American reinforcements were on their way. When pressed by the commodore, Lovell admitted that without an influx of such reinforcements his present force would be unable to effectuate any viable attack upon the garrison. The ultimate question was then proposed: should the siege atop Majabigwaduce be abandoned? Citing the obvious inability of the land and sea forces to sustain a viable fighting capacity, Paul Revere argued vehemently for discontinuing the siege and retreating with the army westward. The futility of standing and fighting with men of poor morale, he contended, required nothing short of raising the siege. In a thirteen-to-eight vote against Revere's position, the frustrating vacuum of the status quo was preserved and the council was adjourned. Revere later recalled, "[T]hey broke up without agreeing to any thing."[52]

With every moment of delay, the confidence and morale of the British troops defending Majabigwaduce increased. "We were always in expectation of their coming to storm us, and were as ready to receive them on the point of our bayonets," a British artillery sergeant recorded in his journal.[53] Captain Mowat and General McLean had optimized their communications and coordinated their efforts, and according to the Loyalist Dr. Calef, ". . . a brotherly affection appeared to unite the forces by sea and land . . . to the honor and benefit of the service."[54]

In stark contrast, Saltonstall and Lovell now returned to their separate posts and conducted actions in furtherance of their own ends, each entirely independent of the other. General Lovell undertook a series of small skirmishes against the enemy with little effect, and he continued the bombardment of the fort and its surrounding areas by Revere and his artillery. Saltonstall, wishing at least to appear engaged, passed the time surveying the ground adjacent to Mowat's ships for possible battery locations, but he made no appearance or attempt of aggression against the enemy.

On one of these forays on the afternoon of the August 7 council of war, Saltonstall, accompanied by several of his captains, was seen by the men of the *Nautilus* reconnoitering a land position beyond a cove on the eastern slopes of Majabigwaduce. As dusk fell, a company of British marines gave chase and, though the captains made their quick escape, Saltonstall himself was separated in the chaos. "They waited, but he came not . . . ," wrote Thomas Philbrook, a seaman aboard the *Providence*. "[I]t began to grow dark, the British boat had returned to the ship; finally, at 9 o'clock, they concluded to leave him to his fate and take care of themselves."[55] For better or worse, the future of the Penobscot Expedition hung in the balance. By sunrise the next morning, however, as a dreary rain blanketed the peninsula, the frayed and insect-bitten commodore was picked up on the shore and whisked back to the *Warren*.

❦ The Massachusetts Council in Boston received General Lovell's plea for reinforcements and began a desperate and politically delicate scramble for men. At the confident start of the Penobscot Expedition, the council had elected not to seek Continental support for the operation; but now, with General Lovell and his men languishing on the heights of Majabigwaduce, that support had become nothing short of imperative. Hat in hand, Samuel Adams was immediately shuttled to Providence, Rhode Island, to apply his shrewd influence on General Gates for the dispatch of four hundred disciplined soldiers and to inform him of the "fatal consequences that must Ensue if this Expedition to the Eastward should prove abortive for want of a few Continental Troops."[56]

Meanwhile, about 150 miles to the south of Majabigwaduce, a fleet of six British warships commanded by Sir George Collier surged forward through the New England fog toward Maine.[57]

❦ The spirit and morale of the Rebel forces had now sunk to desperate levels. "Tumults . . . ran high," remembered Thomas Philbrook. "[T]he General was hissed and hooted at wherever he made his appearance, and the Commodore cursed and execrated by all hands."[58] There was talk from the sailors aboard the Rebel fleet of selecting their own command and storming the fort, independent of support and orders. "It is strange that these spirited fellows were kept peaceable so long . . . A single word of encouragement from any of the captains . . . would have set them in rapid motion," wrote Philbrook.

The weather again had turned stormy and had caused the loss of ammunition and supplies, and this had further eroded the spirit of General Lovell's men. It had become evident to all that a critical moment was at hand; unless some bold and decisive action was undertaken, the Penobscot Expedition must be abandoned.[59] On August 8 the Continental Navy captain of the *Providence*, Hoysteed Hacker, desperate for a solution, proposed a bold plan of joint attack that was forwarded to the commanders and officers for consideration. Hacker requested the immediate convention of a council of war to review and evaluate his plan.

Meanwhile, it had come to Saltonstall's attention that a route existed beyond the reach of Fort George's guns that could be safely taken by his ships through Majabigwaduce Harbor.[60] Upon evaluating this information in conjunction with Captain Hacker's plan and debating his options with the other naval officers, Saltonstall finally determined that he would, in fact, enter the harbor and attack, despite what he professed to be great risk, if Lovell likewise would muster some mode of land assault.

On August 10, another joint council of war was convened to decide whether and how to attack the British forces. Though Saltonstall initially complained that there was little advantage to taking the enemy ships, General Lovell expressed a tentative willingness to attack and attempt to hold the ground to the rear of the fort, thereby cutting off an escape route for the British sailors. Upon the unanimous urging of his men, the commodore begrudgingly agreed to enter the harbor and attack.[61]

Finally, it appeared that the leaders of the American forces at Majabigwaduce would execute their orders to "Captivate Kill or destroy" the enemy.

From Providence, Samuel Adams forwarded a note to Jeremiah Powell and the rest of the Massachusetts Council informing them of the welcome news that Colonel Henry Jackson and a detachment of four hundred men from his regiment were on their way to Boston for transport to Penobscot Bay. Adams had found General Gates "ready, as usual to afford every Assistance in his Power for the Service of the Great Cause . . ."[62]

At midnight on August 11, Jeremiah Powell dispatched his messenger north to Majabigwaduce to inform General Lovell of the news. "Something must be hazarded and Speedily too," warned the council president. "Delay may operate to your destruction."[63]

Earlier that evening, George Washington's letter of August 3, warning of Admiral Collier's departure for Maine, had reached the Council Chamber, and tensions in Boston were running high.

"I think the Enemy does not know my force," lamented Solomon Lovell in his journal entry of August 11. "[I]f they did there's a probability that they would attack me."[64]

Immediately following the joint council of war, the general began having second thoughts. He thought it prudent to first test the character and temperament of his men in some manner before actually putting the agreed-upon plan into action.

Wangling several hundred volunteers from his militia into the open ground between the fort and Majabigwaduce Harbor, Lovell maneuvered the men in a provocative fashion to decoy the British and draw them from their positions. The scheme proved successful and, before long, about fifty Redcoats emerged from their garrison and charged toward the Rebel position. Paul Revere, who had been ordered to the south of the wood with two fieldpieces, recorded that the general's army retreated "in the utmost disorder."[65] Lovell himself noted with despondence that there was such confusion among his men at the first sign of enemy aggression that "it was impossible to form them but retreated in the greatest hurry."[66]

That evening Lovell soberly called a council of war among only the officers of his ground forces, which unanimously concluded that the men could not take and hold a post at the rear of the British fort as had earlier been agreed. "On any alarm or any special occasion," the council minutes reflected, "nearly one fourth part of the Army are skulked out the way and concealed."[67]

At first light, the general, accompanied by Paul Revere, delivered the news to Saltonstall. Ever opportunistic, the commodore feigned surprise and almost giddily taunted that he was ready to lead his ships into the harbor and attack. Predictably, the men agreed to nothing except to convene yet another joint council of war that evening.

Lovell now clearly understood that he was completely out of options. Either the commodore agreed to destroy the enemy's ships or the expedition must fail. In preparation for the latter, Lovell ordered Revere to begin the grim task of removing his artillery pieces from the heights of Majabigwaduce.

As the general and commodore postured for dominance, each waiting for the other to embark upon some resolute stroke, and as the endless string of futile councils of war continued, Boston grew impatient. On August 12, William Vernon and James Warren of the Navy Board forwarded an angry missive to Saltonstall. The time for decisive action was at hand.

> Sir
> We have for Some time been at a loss to know why the Enemy Ships have not been Attacked . . . [W]hy should any business be delayed to another day that may as well be done this.
> Our Apprehensions of your danger have ever been from a Reinforcement to the Enemy. You can't expect to remain much longer without one, whatever therefore is to be done should be done immediately both to prevent Advantage to the Enemy & delays if you are obliged to retire . . . With these Sentiments We think it our duty to direct you to Attack & take or destroy them without delay in doing which no time is to be lost as a Reinforcement are probably on their passage at this time. It is therefore our orders that as soon as you receive this you take the Most Effectual Measures for the Capture or destruction of the Enemy's Ships & with the greatest dispatch the nature & Situation of things will Admit of—
> We are Your Friends & Servants
> W Vernon J Warren[68]

Colonel Jackson's Continental regiment completed the forty-mile trek from Providence to Boston through rain, poor roads, and excruciating heat, arriving by sunrise on August 12 "much beat out."[69] The town came out in full fashion to welcome the troops and immediately presented each of the officers with a hogshead of Jamaican spirits and a cask of wine. As the hours turned into days, the regiment lingered in the gracious confines of Boston treated to public dinners and merry parades. Finally, on August 15, "[h]aving dined and enjoyed a number of songs over the cheering glass, wishing success to the Penobscot Expedition," the regiment boarded the *Rising Empire* and the *Renown* and awaited a fair wind for their journey to Maine.[70]

In Majabigwaduce, meanwhile, calamity had already struck the beleaguered Rebel forces.

Chapter **9** "This Terrible Day"

ON THE MORNING of Friday, the thirteenth of August, another joint council of war was held aboard the *Warren* on the question of whether to end the Rebel siege of Majabigwaduce. For two hours the men cajoled, accused, charged, and blamed one another; yet despite the obvious perils of inaction, they agreed to nothing in the way of strategy. A frustrated and incensed officer aboard the Continental ship *Hunter* recorded in his journal the prevailing mood of the American forces:

> Three weeks have now elapsed since our siege began, and little or nothing is affected to our advantage. In the meantime our opponents are fortifying, and have completed a very formidable citadel, where they are secure against us; which at our arrival was only a breastwork . . . which then, in all probability, we could have reduced very easily, as also their shipping . . . in the course of which time thirteen or fourteen councils of war have been held, resolving one day to attack, and the next day reversing their schemes. The Commodore complaining that the General is backward, and the General that the fault is in the Commodore; the people censuring both, and are determined, unless something is directly done, that is either to attack vigorously or raise the siege (preferring the former) that they would leave the ships, and not risk an attack by a superior force which was daily expected.[1]

Fourteen officers—including Solomon Lovell and Peleg Wadsworth—voted to continue the siege of Fort George, over the objections of Paul Revere, who joined Commodore Saltonstall and eight others urging the immediate evacuation of Majabigwaduce.[2]

Solomon Lovell now reached his fated moment. Clinging to the hope that reinforcements would soon arrive, he resolved that, this day, he would lead his men into battle and would rather die in the attempt than to abandon his duty or to give the commodore one further excuse not to act.[3]

Lovell gathered his men and once again pleaded with them to stand with the "Sons of Liberty and of Virtue"[4] in one last blow against the enemy. Within a thick fog that enveloped Majabigwaduce, General Lovell personally marched four hundred volunteers to the edge of the forest encampment and, through a barrage of enemy grapeshot, skirmished his way to a position at the rear of Fort George. With courage and desperation, the valuable ground between General McLean and his naval forces on the Majabigwaduce River finally had been taken. Now, thought Lovell, if the commodore would just venture his ships into the harbor, he might be able to convince his men to storm the British garrison.

Energized, Lovell dispatched one of his officers to the *Warren* to inform Saltonstall that the time had come for the navy to enter the harbor and destroy the British ships.

By mid afternoon, word had traveled to the American sea captains of a possible excursion, and naval maneuvers began in preparation for attack.

Captain John Allen Hallet, aboard the state brigantine *Active*, peered through the lifting haze for any sign of motion. Several days earlier the commodore had placed Hallet's vessel together with the *Diligent* at the mouth of Penobscot Bay to provide advance detection of the approach of any British reinforcements. Now, at about 2:00 P.M., Hallet spotted through his glass what looked to be a cluster of thin trees towering in the distance above the ocean fog. Unsure of what he was viewing, he asked the opinion of the *Diligent*'s captain, Philip Brown. It was unmistakable, concluded Brown: a fleet of large ships was advancing from the south through the mist of the open seas.

Instantly, the *Diligent* bore away toward the remainder of the fleet with the disquieting news.[5]

From the bluffs to the east of Fort George, General Lovell watched with mounting exhilaration as the mainsails of five American warships caught the remaining breeze of the day and began sailing into Majabigwaduce Harbor. The commodore had, indeed, given the order to proceed, and the attack finally appeared to be under way.

In the harbor, Captain Mowat had armed his remaining transport ship, the *St. Helena*, and arranged it with the other sloops of war in a defensive broadside against the approaching threat. Within the fort, General McLean had turned five artillery pieces toward the American ships and prepared "to salute them as they came in."[6]

Suddenly, the *Diligent* was seen surging briskly from the bay. From above, General Lovell observed the attacking Rebel fleet abruptly heave to and seemingly hold its position. The late afternoon winds had been diminishing, and Lovell surmised that the naval assault had been delayed until sailing conditions improved. By dusk, however, he knew that something was wrong, and when the fog began to lift, Lovell and his men could see the faint silhouette of ships emerging on the southern horizon.

At about 10:00 P.M., a messenger from the *Warren* approached the newly held Rebel position and handed the general a message from Dudley Saltonstall. Six enemy ships had been spotted through the fog approaching from the south of Penobscot Bay.

"If you mean to order the Transports up the River, I think they ought to be under way—as soon as possible," wrote the commodore.[7]

Without naval support, Lovell had no other option but to order a retreat of his army. That night, anticipating the political firestorm to come, he wrote to the council, "I hope the Public will suspend their Judgment till a fair and Candid hearing can be had—The two Fleets are now closing together what will be the Event God only knows . . ."[8]

Through the rain-soaked night and into the predawn hours, vacant-eyed troops stoically packed equipment and munitions and quietly made their way down the cliffs of Majabigwaduce that, seventeen days earlier, had been so valiantly conquered with American blood. Finally granted what he had advocated for some time, Paul Revere dutifully collected his regiment and oversaw the swift removal of each piece of artillery remaining in the various Rebel batteries surrounding Fort George.

By sunrise, every man, musket, cannon, and store—amassed by the good intentions of Boston to fulfill the glorious purposes of the Penobscot Expedition—had been cleared from the heights of Majabigwaduce and crammed into the transports waiting at the shore. "This morning," wrote the general in his diary, "I completed my retreat . . . without the loss of a Man."[9]

When the "brave, vigilant and indefatigable seaman"[10] Sir George Collier finally set sail on August 3 aboard HMS *Raisonnable* from Sandy Hook, New York, toward New England waters, he was battling a terrible illness that he privately thought might be his last. "The raging fever . . . grew to that height, as to make me believe I was on the point of setting out on a much longer voyage than to Penobscot," he would write to Henry Clinton.[11]

Mounting 214 guns in total, the Royal fleet heading for Majabigwaduce presented an imposing naval fighting force.[12] The *Blonde, Greyhound, Virginia, Galatea, Camilla,* and the *Otter* joined the *Raisonnable* in the ten-day, fog-enshrouded journey; and though they were temporarily separated in the darkness, all but the *Otter* found their way to a rendezvous point at Monhegan Island north of Falmouth, Maine.[13]

Sailing against the better judgment of his physicians, Collier had found the voyage a difficult one. As his fleet cruised safely into the southern waters of Penobscot Bay in the late afternoon of August 13, however, the Admiral could feel his fever showing signs of breaking.

In the forests surrounding Fort George, an eerie calm prevailed. As dawn approached, the British sentries noticed "an unusual degree of quiet" on the Rebel lines and, upon investigation, found that the positions had been abandoned.[14] General McLean immediately sent eighty men from the Hamilton Regiment to cut off the American retreat, but they found only litter-strewn trails heading from the heights, devoid of men and artillery.

With the bulk of his fighting force huddled safely aboard the unarmed transport ships in the waters off of Dyce's Head, General Lovell now ordered a swift retreat north into the Penobscot River, where, under the command of General Wadsworth, they could erect a defensive fortification. Once within the twenty-mile stretch of narrow but passable river waters, the sloping terrain of the valley would, they hoped, offer refuge as well as strategic sites for the mounting of cannon to impede the advancing British warships.

As Lovell's transports embarked upon their escape, Commodore Saltonstall conducted yet another council of war aboard the *Warren* to consider what action the Navy should take regarding the approaching enemy. With the arrival of further intelligence regarding the fleet's size and strength, the captains summarily agreed that the American force was "vastly inferior" to that of the enemy; and upon a vote exhorted by the commodore, they unanimously determined not to directly engage the British warships.[15] Some of the captains advocated slipping through the west side of Long Island at the center of Penobscot Bay to make their escape, while others wanted to navigate up the river and make a stand.[16] Following the meeting, Titus Salter, captain of the New Hampshire privateer *Hampden*, approached the commodore and requested orders. A confused and bewildered Saltonstall turned to the captain and muttered, "[W]e must all shift for ourselves . . ."[17]

As the transports moved north through the bay, General Lovell realized that three Rebel cannon remained in the previously captured battery on Nautilus Island. With British soldiers and sailors already swarming though the area, it was clear that decisive action had to be taken to rescue the guns for the establishment of artillery positions upriver.

Lovell would later record that he "used every endeavor to secure them, by ordering a party for that purpose, but . . . time was too short."[18] The "party" referred to by the general was Paul Revere—and perhaps his characterization of the reasons for failing to safeguard the Nautilus Island cannons had been overly charitable.

Through the bellowing chaos of retreat, William Todd had delivered the general's order to Revere to gather his men and remove the three cannon from the island battery. Despite the obvious gravity of the situation, Revere paused to evaluate Lovell's order; then according to Captain Gilbert Speakman, the commissary of ordnance who witnessed the encounter, Revere curtly replied that compliance was quite impossible and that all available craft were employed elsewhere in the course of the retreat.[19] Later that morning, according to Speakman, Revere admitted that he simply chose not to risk his men on such a mission. He then fished out his original orders given weeks earlier by the Massachusetts Council and began to scrutinize them legalistically to determine whether he was compelled even to obey the general's directives at that point in the mission. "[He] said his Orders were to be under the Command of General Lovell during the Penobscot Expedition," declared Speakman, "and as the Siege was rais'd he considered the expedition at an end, and therefore did not consider himself any longer under General Lovell's Command."[20]

Despite the timidity of the Rebel navy and its waffling and irresolute commodore, the American warships managed to form themselves temporarily into a defensive crescent across the river mouth to allow time for the transports to begin their flight. The Rebel ships at first "seemed inclinable to dispute the passage," noted Admiral Collier.[21]

With Saltonstall holding his position in the bay, the transports ventured about seven miles upriver to the jut of land housing the abandoned Fort Pownal, a British stronghold during the Seven Years' War. Then, against an ebbing tide and calming breezes, they were forced to halt and drop anchor. To the south, the winds driving Admiral Collier's fleet remained brisk, and by late morning as the British warships approached, word came to General Lovell that Saltonstall "was very much dejected."[22]

Fearing the stability and judgment of the naval commander, Lovell felt compelled to navigate downriver to the *Warren*, where he found the commodore "in low spirits" and on the verge of abandoning the fleet's defensive position.[23] Perceiving that Saltonstall's seventeen warships provided the only chance of survival for his beleaguered troops and their unarmed transports, Lovell pleaded with the commodore to stay the course and fight the enemy. Receiving nothing but steadfast refusals, Lovell angrily departed the *Warren* and rushed back toward Fort Pownal to warn his men of their pending fate.[24]

By 1:00 P.M. the imposing mainsails of six fast-closing, square-rigged

British vessels could be seen commandingly unfurled in the open waters of Penobscot Bay. Panic immediately infused the Rebel warships, and in the words of George Collier, "an unexpected & Ignominious flight took place."[25]

Sensing chaos and weakness in their enemy, the British instantly gave chase "with all the eagerness which a desire of destroying the enemy could inspire,"[26] and the bulk of the American warships hove sharply to port and began racing into the mouth of the river.

In a desperate attempt to elude the marauding British vessels, the captains of the privateer *Hunter* and the brig *Defence* banked hard and sailed to the west seeking passage through the bay behind Long Island. As the rest of his ships began their methodical corral of the American fleet, Admiral Collier immediately dispatched the *Blonde* and the *Galatea* in pursuit. The *Hunter* would quickly be run aground with every sail raised and her men taking to the woods without a fight, while the *Defence* attempted to evade capture by anchoring in a small inlet. Collier later ordered his ship, the *Camilla*, to take the brig with its sixteen guns, "but she prevented that measure being carried into execution," he wrote, "by blowing herself up."[27]

Now Captain Mowat and his three sloops of war rearmed themselves with the cannon previously sent to Fort George, slipped their moorings, and eagerly joined in the chase. First Lieutenant George Little, who served on the Massachusetts State Navy brig *Hazard*, would later note the delicious irony of the ships, which the commodore had seen no advantage in destroying, now pursuing him up the river.[28]

Captain Titus Salter raised every available sail on the *Hampden* and attempted to break free of the coming onslaught, but she was "sailing heavy"[29] and the fast-moving *Blonde* and *Galatea* were closing upon her. Soon followed by the *Virginia*, each British ship began firing its guns at the hapless vessel. During every council of war, Salter had consistently urged attacking the enemy. Now, as the *Hampden's* mainsail, flying jib, and foresail were shot away and fell about her deck in a twisted mass of cloth and rigging, Captain Salter turned his crippled ship broadside and returned fire as best he could. Heavily outgunned and with men lying wounded upon the deck, the captain soon realized that he had little chance of escape. Against his every instinct to stand and fight, Salter reluctantly struck his colors and surrendered the *Hampden* and her crew of 130 to his British pursuers.[30]

By mid afternoon, the upriver breezes began to stir, and the transports once again drifted north toward the narrows of the Penobscot River. With the same wind in their sails, the Rebel warships now took flight from the bay as well and, with four of Admiral Collier's frigates in close pursuit, bent every sail toward Fort Pownal.

As the transports approached Orphan Island (present-day Verona Island), which divided the Penobscot into east and west narrows, Saltonstall's fleet quickly approached from the south. Anticipating that their armed vessels would heave to and finally make a protective stand allowing the clustered transports to escape up the river, the men hailed the ships and welcomed their arrival. To their "great mortification," however, the warships frantically signaled the transports to clear the way and allow them to pass. "Without any notice or assistance," the American warships shoved and heaved their way forward through the westward narrows and past the huddled and helpless transports.[31] "With every endeavor [they] strove to keep way," wrote General Lovell, "but the Armed Vessels run by and left them to the power of the Enemy . . ."[32]

As Saltonstall's panic-stricken fleet pushed its way past the transports without even the pretense of defensive fire, the stunned and unprotected troops looked about half a mile south toward Collier's ships, which drew menacingly closer by the moment. With dusk approaching, and with the boats struggling against the adverse tide and a dying wind, fear ran through the Rebel army like a corrosive thread.

The captains of the transports were now faced with the unenviable choice of scuttling their vessels or surrendering them to the enemy. Though the men had gallantly attempted to tow their sloops and schooners upriver with rowboats, movement against the tide had become all but impossible and capture by the approaching enemy seemed inevitable. As dusk settled on the Penobscot, the transport captains, seemingly out of options, began purposely running their vessels aground. One after the other, they set them ablaze, while from a distance, Admiral Collier and his crewmen looked on with astonished pleasure. The panic-stricken Rebel troops gathered their muskets and what provisions they could. With all semblance of order or command now lost, they abandoned all but four of the twenty-one transport ships and, in the throws of "utmost confusion,"[33] dashed for the forest to avoid capture.

Prior to the retreat of Saltonstall's warships from Penobscot Bay, Paul Revere had joined General Wadsworth in an effort to rescue some of the sick and injured from the makeshift American hospital near Fort Pownal. Just as they returned to a point below the narrows, the men witnessed Saltonstall's warships retreating through the helpless transports. Amid the turmoil Revere sought out the ordnance brig. Wadsworth took to his boat and began moving among the various transport ships, many aground, some not yet on fire, and exhorted his men to stay on board and not abandon their ships unless forced to. "No Pains were spared to collect the Troops, to save the Stores & Ordnance on board the Transports then on fire, but neither Men nor Officers were under the least control . . ." Wadsworth would later write.[34]

As he passed the *Samuel*, Wadsworth shouted orders to Revere to place a twelve-pound cannon on a flatboat to be held in readiness while he scouted the narrows for a place to land the gun and halt the enemy's progress. Quickly surveying the upriver grounds and discovering an appropriate fortification site, Wadsworth soon returned in a birch canoe navigated by two Indians only to find, to his dismay, the bulk of the transports clustered together and in flames—and the *Samuel* abandoned with her sails unfurled and her bow bumping into the river bank. There was no sign of the ordered cannon or the artillery commander who was to secure it.

Undaunted, the young general heroically attempted to gather his troops scattered in the bush along the shore, many of whom by that point had already decided on the futility of further resistance.[35] During the siege of Fort George, Wadsworth had implored General Lovell to consider the creation of some rendezvous point up the Penobscot River, where the men could meet and a fortification could be established in the event a retreat was deemed necessary. "[T]he General would hear nothing of the kind; alleging that it would dishearten our Army & show them that we did not expect to succeed," Wadsworth would later muse.[36] Now, with the flames from the burning transports lighting up the evening sky and the troops flailing about the water and along the riverbank in disarray, Wadsworth ordered whatever men he could find to retrieve any salvageable provisions and to prevent what remained of the boats from falling into British hands. The task would prove demoralizing. "The troops were chiefly dispersed or gone back into the Woods & the rest not to be commanded," recorded Wadsworth. "By the help of a few Individuals, chiefly Officers, a small Quantity of Provisions & Ammunition was got on Shore."[37]

While General Wadsworth courageously attempted to buoy his men, Paul Revere seemed to have concluded that his cooperation was no longer required.

With the timbers of the burning transports littering the narrow waterway, the general's attention was at once drawn to a small schooner drifting helplessly in the ebbing tide toward the enemy ships. The vessel, Wadsworth understood, contained a crew of men and a large supply of remaining provisions. A rescue of the craft had to be attempted.

Wadsworth immediately spotted Revere's Castle barge bobbing near the shore and ordered several of the artillerymen to quickly "tough [the schooner] across the stream & . . . take out her crew."[38] Nevertheless, amid panicked shouts for help from the beleaguered seamen, Revere instantly bristled at the young general and, turning to his men, forbade them from following the order.

Incredulous at the lieutenant colonel's obstinate refusal of orders, Wadsworth angrily overruled Revere's denial and once again sternly ordered the artillerymen to launch the barge. As the men leaped into action, Revere indignantly turned to the general and grumbled that his personal baggage and other belongings were stowed on the vessel. "Who would thank [me] for loosing *that*, in attempting to Save the Schooner to the State?" Revere demanded. Wadsworth glared back in disbelief at the pugnacious officer and hissed, "Have you come to take care of [your] private baggage, or to Serve the State?"

With that, the man whose grandson would one day immortalize the name of Paul Revere now promised his immediate arrest as soon as the army could be collected.[39]

🐝 With darkness shrouding the river narrows and the presence of burning transports preventing further safe passage, Sir Collier's frigates anchored downriver and bided their time. Following his last futile encounter with the commodore, General Lovell had gone aboard the *Hazard* and unwittingly joined the frenetic rush past the besieged transports. Now, as seventeen American ships of war lay scattered for miles in the calm evening waters north of Orphan Island between Marsh Bay and Bald Hill Cove, Lovell contemplated the question of how to salvage the Penobscot Expedition.[40]

Just to the south, a dejected Captain William Burke stood alone in the darkness at the helm of his warship, *Sky Rocket*. The vessel earlier had run aground, and her crew had darted into the woods heading for home. With no other choice seemingly available to him, Burke fashioned a trail of powder that led from the ship's rope ladder to the holds below where barrels of gunpowder were stored. Then, as the nighttime mist began to settle on Marsh Bay, he ignited the trail and dove into the woods for cover. Instantly, a blast ripped through the ship's massive hull illuminating the night sky and shattering the relative quiet of the Penobscot River. Through the night, similar explosions would bring the same fate to three other warships in the fleet, though no order or authorization allowing their destruction had been issued.

Aboard the *Pigeon*, one of only several transports to escape the inferno near Fort Pownall, Paul Revere slept comfortably. He insisted that earlier, while the Castle barge "was getting some men from a Schooner," he had been separated from the rest of his regiment and spent the remainder of the evening searching for them as he moved upriver.[41] Captain Cushing, however, would later recollect that Revere had left him on the beach, telling him that he would be back in a few minutes, "but I saw no more of him . . ."[42]

Awake in his cabin aboard the *Hazard*, a crestfallen General Lovell replayed the events of the day over and over in his mind. Years later, Peleg

Wadsworth would describe the general as "a Man of Courage & proper Spirit, a true Roman Character, who never would flinch from Danger; but He had not been accustomed to the Command of an Expedition in actual service."[43] Though clinging to the hope of generating some opposition to the British naval force pursuing him, Lovell knew that the retreat from Majabigwaduce would be viewed as nothing short of a catastrophic and humiliating defeat for the Rebel cause.

"To attempt to give a description of this terrible Day is out of my Power," he wrote in his journal entry of August 14. "It would be a fit subject for some masterly hand to describe it in its true colours, to see four Ships pursuing Seventeen Sail of Armed Vessels, nine of which were Stout Ships, Transports on fire, Men of War blowing up, Provisions of all kinds . . . throwing about, and as much confusion as can possibly be conceived."[44]

By daybreak, Paul Revere had sent one of his officers to scout the river in the Castle barge for his artillerymen with orders that they join him upriver if found.

General Lovell, who had made up his mind to collect whatever troops he could to make a stand against the British fleet, was already on a small boat rowing south with a group of other like-minded officers. As the boat passed the *Pigeon*, Lovell spotted Revere on the deck and shouted for him to gather his men and retrieve the artillery from the *Samuel*. "[H]e told me, he was going to bring up his men, to make a Stand,"[45] Revere later recorded. Without hesitation, Revere informed the general that an officer already had been dispatched in search of his men and that the *Samuel* and all its armaments had been destroyed with the other transports.[46] Undaunted, Lovell continued on, intent on securing his artillery from whatever ships remained. The commander of the artillery train, apparently content with his contribution to the cause, then proceeded upriver as far as Grant's Mills to join others who had been ordered to assemble and refortify. "There I landed to wait for my boat . . . I stayed there all that day," Revere wrote in his journal.[47]

It was true that Revere had moved north along the river and that his men had scattered through the Maine woods, but his ordnance brig was, in fact, alive and well, contrary to what he had informed the general. Upon running the *Samuel* ashore a day earlier and abandoning her on the western side of the river narrows between two burning transports, the ship's captain, James Brown, thought surely, as perhaps Revere did, that the heavily armed vessel would catch fire and explode into cinders. Instead, the brig somehow survived and, through the night, drifted aimlessly north along the narrows of the Penobscot River with its full store of artillery still aboard.

When Lovell and his officers arrived at Marsh Bay, they discovered the *Warren* run aground and its crew reeling and confused. In the commotion, Commodore Saltonstall informed the general that, in fact, the *Samuel* and its valuable armament were intact but perilously ensconced upon a sandbar about three miles downriver. Lovell, at once, directed his trusted militia captain, Waterman Thomas, and the salty George Little, first lieutenant aboard the *Hazard*, to gather some men and free the *Samuel*.

As Lovell sought out the assistance of barges to tow the *Warren* to safety, Little and Thomas encountered the *Samuel* and began the task of leveraging her back into sailable waters. "After much difficulty,"[48] and with pensive eyes scanning downstream for any sign of the British fleet, the two officers, assisted only by a few spirited sailors and a flooding tide, managed to free the brigantine and begin navigating the ship north in the light breezes.[49]

With the *Samuel* and her makeshift crew limping back toward friendlier waters, it would not be long before two quick-moving and agile British sloops of war were spotted in pursuit at the river bend just north of Orphan Island. Lieutenant Little, not a man to surrender without a chase, unfurled every sail on the brigantine and raced north as quickly as the breeze would take him. The valuable cargo of artillery upon the *Samuel*, he knew, would be instrumental in the general's plan to stop the British and to refortify farther up the river.

By noon, however, after nearly nine miles of pursuit, the tide again began to shift, and the *Samuel* slowed in the water. With the *Warren* now freed from the sandbar and in plain sight ahead of them, Little dropped anchor and nervously watched as the sloops of war edged closer from the south. He thought that if he could only drift nearer to the *Warren*, the commodore would spot the scene downriver and surely turn several of his thirty-two guns on the approaching British ships. As all hope seemed to fade, a southwest wind again began to stir and, against the ebbing tide, the lieutenant weighed anchor and steered the ship gradually forward.

By the time the ordnance brig reached the *Warren*, it was painfully clear that Saltonstall had no intention of rescuing the besieged vessel. Little and Thomas could clearly see the *Warren*'s crew fleeing the ship in droves and running into the forest under the direction of the commodore. With the British sloops steadily making their way upstream despite the ebbing tide, and with no chance of Saltonstall ordering a defensive stand, it was clear that the *Samuel* would have to be scuttled to prevent it from falling into enemy hands. After hurriedly off-loading two barrels of flour and whatever entrenching tools and ammunition they could, Little and Thomas ignited the powder hold and burned the *Samuel*. In seconds, the intrepid crew was huddled in a small rowboat headed for the safety of the *Warren*.

With the brigantine ablaze in the middle of the narrow waterway, the captains of the approaching sloops of war dared not risk further pursuit for fear of detonating their own powder-laden ships, and so they dropped anchor and waited for the flames to subside. Aboard the *Warren*, Lieutenant Little could hardly believe what he was hearing. "I found General Lovell Begging the commodore not to Burn his Ship," recalled Little.[50]

In solicitous tones, Lovell pledged to Saltonstall that, if necessary, he would remain on the ship with him and be of service in any way that he could in defending her, and that he would direct the captains of each remaining ship in the fleet to send a barge in order to tow the *Warren* to safer waters. Lovell extolled and lauded his plan to create a fortification upstream, arguing that the vessel and its crew could play a vital role in that fortification, and he *pleaded* with the commodore to spare the flagship of the Penobscot Expedition. Saltonstall just shook his head and, turning to Lieutenant Little, vacuously inquired what more could he have done.

With that, George Little flew into a defiant rage.[51] He cast an accusatory glare on the commodore and, with fury resonating in his voice, shouted that he had done absolutely *nothing* as of yet. Little then edged closer to Saltonstall and balefully questioned "why he did not fire his Stern Chasers Coming up the River to Cover the Transports."

"What good would It [have] done, the Enemy would fire again," replied the commodore.

Seething with anger, Little charged that with the slightest show of resistance from the warships—just a defensive line formed at the narrows—the transports could, perhaps, have survived the retreat and made it up the river. The defiant lieutenant now looked across the water to the burning *Samuel* and to the two menacing sloops of war beyond and advised the commodore to swing all of the eighteen-pound guns portside in defense of his ship. Again Saltonstall protested that if he fired the guns "the Enemy would git the Ship by that means . . ."

At that point, the *Warren's* second lieutenant came to the commodore's aid, telling Little that there were men aboard the ship "as good or better" than he and that if the commodore ordered the *Warren* to be burned he would follow those orders. The second lieutenant than glared defiantly at Little and asked if he knew what ship he was on and that he should watch what he said aboard her. As the men verged upon blows, General Lovell put a stop to the matter and once again assured Saltonstall that the *Warren* could be saved and that the other ships in the fleet would send men and boats to aid her.

For the moment, the commodore acquiesced.

The general and his band of willing sailors and officers then parted from the *Warren* and journeyed back upriver to consult with each of the sea captains, but the news was not good. Aboard the *Vengeance*, Captain Thomas almost scoffed at the appeal to assist the commodore. His men had all gone ashore, and Thomas was preparing to burn the privateer. Upon the general's protest and his order to head north to refortify, "Replied Captain Thomas you may have my Ship—on Answer the General Said he would accept her Rather than have her Burnt."[52] As Lovell searched in vain for men to commandeer the *Vengeance*, however, he soon recognized that Captain Thomas would have to be left to his own devices.

One by one, Lovell came alongside the hull of each ship and begged the captains not to destroy them. The valuable cannon aboard the vessels, he urged, could be sailed north and offloaded at a point of fortification. He assured them that reinforcing troops were on their way and that the French would, no doubt, be sending ships. It was "shocking," claimed Lovell, "to think of destroying such a fleet when it might easily be defended."[53]

As General Lovell frantically endeavored to rally his men into some form of defense, Paul Revere had made up his mind what to do next. By nightfall he had taken refuge on the beleaguered *Vengeance* and was told by Captain Thomas that the ship was to be burned by morning.[54] Major Todd, Captain Williams, and several others passed by the vessel and saw the men on the deck busying themselves with tasks. "[T]hey told us that they were going to set fire to their shipping and were preparing for the Same," Williams recalled.

"Colonel Revere Told me he was going home."[55]

Dodging burning Rebel ships and toiling against calm winds and shifting tides, Captain Mowat and Admiral Collier slowly made their way up the Penobscot River. Despite the remonstrations of General Lovell and the best efforts of several sea captains to maintain order and to gather their men in defense, the crews of the American fleet, aware that the enemy was at hand, had lost heart, and most abandoned their ships and fled into the woods.

By the early morning of Monday, August 16, the faithful captains and fairly intact crews of the Continental vessels *Diligent* and *Providence*, and the state brigs *Tyrannicide*, *Active*, and *Hazard*, were still prepared to make a stand and defend their ships. Lovell had informed them, perhaps falsely, that the commodore was willing to save the *Warren*, and according to Captain Philip Brown of the *Diligent*, the news had "put new Life in [the] Officers, & men."[56]

Many of the American warships had, by now, congregated in an area south of a waterfall about twenty miles upstream in the Penobscot— a point beyond which the vessels obviously could not pass.[57] At about

8:00 A.M., to the dismay of the remaining captains, the privateers *Hector* and *Black Prince* were set ablaze without any orders or prior notice, "not half pistol Shot from Many ships."[58]

With the guns in each of the surrounding vessels fully loaded and with stockpiles of explosive powder stored in their hulls, panic and chaos now enveloped the remainder of the fleet. "I thought myself in as much Danger as if I had an Enemy to Engage," recalled Philip Brown.[59]

Waterman Thomas and George Little, who had earlier attempted the valiant rescue of the *Samuel*, now sprang into action. They leaped into a flatboat and immediately rowed for the shore to warn the gathering hoard of men to run as fast and far as they could. Meanwhile, the crew of the *Hazard* was "crying out for god sake to Fetch them off . . . [the] boat . . . expect[ing] every moment to be set on fire by the two ships."[60] In the panic, Captain Brown was heard shouting in vain for someone to assist him in getting a boat over to the stricken ship. Finally, General Lovell himself rowed to his aid and began removing the men.

Suddenly the *Hector* and *Black Prince* exploded, shooting grapeshot and timber into the Rebel fleet and across the river. Flames blanketed the ships, and panicked men dove into the water and swam for their lives. Though many of the sea captains had resolved to defend their ships until reinforcements arrived from Boston, it was now clear that the fleet could not survive. John Cathcart, captain of the *Tyrannicide*, later wrote, "I was Compelled to share the fate of the other Vessels."[61]

One after the other—the *Providence, Hazard, Active, Diligent, Charming Sally*, and others—all comprising the pride and promise of the Penobscot Expedition—were abandoned by panic-stricken crews and burned in the river narrows. Barely escaping the blistering inferno, Lieutenant Little and Captain Thomas rowed frantically downstream rendering aid and assistance where they could. Lamenting the hulking remains of the American fleet as they passed, the remnants of exploded powder and burning timbers suffused the air and scorched their lungs.

With the British fleet now upon them, the men rowed for shore and disappeared into the woods, leaving behind the smoldering skeleton of the *Warren* settling in the water and sighing its last.

Chapter 10 Outrage and Allegations

GEORGE LITTLE could not believe his eyes. Hours earlier, he had brazenly scolded Commodore Dudley Saltonstall on the deck of the *Warren*, pressing him to take *any* defensive action against the approaching enemy. Now, as the timbers of the entire American fleet burned behind him, the young lieutenant watched with incredulity and contempt as Saltonstall committed his last act as commodore — slinging his pack over his shoulder and setting out on foot into the wilderness — abandoning his command, and with it the last chance of expelling the British from Majabigwaduce.

The defeat had been absolute and overwhelming. In a letter of August 23 to General Henry Clinton, the commander in chief of British forces in North America, Francis McLean wrote, "I am happy to inform your Excellency that their destruction has been complete not one having escaped being either taken or burnt."[1]

What had begun as a concerted effort to remove a single British outpost from the strategically valuable coastline of Maine had become a military and economic disaster for the Province of Massachusetts and the Rebel cause. With the rout complete, the ugly process of retreat would become the final affront to the doomed mission.

Though Generals Lovell and Wadsworth continued in their attempts to rally the troops, Saltonstall joined more than one thousand Rebel soldiers and sailors in a desperate trek through the Maine woods. Rank and military honor rapidly disintegrated into a battle of personal survival. The escape from the blazing ships and exploding armaments had left them little if any opportunity to gather provisions for the journey home. Though the Kennebec River — the route south to Boston — lay forty miles due west of the Penobscot, confusion and lack of guidance caused many who were unfamiliar with the area to walk aimlessly for days through marshes and thick brush, some barefoot and without food, searching for routes homeward.

"Our retreat," wrote one soldier, "was as badly managed as the whole expedition had been. Here we were, landed in a wilderness, under no command; those belonging to the ships, unacquainted with the woods, and only knew that a west course would carry us to the Kennebec."[2]

Even before the final destruction of the American fleet, Paul Revere had set up camp with a small group of his artillerymen in the relative safety of the woods about a mile from shore. The men cursed the commodore and, lamenting the loss of the entire naval fleet, convinced themselves of the hopelessness of a further stand. There was no sense, they rationalized, in risking lives and property when most of their comrades were giving up the fight and disappearing into the wilderness.

Huddled among the defeated Rebel soldiers, Revere's thoughts no doubt turned to home and to the comforting arms of his wife, Rachel. A year earlier, while in Newport for the second Battle of Rhode Island, he had written to his "dear girl" how "very irksome [it is] to be separated from *her*, whom I so tenderly love, and from my little lambs."[3] With eleven young mouths to feed back in Boston, Revere's priorities were starkly clear. Hours earlier as Revere lodged aboard the *Pigeon*, General Lovell had informed him that he intended to gather what men he could to establish defensive positions against the enemy. Now, plainly believing that all was lost, Paul Revere began the slow journey home.

As Revere and his men melted into the Maine woods together with the majority of the American force, Peleg Wadsworth tried to gather whatever remaining troops he could collect in a final stand against the British marauders. He had intended to rescue what was left of the Rebel artillery and ammunition and to position it against Collier's fleet as it made its way up the river in an attempt, perhaps, to salvage the expedition. The effort proved difficult. "[S]ome of the Militia had passed before I came up," Wadsworth would later write. "[O]thers had sheared off to prevent being Stopped; and the rest although: much fatigued had not lost their Eagerness for returning home, & in spite of every Order & precaution, after drawing provisions skulked off . . ."[4]

Wadsworth now recognized that his efforts on the Penobscot River were fruitless. Unable to locate General Lovell for further orders, who was at that time four or five miles upriver, and powerless to gather his scattered troops, he decided to make his way west to Camden to set up headquarters and regroup his army. Along the way, Wadsworth came upon hordes of Maine militiamen who did their best to avoid him. Despite maddening difficulties in rallying the exhausted men, he was, astonishingly, able to gather the officers of five companies who, in turn, influenced their troops to establish defensive posts at the surrounding towns of Belfast, Camden, and Townsend. There the militia provided local inhabitants with much-needed protection against Tory incursion, and they encouraged the population to organize and stand against the enemy.[5]

Meanwhile, the hapless American retreat had left General Lovell nearly despondent. He had felt it his duty to remain and fight while most of his army had fled; but with the burning of the entire navel fleet and the dispersal of his men from the shores, he soon grasped the hopelessness of the situation and dejectedly ordered "every man to shift for himself."[6]

Still, conscience did not allow Lovell to leave the area without achieving *some* material success. He had learned that the Penobscot Indians, who had by and large sided with the American effort at Majabigwaduce, were now "in a fluctuating mood"[7] by what they felt was a dishonorable flight and had begun to switch sides and turn against the Rebels. Lovell accordingly traveled north up the Penobscot River with eight of his remaining officers in an attempt to confer with tribal leaders and negotiate a permanent truce in the region. Finding that the majority of the native population had fled ninety miles north of the river mouth to their upper villages, Lovell followed undeterred and soon met and successfully reestablished peaceful relations with the local tribes.[8] Despite Lovell's puzzling decision to travel upriver to negotiate with the Indians without consent or order from the council while the bulk of his army toiled in the Maine wilderness, he considered these pursuits to be "a matter of utmost importance."⁹ Deeming that nothing further could be accomplished militarily on the Penobscot and discovering "a universal uneasiness among the Indians" that had led to "outrages which drew terrible Apprehensions on the Inhabitants," Lovell felt compelled to "negotiate matters with them, and effectually [secure] them to our Interest."[10]

As Wadsworth labored to defend the towns and villages of the eastern country and Lovell sought out peace with local Indian tribes, the bulk of the American force scattered westward through an untamed and trackless wilderness toward the settlements along the Kennebec River. Without adequate provisions or guidance, many of the men found themselves starving and lost in the wilderness for days—and some perished during the ordeal. Some of the local militiamen knew the country well, but in the confusion of flight, few were employed as guides. "We had no one to direct, so every one shifted for himself," wrote Thomas Philbrook. "Some got to their homes in two days, while the most of us were six or seven days before we came to an inhabited country."[11] Paul Revere and several of his artillerymen had joined a large party of other soldiers and sailors in the Maine woods and stumbled their way on foot through the backcountry. With dwindling food and supplies, Revere arrived on the night of August 19 at the makeshift refugee camp that had taken hold at Fort Western on the banks of the river.

An early staging point for Benedict Arnold's 1775 assault on Quebec, Fort Western, built at the head of the river's navigation on the site of present-day Augusta, served more as a storehouse in support of nearby Halifax than a military or tactical station. As hundreds of starving, exhausted refugees of the Penobscot Expedition poured into the outpost, those manning its galley struggled to feed them.

The forty-four-year-old Revere was unaccustomed to the rigors of frontier existence. He had spent nearly all of his life in the bustling city of Boston and had dedicated himself to the trades and social clubs of Boston's North End. With little or no experience as a trapper or backwoodsman, Revere staggered into Fort Western after the grueling three-day journey, insect bitten and limping badly. Revere would state that "he was so lame he could walk no further . . ."[12]

At Fort George, celebratory volleys of cannon fire filled the air as word spread of the destruction of the American force. With the Rebel guns now silent, jubilant soldiers and sailors of His Majesty's service paused in reflection of the occasion. Sergeant Lawrence of the Royal Artillery triumphantly wrote in his diary, "Now the Siege is raised, our fears are ended, we will return thanks to God that he has delivered us from outrageous men, and Rebels, such that was commanded by General Lovell."[13] John Calef, the Penobscot Loyalist who actively assisted the British cause during the entire siege, added his gloating punctuation mark:

> Thus did this little Garrison, with three Sloops of War, by the unwearied exertions of Soldiers and Seamen whose bravery cannot be too much extolled, under the judicious conduct of Officers whose zeal is hardly to be paralleled, succeed in an enterprise of great importance, against difficulties apparently insurmountable, under circumstances exceedingly critical, and in a manner strongly expressive of their faithful and spirited attachment to the interests of their King and Country.[14]

Sir George Collier did not join in the approbation of Fort George, or even the rationale for its initial founding. "I can't perceive one single end a settlement here will answer," wrote Collier as he recovered from the fever that had besieged him during the journey from New York. "[A]ll the inhabitants are rebels who take an oath to the King today, and another to Congress tomorrow . . . The face of the whole country is as dreary as can be imagined . . . the fort too I think ill placed & I fear won't be in a state of defense by the time the winter sets in. That fellow Nutting . . . I asked . . . what could possibly induce him to recommend . . . a settlement in such a place, & what advantages might be expected from it? He denied his having ever recommended the measure to Lord Germaine, nor could I learn from him what particular benefits would accrue to us, by keeping possession of so infernal a spot."[15]

Despite Collier's misgivings, on August 23 he and General McLean issued a new proclamation to those local inhabitants who had assisted the Rebel cause during the Penobscot Expedition through compulsion or otherwise. Being persuaded by the king's "most gracious and merciful inclination towards his American subjects," McLean and Collier promised the continued peaceable possession of lands under the protection of British forces, *provided* that full and unconditional allegiance again be sworn to the Crown, demonstrated by a joining of arms with the British cause. The beneficent decree also demanded the assistance of all able hands in the completion of Fort George.[16]

His penchant for compelling the allegiance of colonists notwithstanding, General McLean was, by and large, considered a decent and humane officer who honored the ethics of warfare. At Majabigwaduce, he allowed Colonel John Brewer of the local militia to arrange safe passage for the sick and wounded Rebel soldiers who were unable to escape with their army—and even provided them with food and medical supplies for the journey home.[17]

Other examples of his compassion followed. Soon after the American retreat, a British ship ominously sailed into Portsmouth Harbor, New Hampshire, as terrified local inhabitants looked on. Expecting an attack or demand for immediate surrender, the townspeople were quickly relieved to see the crew of the captured New Hampshire privateer *Hampden* released into the joyous and relieved arms of Portsmouth. General McLean had humanely allowed the Rebel seamen to escape imprisonment and to return home to their families.[18]

Nevertheless, respect and admiration for the general was far from universal. Back at Penobscot Bay, the actions of the British army in the wake of the American defeat were described in a petition from the inhabitants of Lincoln County as "the wanton depredations of an insolent & triumphant enemy . . ."[19] McLean's loyalty proclamation was considered more of an invitation for servitude than a peace offering, and most fled the area with their families. "[T]he inhabitants, men, women & children having fled thro' the wilderness to the Western parts of the State; leaving behind them their stock, provisions, crops & all they had . . . know not where to set their heads, being destitute of money & every resource of supply to their families, & must cast themselves on the mercy of the country in general, or expect to terminate their present calamities by a miserable death; Many more are following them in similar circumstances," pleaded the county residents.[20] Of those who felt compelled to take the "impious & profane oath contrary to their consciences," they were, according to a petition for assistance filed with the Massachusetts Council by the residents of Lincoln County, Maine, "driven in like slaves to work . . . & in the meanwhile obliged to find their own supplies & subjected to be cudgelled, kicked, & abused by every petty officer that is set over them."[21]

Several inhabitants who had been loyal to the Rebel cause saw their homes and barns burned and their cattle plundered, and soon a wail of despair would rise and find its way to Boston. "Our case is very bad," wrote Reverend John Murray to the Massachusetts Council. "[Hundreds] of families are now starving in the woods—their all left behind them—all will despair—& the Majority will Quit the Country & the rest will revolt if something vigorous be not done to protect them from the insolence of the triumphing foe, who are carrying fire & desolation where they come."[22]

Back at Fort Western, Paul Revere happened upon many of his fellow officers and artillerymen who had fled the interno on the Penobscot River. The men were exhausted and short on provisions, and they still faced a long and grueling journey home. Unlike the five companies of militia that had traveled to Belfast, Camden, and Townsend at the behest of General Wadsworth to establish defensive posts, the men who stumbled into Fort Western had long abandoned any thought of further battle or fortification.

Revere, who had been limping badly from his westward slog, insisted that he could never complete the trek on foot. He negotiated the purchase of a small boat for the trip back to Boston with several other officers, supplied his men with what money he could spare, and ordered them to march the remaining hundred and fifty or so miles home. He then surrendered command of his company to Captain Perez Cushing.

It would be his last official act of the American Revolution.[23]

As the gaunt and demoralized survivors, many barefoot and starving, staggered out of the Maine woods and slowly trickled south, word of the disaster began to spread through the towns and villages between southern Maine and Boston. Individual acts of kindness on the part of local citizens eased the despair of a growing flow of refugees, but the resulting burdens on families and villages sorely tested the endurance of the people. Entire settlements became staging grounds for the sick and wounded.[24]

But despite personal hardship and fear of pending attack, local residents offered care and comfort to the refugees as their patriotic duty. Meanwhile, Committees of Safety, created as a means to communicate concerns and coordinate defenses between towns (among which Paul Revere had been so actively engaged in earlier years), now passed word of the disaster throughout the region.

Soon local militias and entire towns rallied in defense of expected British reprisals. Reverend John Murray, perhaps in imitation of Revere himself, immediately journeyed around the region "in order to rouze the Country from their present idle despair."[25] He warned citizens and officials of possible British reprisals and engaged local militia units to rally and stand from Portsmouth and Townsend to points as far north as Falmouth, Maine. Georgetown, Massachusetts, was refortified with three hundred armed and ready soldiers from interior sections of the state,[26] and despite lack of formal training or accoutrements, militia units rose and stood ground along these vulnerable coastal towns.

Not sixty days earlier, Boston had brimmed with confidence that the coming expedition would drive the British from Majabigwaduce. Massachusetts had assembled the most daunting naval force of the entire war with only a limited appeal for assistance from the Continental Congress in Philadelphia, and privateers cheerfully had accepted bids from investors for a share in what was most assuredly to be the bountiful treasures of conquest.

Now, as the first bandaged and blood-soaked survivors of the failed expedition wearily limped into the unsuspecting Town of Boston, early word of the disaster began to spread like a venous web throughout the town. Wild reports of vast loss of life, as well as sick and dying men streaming into seaports from Maine to Massachusetts, circulated among citizens and local officials. And soon the names Saltonstall and Revere were whispered in angry and resentful tones. "I have not the least doubt," Revere later wrote, "but Captain Todd procured [an order for my reprimand] and then sent it to Boston. For my friends, tell me, that they heard of the Order, before I got home, and they have no doubt it came from him."[27] The Penobscot Expedition, wrote one historian, "resulted in disaster so complete, so utterly without excuse, and so thoroughly discreditable to American arms as to make its contemplation without feelings of shame and humiliation impossible."[28]

The first *official* word of the retreat from Majabigwaduce reached the Massachusetts Council on the morning of August 19, three days after the retreat. The dispatch soberly announced that the enemy had been reinforced, demolished the American fleet, and dispersed the Rebel forces into the countryside.[29] Immediately, the bewildered councilmen frantically sought to establish communication with General Lovell, unaware of his specific location or his ongoing efforts to secure Indian alliances. They issued orders via carriers charged with locating the general that he establish a post in the area and that he call on local militia units to "secure the Eastern Counties [of Maine] from being plundered and ravaged by our merciless Enemy."[30] Also included with Lovell's orders was a proclamation written by Samuel Adams urging the freemen of the counties of York, Cumberland, and Lincoln to "Rouse and Stand upon their defence."[31]

While the Massachusetts Council grappled with the initial accounts of the Penobscot defeat, Peleg Wadsworth, now stationed at Thomaston (south of Camden, Maine), took quill to paper and issued what the council would later describe as the most authentic account of the siege and the humiliating Rebel retreat.[32]

"Being uncertain whiter you have yet been informed of the sad catastrophe of your Armament against the Enemy at [Majabigwaduce]," began Wadsworth, "[I] am under the disagreeable Necessity of informing your Honor that . . . the destruction of your Fleet was completed on the forenoon of the 16th Instant and that the army five Companies excepted, are dispersed to their several homes."[33] What then followed was an eloquent and sorrowful chronicle of the American defeat at Penobscot and Wadsworth's continuing efforts to defend the local inhabitants against British aggressions.

"Your Honor is doubtless informed," wrote Wadsworth, ". . . of the Evacuation of the Heights of [Majabigwaduce] by your troops . . . on the approach of a Fleet up the Sound . . . The Wind being very faint and much against us prevented our getting far up the River on the Tide of Flood, till the coming in of the Sea Breeze in the Afternoon which brought in the Enemy's fleet along with it . . ." Wadsworth then described his dismay at the grounding and burning of the transports. "I had been up a little past our foremost Ships Just at the narrows to find a place for landing . . . but on returning to my great surprise found many of our Transports on fire all deserted & our troops Scatter'd in the Bush in the Utmost Confusion." Describing the final conflagration of the fleet, Wadsworth wrote, "Our army by this time was thoroughly dispers'd in the Wood and our Ships of War not able to hold their Ground began to Blaze."[34]

Final confirmation of the council's worst fears was sent from Portsmouth on August 22 by Colonel Henry Jackson, whose Continental regiment earlier had been ordered north to reinforce the faltering American expedition. "Lt. Col. Revere this moment arrived from Penobscot . . . ," wrote Jackson. "[H]e informs us that the whole of our shipping is destroyed, with all the Provisions Ordnance & Ammunition & the whole Army Deserted and gone home—I refer you to him for particulars who sets off for Boston this evening."[35]

❧ The depth of loss suffered at Majabigwaduce would permeate the region with a pall of outrage. "A prodigious wreck of property,—a dire eclipse of reputation,—and universal chagrin—were the fruits of this expedition," wrote Maine historian William D. Williamson. "So great pecuniary damage at this critical period of the war, and of the State finances, was a severe misfortune. In short, the whole connected was sufficiently felt; for it filled the country with grief and murmurs."[36] In a letter to James Lovell, a Massachusetts delegate to the Continental Congress, Abigail Adams lamented what she called "disgrace, disappointment and the heaviest debt incurred by this State since the commencement of the war."[37]

While the final official tally of financial loss to Massachusetts as a result of the failed Penobscot Expedition would later be set at £1,739,174,[38] a true and accurate accounting of American lives lost at Majabigwaduce seemed to be an elusive measure. High rates of desertion during battle, and the scattering of local militia units through the backwoods of Maine following the retreat, would result in widely varying casualty counts. Though initial reports of a Rebel bloodbath mercifully proved inaccurate, it appeared that no fewer than 150 men had been killed or wounded during battle, with dramatically higher losses occurring during the perilous journey home.[39]

Though actual casualties would never be tabulated, the loss of property and armament became all too clear. Massachusetts, the maritime pride of colonial America, had lost her *entire* naval fleet of forty seafaring vessels.

The Penobscot Expedition, which had begun with infinite promise, now had become an insupportable burden on the Cradle of Liberty. Massachusetts had assumed nearly complete responsibility for the endeavor without consent or approval from the Continental Congress. Insurance of private ships, provision of men and weaponry, payment of crews, and (with the exception of three Continental ships) the supply of a naval force all had fallen into the willing lap of the Massachusetts colonial government. With reminders of the dismal failure at Majabigwaduce now pouring into Boston on a daily basis, the entire colony faced the bleak reality of fiscal insolvency. "The Failure of the Expedition . . . to dislodge the Enemy from Penobscot . . ." wrote Jeremiah Powell to the Continental Congress, "keeps our Treasury exhausted."[40]

Adding to this burden were the ceaseless appeals of those directly affected by the disaster. Measures taken by towns and villages from Maine to Massachusetts in the care of soldiers and refugees, and in the growing fear of counterattack by an emboldened British force, resulted in enormous outlays of money and resources—all of which Massachusetts had agreed to assume to preserve the public credit and confidence. Rhode

Island and Connecticut each appealed to Massachusetts for defensive troops and supplies, and a petition to the Massachusetts Council from the Town of Falmouth, Maine, starkly expressed the remaining sentiment of the region: "New applications of various kinds are daily made to us; & new difficulties arise . . . In short affairs here are in the wildest Confusion."[41]

Even the Penobscot Indians petitioned Boston for aid. Their tribal representative wrote, "Brothers We rejoice at the Great Spirit which has brought us together at this place . . . I am destitute of Clothes . . . You know [what] the situation of our Families is. We hope you will grant us some Assistance for them."[42]

As the economic and psychological impact of the military debacle came into focus, anger began to spread through the streets of Boston. Answers were demanded.

And fingers were pointed.

On August 26, Lieutenant Colonel Paul Revere drifted through the harbor islands in his worn and weather-beaten boat and into the storm of outrage that had rolled over the port of Boston. He was the first of the expedition's senior officers to find his way home, and despite mounting gossip about Revere's conduct at Majabigwaduce, the Massachusetts Council ordered him to resume command of Castle Island.[43] Telltale rumors as to the cause of the defeat had preceded Revere, and whispers of scandal and disgrace already had begun circulating among his countrymen. General Lovell had been especially angered that Revere had returned home after the retreat without orders, and according to Revere himself, his nemesis William Todd had sent early word to Boston of the allegation.[44] Penobscot, Revere would later complain, would provide ample basis for his enemies to plot against him.

On his return to Boston, Revere would discover that the ill will that had developed against him in the prior years at Castle Island had multiplied in his absence, and he quickly came to believe that a conspiracy to tarnish his character had erupted as a result. "They ordered me to take the command of the Castle again . . . But the plan was too deep laid for me to stay there long," Revere wrote to a friend.[45]

With the removal of the company and artillery from the Castle during the Penobscot Expedition, town officials deemed it an appropriate opportunity to repair and refortify the island garrison. After Revere's departure for Maine, a committee had been formed for that purpose, and John Hancock, who was at the time not only speaker of the Massachusetts House but also major general of the Massachusetts Militia, was appointed to the team. In early August, Hancock arrived at the island for initial inspections and, after consultation with committee members, reported that conditions at the fort were deplorable and indicative of failed leadership.[46]

According to Revere, Hancock "found fault with everything there . . . [and] when he went to Boston he told all companys that none but Col. Revere would have left the Castle in such a situation."[47] Having had no prior acrimony or known disagreement with Hancock, Revere believed that the speaker had been urged on by his Masonic rival Colonel William Burbeck, who in 1773 had been suspended from the Massachusetts Grand Lodge of Ancient Masons in a bitter battle spearheaded by Revere. Burbeck, a former member of Richard Gridley's Massachusetts Artillery Regiment, was now the commandant of the laboratory at Castle Island and keeper of its ordnance and, accordingly, had close dealings with Hancock during the restoration work at the Castle.

Buttressed by Colonel Burbeck, Hancock publicly grumbled that Revere had allowed a commissioned fort to remain in an appalling state. He complained that Revere had left mismatched artillery equipment— thereby rendering useless the remaining armaments—and had allowed ankle-high piles of gunpowder to lie dangerously near the magazines. He alleged that certain wheelbarrows and handbarrows, together with fortress cabins, had been burned without Revere's knowledge and that no one had been punished for the offence. And he claimed that certain cannon had been taken from the island without orders or authorization. In short, John Hancock and William Burbeck implied that the fortress commander had been guilty of public malfeasance in the maintenance and organization of the Castle Island assets.[48]

Public sentiment in and around the Town of Boston now turned decidedly against Revere. William Todd and Thomas Carnes had brought back from Maine rumors and allegations of Revere's inattention to duty, refusal of orders, and downright cowardice while on the Penobscot Expedition, and gossip began to envelop the artillery commander. Stories of questionable conduct at Majabigwaduce joined rumors of command incompetence, and soon the once-heralded "Messenger of the Revolution" found himself shunned by many of his countrymen.

By late August of 1779, a team of citizen volunteers was assembled to make improvements to the fortress at Castle Island in accordance with the committee's recommendations. In a letter to General Horatio Gates, a fellow officer, Major John Rice, boldly recorded that Revere's homecoming had "so disgusted the Volunteers who subscribed for repairing and completing the Works, in and about this Town, that they have refused to proceed in this Business until he is removed; they allege that his Conduct upon the Expedition, was very unsoldierlike & very reprehensible . . ."[49]

Unrepentant and pugnacious as ever, Paul Revere bristled at the growing chorus of condemnation. "I don't think ever one person suffer'd so much abuse as I have with so little reason."[50]

As Revere languished under a pall of condemnation in Boston, General Lovell continued his efforts to mollify the region following the devastating defeat at Majabigwaduce. After a long and exhausting journey through Indian tribal country, Lovell made his way by canoe with the help of native guides back down the Penobscot River and through a system of tributaries to the Kennebec. Arriving in Georgetown, Massachusetts, on August 28, nearly two weeks after the defeat at Majabigwaduce, he finally wrote to the council. As Peleg Wadsworth had done, Lovell provided a detailed account of the American retreat as well as a description of his efforts to pacify the Penobscot Indians. But more important, he assured the colony that he had not been killed or taken prisoner by disgruntled natives. "You may depend I shall do everything in my power for the Good of the State," he wrote in closing.[51]

On August 29 Lovell traveled north to Townsend to establish his headquarters. Having received orders from the council to defend and rally the populace, he once again wrote to Jeremiah Powell and provided a detailed plan of action for the protection of the region. Noting that the British were diligently working to fortify their encampment at Maja-bigwaduce and continually sending expeditionary forces to plunder the area of food and supplies, he insisted that bold defensive action was required. Believing that follow-up British attacks against the surrounding towns were imminent, he rallied local militias in Falmouth and Camden, as well as in Pemaquid and Belfast, for readiness against aggression. He finalized plans for the fortification of Townsend Harbor and the Kennebec River and sought engineering and supplies for the effort. Until these matters were accomplished, Lovell felt compelled to delay his journey home. "The duty of my country has detained me," he would write to the council.[52]

Lovell then set forth a requisition of needs, including men, tools, and weaponry, all of which would be required to raise "a considerable Fortification" at the mouth of the Kennebec River. And noting the pressing need for artillery companies to support his defensive batteries, the general closed his dispatch home with a plea that Paul Revere's detachment be redeployed back to the area "with all speed."[53]

"I should likewise beg," continued Lovell, "you would give Lt. Col. Revere a very strong reprimand for his unsoldierlike behavior in returning home without orders."[54]

On August 31 Commodore Saltonstall crept into the Town of Boston like a spectral presence. He refused to give any account of his actions at Majabigwaduce, and he denied the authority of colonial "white-wigs" (who had never fired a musket in anger) to question any aspect of his conduct.[55] With sullen contempt, Saltonstall quietly repaired to his quarters, disdainfully eyeing the gathering storm and disinclined to acknowledge its fury.

The fiscal and political situation in Massachusetts quickly degenerated into a firefight of accusations and finger-pointing. The massive losses of the failed expedition left the state with an enormous emotional and economic time bomb, which the Massachusetts Council sought mightily to defuse. Though the operation had been undertaken without federal assistance, Massachusetts now turned, hat in hand, to the Continental Congress for subvention.

"With disagreeable Sensation I now acquaint you that the Expedition to Penobscot (of which we had formed pleasing prospects of great good accruing to the United States) has proved abortive," wrote Jeremiah Powell to John Jay.[56] Asserting a strong national interest in dislodging the British from the strategic ground of Majabigwaduce, the petition claimed that the operation was "of such Importance to the United States as well as to our allies that . . . we doubt not it will meet the Approbation of Congress although it has proved unsuccessful."[57]

It would be the first in a series of pleas to the national government that would continue for years.

Paul Revere would maintain steadfastly that his enemies were eager to provide Massachusetts with a ready scapegoat for the devastating failure of the Penobscot Expedition. The economic loss and festering public anger would demand no less. He believed that the committee in charge of the Castle Island cleanup would stop at nothing to have his command revoked, and he confessed bewilderment at the events unfolding before him. "[I]n short," he would write, "every thing that could be said to my disadvantage was said, when the very reverse was true."[58]

One morning in early September, as the bulk of the remaining Rebel forces arrived home from Maine, Captain Thomas J. Carnes brazenly ascended the steps of the Massachusetts Council Chamber armed with a provocative and explosive accusation. In an informal meeting with council members, Carnes insisted that Paul Revere had personally failed to come ashore with his men at Majabigwaduce and that his overall conduct during the Penobscot Expedition had been nothing short of deplorable. Sanctions, Carnes implored, should be imposed against him.

Captain Carnes, a battle-tested former artilleryman in the Continental Army, was perhaps the perfect candidate to level the incendiary charges. He had been captured by the British at Fort Washington in

1776 and endured brutal captivity before being released in a prisoner exchange. He was present during Bunker Hill and the British siege of Boston, and he had borne the hardships of Valley Forge.[59]

At Majabigwaduce, Carnes had led his company of Massachusetts
Marines up the ragged heights north of Dyce's Head, and after taking
possession of the high ground and setting up defensive positions, he had
occasion to observe Colonel Revere's actions. With activity between the
beachhead and the heights becoming furious and with men and equipment shuttling back and forth among positions, Carnes had watched
with mounting incredulity as Paul Revere left his men and went on board
a transport vessel at breakfast and dinner time.[60] The incident would fes-
ter in the marine captain's mind, and he watched Revere intently for the
remainder of the expedition.

Revere still had friends in positions of government, though, and no
sooner had Carnes leveled his indictment than word traveled to the accused. Revere seethed with anger and fixed his mind on the full range of
possible foes capable of stooping to such depths. He would claim that
Carnes was nothing short of the vengeful spearhead of a conspiratorial
plan to disgrace him.[61] He carefully deliberated on his actions at Majabigwaduce and, though confessing to little if any sharp military engagement during the siege, indignantly concluded that the failure was not
his to bear. "[B]efore we sailed," he would later write, "[the Council was]
advised . . . to send at least 3,000 men, and they were advised to apply for
continental troops. But the most they ordered was 1,600, and there never
was 900, and one third of them were boys and old men."[62]

The brazen attack upon his character—Revere's most cherished possession—could not be permitted to stand without challenge. In a sharply
worded yet obsequious statement to the council, Revere protested his
innocence and demanded the opportunity to confront his accusers in a
formal setting.

"I feel the highest obligations to Your Honors for Your Candor to
me, when the popular clamor, runs so strong against me," Revere began.
"Had your Honors have shown as little regard for my character as my
Enemies have done; Life would have been insupportable. Were I con-

scious that I had omitted doing any one thing to Reduce the Enemy, either through fear, or by willful opposition, I would not wish for a single advocate," he continued. "I beg your Honors, that in a proper time, there may be a strict enquiry into my conduct where I may meet my accusers face to face."[63]

The council recognized that the off-the-record sparring regarding Revere's conduct at Majabigwaduce amounted to little more than idle gossip. Formal charges, if there were to be any, had to be drawn and placed before an authoritative body in order to join the issues; and accordingly, Carnes was instructed by the council to file his written complaint or, alternatively, let the matter die.

The response was swift. On Monday, September 6, Captain Carnes delivered his official statement of charges against Paul Revere.

Gentlemen

Being Requested to Lodge a complaint against Lt. Colonel Paul Revere, for his behavior at Penobscot—Which I do in the following manner Viz:

First. For disobedience of orders from General Lovell in two Instances, Viz, when ordered to go on shore with two eighteen pounders, one twelve, and one four & One howitzer, excused himself.

Second. When ordered by Major Todd at the retreat to go with his Men and take said Cannon from the Island, refused, and said his orders were to be under the Command of Gen. Lovell during the expedition to Penobscot, and that [when] the siege was raised, he did not consider himself under his Command.

Thirdly. For neglect of Duty in Several instances.

Fourthly. For unsoldierlike behavior, During the whole expedition to Penobscot, which tends to Cowardice—

Fifthly. For refusing Gen. Wadsworth, the Castle barge to fetch some men on shore from a Schooner, which was near the enemy's ships on the retreat up the River.

Sixthly. For leaving his men, and suffering them to disperse and taking no manner of Care of them.

T. J. Carnes

Sept 6, 1779[64]

Within hours of Carnes's official filing, Lieutenant Colonel Paul Revere received orders, attested by John Avery, secretary of the Massachusetts Council, to resign his command of Castle Island and the other fortresses of Boston Harbor immediately, to confine himself to his home in Boston, and to remain there by order of law until a full investigation of the charges was completed.[65]

Chapter II "Great and Universal Uneasiness"

ON SEPTEMBER 9, the *Independent Chronicle*, one of Boston's leading republican newspapers, articulated in acerbic prose the mood of Massachusetts. "We have waited long enough to have . . . a particular account of the Penobscot expedition," its editors wrote. "From the various accounts we have had, the general report stands thus . . . [O]ur irregular troops made an irregular retreat . . . in imitation of an irregular Brigadier, and a new-fangled Commodore, without any loss, excepting the whole fleet." Then, in a portentous flourish, the editorial concluded, "The question now is, Who is to blame?"[1]

The Great and General Court of Massachusetts, unquestionably in accord with the local press of Boston, was pondering the same question. Within hours of the appearance of the *Independent Chronicle* perspective, John Hancock, speaker of the Massachusetts House, sent up to the Council Chamber a resolution, premised on the "great and universal Uneasiness" occasioned by the failure of the Penobscot Expedition, creating a committee of inquiry to investigate the "causes of the said Miscarriage."[2] Privately irate over the timidity of the mission leaders in failing to vigorously pursue the enemy at Majabigwaduce, the council members were eager to interrogate, through their appointed committee, the land and sea officers of the expedition. Confidence in the efficacy of such an inquiry, however, was not universally shared. "What will arise from ignorant militia-men being examined by an ignorant court 'tis impossible to tell," wrote Israel Keith, a former deputy adjutant-general to William Heath.[3]

Nine legislators and military officers were appointed to the committee, with each given broad investigative authority to summon and examine any person or document thought necessary to further the assigned purpose of the body.

Chairing the committee was fifty-one-year-old Artemas Ward. As the first major general in the Continental Army under George Washington, Ward had become a well-known political force in the Massachusetts legislature, serving for many years in the House of Representatives and, by 1777, in the Executive Council. "A plain man, a solid citizen, upright and conscientious, one who did his duty modestly and effectively," wrote *Scribner's Monthly* years after his death. "[H]is life offers little to fascinate and much to respect."[4]

As Paul Revere languished under house arrest, he churned with anger and brooded over the audacity of his enemies to levy such scurrilous allegations against him. And he wasn't alone in his sentiments. Though public opinion had turned against him, some in the town believed that his removal from command had been a miscarriage of justice perpetuated by those in government. "The indelicacy with which Col. Revere was treated by the Council in the manner of his arrest," wrote Israel Keith, a supporter of Revere, "would have disgraced a sergeant in the army of General Washington."[5] On the day that the council formed its committee of inquiry, however, it discharged Revere from his previous house arrest order and commanded him to stand in readiness to appear before the body for the purpose of offering testimony regarding the Penobscot Expedition.[6]

Immediately following his release, Revere stalked about Boston in a near-frenzied quest to distinguish friend from foe. Many members of the Massachusetts Artillery Train remained loyal to their commander and offered their assistance in the upcoming inquiry, while others on the expedition, mostly those included in General Lovell's camp and in alliance with Todd and Carnes, would clearly be acting against him. Revere sought out his friend William Heath, who was at the time a major general of the Continental Army; and though he asked for no influence or favor, he wrote in great detail about the specifics of the mission, the reasons for its failure, and his poor treatment upon arriving home. "I am left in a worse situation than if I had always been a friend to government," confided Revere.[7] While the council members and the Massachusetts government as a whole grappled with the overall causes of the military defeat and how the attendant financial burdens would be defrayed, Revere was consumed, perhaps justifiably so in light of the allegations against him, with squarely confronting his accusers and clearing his name. The inquiry into the Penobscot Expedition would be, to Paul Revere, a referendum on his personal character as well as the malevolence of his enemies.

In the ensuing weeks, summonses were delivered by the Massachusetts Council to virtually every sea captain and land officer of the Penobscot Expedition, compelling their attendance before the committee of inquiry, which was to convene on September 22 at Faneuil Hall in Boston. Such was the level of concern for the preservation of order and decorum during the inquiry that the Council appointed a band of civil officers, deputies, and constables from Suffolk County and the Town of Boston to stand guard during the proceedings.[8]

Even before the first witness was called—indeed, even before he was appointed by the council as chairman of the committee—Artemas Ward had given ear to the pervasive rumors floating about Boston and had drawn some conclusions regarding the major players in the ill-fated expedition to Maine.

"[O]ur friend Wadsworth's conduct," he wrote to a colleague, "is spoken of with universal applause, as judicious and brave. Brigadier Lovell is well spoken of, that he did everything in his power. The commander of the fleet is cursed, bell, book, and candle by many . . . Lieut.-Col. Paul Revere is now under an arrest for disobedience of orders, and unsoldier-like behavior tending to cowardice, etc. As soon as the siege was raised, he made the best of his way to Boston, leaving his men to get along as they could (as it's said). I hope the matter will be thoroughly enquired into, and justice done to every individual officer."[9]

For Paul Revere, justice would prove to be an elusive ideal. Though an incendiary complaint had been lodged against him, there was no talk of, nor had he requested, formal court-martial proceedings to inquire specifically into the charges. For the time being, *individual* justice would have to be found within the constraints of the state-ordered inquest into the Penobscot Expedition as a whole.

It has been argued that, perhaps, Massachusetts harbored a self-seeking interest in the political demise of Dudley Saltonstall. If blame for the failure of the expedition could be foisted upon the commodore—a Continental officer—then, went the argument, responsibility for the massive attendant financial loss could justifiably be placed on the shoulders of the United States government.[10] Whether aware of this proposition or not, on September 7, 1779, the Navy Board Eastern Department issued a warrant for Saltonstall's court-martial.

On September 14 Saltonstall and a bevy of compelled witnesses gathered in the forecastle of the frigate *Deane* anchored in Boston Harbor, prepared to give testimony on the commodore's conduct during the Penobscot Expedition. As the hearing was about to begin, however, an unexplained "requisition" from the Navy Board together with a resolution of the General Court arrived demanding an adjournment of the proceedings to September 28.

Angered by the irregularity, Saltonstall complained that such a delay would prejudice his defense, since several of his key witnesses, each naval captains, were "ready for the seas and resolved to embrace the first wind." The president of the court-martial, Captain Samuel Nicholson, granted the adjournment. However, out of a willingness "to show every indulgence to Captain Saltonstall, and wishing the whole of their proceedings might evince a spirit of impartiality," Nicholson petitioned the legislature to retain the witnesses in Boston through the extended hearing date.[11]

Mysteriously, Captain Nicholson's statement on the subject remains the last official record of proceedings against Saltonstall arising out of his conduct on the Penobscot Expedition. As Gilbert Nash points out, "The most careful search among all known sources of information fails to discover any further traces of this court-martial, although several of the accredited histories, and general tradition, state that he was cashiered and pronounced forever incapacitated for holding governmental office . . . That such was the result in his case there can be little doubt . . . from the fact that he disappears from that time, and is never heard of afterwards in the public records."[12]

Whether Dudley Saltonstall was ever formally convicted in the court-martial proceedings against him seems to be an academic question. What is known is that he never served on another government vessel, and following the inquiry into the Penobscot Expedition, the Massachusetts General Court decreed him to be "incompetent ever after, to hold a commission in the service of the State."[13]

🐝 Since its construction in 1742, Faneuil Hall had long been a focal point of Boston politics, commerce, and entertainment. Donated to the town by Peter Faneuil, whose full-length portrait still adorns its walls, the building served as the backdrop for nearly every celebration, oration, or angry mob of revolutionary-era Boston. "In old Faneuil," wrote William Babcock Weeden, "that guild of temple traders and aldermen, butchers and clerks, hucksters and civic magistrates, the spirit of the people conceived an embryonic nation."[14]

On Wednesday, September 22, 1779, the various officers of the Penobscot Expedition—thirty in number—nervously gathered in the capacious amphitheater of Faneuil Hall. Dressed in the same military waistcoats, breeches, and boots they had worn throughout the arduous journey to and from Maine, the men presented at once a sight of both honor and indignity. The voices that filled the hall, Paul Revere's included, were distinctively Bostonian. With a characteristic suppression of the Yankee "r" that derived from generations of East Anglian immigrants,[15] the officers spoke in hushed and reverent tones befitting the circumstances.

Sworn written statements, or "depositions" as they were called, were required earlier from the men to ensure that their respective narrative accounts were memorialized in the event that travel or domestic obligations prevented their appearance at the hearing. Without the assistance of lawyers, who were generally discouraged in such proceedings so that costs could be minimized, each witness was expected to read his deposition into the record in open court and then be questioned by the committee members or other witnesses.[16] Because the early expectations of the Penobscot Expedition had been so lofty and since the results had been so distressing, the mood at Faneuil Hall was tense and heated.

The panel members, likely adorned in satin robes and powdered wigs, as was the custom, filed into the hall and took their places before the collection of witnesses and interested observers. Artemus Ward, Francis Dana, Timothy Danielson, Brigadier General Jonathan Titcomb, the Honorable James Prescott, the Honorable Major General Michael Farley, Colonel Moses Little, and Major Samuel Osgood, came from a broad and distinguished spectrum of legislative and military backgrounds and brought a clear understanding of the legal and martial issues that would be the subject of the inquiry. Chairman Artemus Ward gaveled the proceedings into order and called the committee's first witness to the chair. Recently home from his travels through Indian country, a grim and wary Solomon Lovell approached the erudite panel, raised his right hand, and swore to tell only the truth of what he knew.

The chairman began the examination by reading into evidence the council's orders to the general given at the outset of the expedition. "You being appointed by the General Court of this State to the Command of the land forces raised and to be raised for the purpose of Dislodging the Enemies of this State who have taken Post at Penobscot . . ." Ward's voice reverberated throughout the hall, each word no doubt piercing Solomon Lovell with somber remorse. "You will in all your operations consult with the Commander of the fleet . . . in Endeavoring to Captivate Kill or destroy the whole force of the Enemy there both by Sea & Land."[17]

Upon acknowledging that he had, in fact, received such orders from the council, Lovell then delivered a day-to-day account of the Penobscot Expedition from its inception to the final defeat nearly a month later. His narrative was rendered reflexively and without hyperbole, stating only salient facts in an impassive manner befitting his position as a general. On several occasions, the committee interrupted Lovell in order to hear the testimony of other witnesses who could not linger, and thus he delivered his statement in sporadic fashion over three separate days.[18]

Lovell began his testimony by pointing out the deficiency in the number of troops available to him for the expedition. He stated that on his arrival at Townsend on July 21 there were only 873 rank-and-file infantrymen on hand, and accordingly he requested that his militia officers scour the countryside in an effort to augment the numbers. "Notwithstanding," he testified, "I concluded to go on to Penobscot."[19]

Lovell explained that upon taking the heights of Majabigwaduce on

July 28, he had learned from prisoner accounts that the British at Fort George numbered approximately one thousand. "Upon this, I ordered lines to be thrown for our defense in case of an attack."

"Did you request the Naval Commander to co-operate with you at the time you effected your landing, or during that Day or any time after?" a member of the committee asked.

"I did not at the time of my landing or during that day—except to furnish the Marines."[20]

Buttressed by the minutes of the respective councils of war and by copies of various letters among the officers, however, Lovell went on to express his unambiguous opinion that Commodore Saltonstall did not exercise sufficient fortitude in the implementation of the council's orders. "I think there was a rational probability of success if the navy had cooperated with me after I had taken possession of the Heights of [Majabigwaduce]," testified Lovell.[21] The ultimate illogicality of the dual co-equal land and sea leadership roles was unequivocally articulated by the general: "I requested Commodore Saltonstall to destroy the Shipping. He asked me if he destroyed the enemy's Ships whether I could storm the Enemy's Main Fort. I told him I could not with my land forces only . . . He then replied, his Ships might suffer."[22]

During the second day of Lovell's testimony, Captain Nathan Brown of the privateer *Hunter* was called by the committee and asked whether the enemy ships could have been destroyed without General Lovell first taking the fort.

"In my opinion they could," replied Brown.

"Why was the attack not made?"

"My Opinion was [that] our Shipping would receive more damage in the attack, than we could reap benefit by the destruction of [the] enemy Shipping—The damage we should have received would have been mostly from the Fort, as it is probable the enemy's Shipping would not have fired more [than] once or twice."[23]

After the completion of Brown's testimony, John Carnes, captain of the privateer *Hector*, was called and promptly swore that "[f]rom the time we arrived 'till the enemy's reinforcement appeared in sight our Ships lay almost inactive . . ."[24] Though Carnes admitted that a naval attack could only have been undertaken at great risk of fire from Fort George, he adamantly opined that "our Navy might have destroyed the Enemy's fleet at any time before the arrival of . . . reinforcement[s]."

Carnes went on to state that on the first appearance of enemy ships in Penobscot Bay, the American fleet might have been saved had clear and unequivocal orders been given by the officers. "I don't know that any orders were given for Burning our Fleet," said Carnes. "I burnt my own Ship without."

In a stolid procession over the next seven days, each of the naval captains and land officers commanding the expedition took the witness chair and provided a disturbing image of indecision and neglect. One by one, the men described in vivid detail the perils and follies of their mission — from the Nantasket departure to their fiery retreat — and uniformly condemned Dudley Saltonstall for the failure of the Penobscot Expedition. "[I]t was always in the power of Our Fleet to have destroyed the Enemy's Shipping without any assistance from the land Army until the arrival of their Reinforcement," stated Titus Salter of the *Hampden*.[25]

Concurring, John Williams, captain of the Brig *Hazard*, testified that if the enemy ships had been attacked and destroyed, Fort George "must have surrendered." Williams insisted that the commodore had been informed of this opinion by several officers; yet, on every occasion, he refused to press the attack though frequently urged of the dangers of delay. "Whenever any proposition was made for attacking the enemy's ships," claimed Williams, "the Commodore opened his Council by Preaching Terror."[26]

And on it went. Captain Allen Hallet of the brig *Active* testified, "During the four days that I continued in the Harbor of [Majabigwaduce], it is my opinion we might have attacked & destroyed the enemy's fleet without any assistance from the land Army, & I was surprised that they did not go in during that time."[27] Hallet informed the committee that when he questioned the commodore on his unwillingness to act, "He made me no answer, but turned from me."[28]

First Lieutenant George Little, who had brazenly confronted the commodore on the Penobscot River, stated in meticulous detail the specifics of the altercation and, when asked if it had been in the power of the

Rebel navy to destroy the enemy fleet without the assistance of General Lovell, he unflinchingly responded, "Yes, with the greatest ease at any time before the arrival of the reinforcement."[29]

John Cathcart, captain of the *Tyrannicide*, was asked the same question and retorted, "It was, and the Grand forts too . . ."[30] And Joshua Davis, commander of the transports, informed the panel that he "to My great Surprise Saw the Explosion of Several Armed Ships—they might have been Very Easily Defended."[31]

Though Dudley Saltonstall's name appeared on the list of witnesses summoned to testify at the committee of inquiry, there is no record of evidence offered by him or on his behalf. His formal account of events, if it ever existed, is lost to history.

Paul Revere attended every day of the inquest at Faneuil Hall. Wearing the formal officer's uniform of the Massachusetts Artillery—a blue woolen waistcoat trimmed in red with white cross belts, vest, and breeches—he listened intently to the testimony, broodingly awaiting the attacks on his character that he was sure were coming. While the committee grappled with the root causes of the expedition's failure, Revere, fixated on his own reputation, ruminated on the motivation of his enemies and, without the benefit of a lawyer or legal training, evaluated witnesses and formulated his defenses.

As Revere's adversaries clearly had collaborated against him, a fact later admitted by Carnes when he stated that he was "desired" by others to file his complaint,[32] so too had Revere sought out the assistance of perceived allies and solicited their supportive statements for the hearing. Thus, on September 24, Phillip Marett, the acting lieutenant aboard the *Sky Rocket*—and Revere's first cousin—informed the committee that while on shore at Majabigwaduce he "saw Colonel Revere who always appeared as he always did . . . as an Active and Diligent officer." Marett further testified that, upon the retreat up the Penobscot River, Revere was asked one evening by the captain of the *Sky Rocket* to come aboard and "drink some Grog," but Revere had refused. "[H]e told him he could not stop for he was trying to Collect his men."[33]

Joseph Whipple, a surgeon in Revere's artillery regiment, specifically responded to Thomas Carnes's complaint addressing the allegations charge by charge as best he could. "[I] saw an order, for Colonel Revere to send Cannon etc, properly Officered and manned, which was Obeyed . . . ," said Whipple. "[As to] neglect of duty . . . I don't know an Instance of . . . [As to] Unsoldierlike behavior I was not a judge of, And I never knew that Colonel Revere had any trial of his bravery."[34]

And Andrew McIntyer, lieutenant of artillery, provided a glowing account to the committee of Revere's leadership during the assent of Majabigwaduce. In direct opposition to Carnes's charge that Revere was not engaged in the hauling of cannons to the heights, McIntyer testified, "Colonel Revere was constantly with us giving directions. [The] afternoon we Opened the Battery, [he] was there most of that afternoon, giving directions; he Visited the Battery, several times a day, every time I was on duty, which was almost every other day. Whenever there was an alarm I always found him there. I never Knew him absent from Camp, without he left word where he was gone . . . I do declare that during the whole expedition, in my opinion, he behaved himself like a good Officer.[35] And, in an obvious swipe at Carnes, McIntyer informed the committee that during the attack, several of Carnes's marines approached Revere and told him they could not locate their commander. Later, according to McIntyer, Carnes came upon the artillerymen and "he went up to Colonel Revere, and shook hands with him . . ."[36]

But by and large, the testimony presented to the committee weighed heavily against Paul Revere. After Phillip Marett had bolstered his artillery commander, Captain Perez Cushing castigated him. Painting a picture of a petty and resentful malcontent, Cushing described to the panel an occasion where General Wadsworth had directly ordered him (Cushing) and a number of artillerymen to deliver three cannon to the mainland battery in an attempt to reach Captain Mowat's ships from the north. As he prepared for the task, Cushing's testimony continued, he informed Revere of the general's order and immediately saw the indignation rise in his commander. "[H]e said he thought he ought to have been consulted by the General before a detachment was made from his Corps,—but said get your Men."[37]

Directly contradicting Revere's assertion that he had searched des-

perately for his company during the disordered retreat from Majabigwaduce, Cushing angrily testified that Revere had abandoned him and
his men on the shores without orders or direction. "I tarried at the place
where he left me . . ..'till near Dark, waiting for Colonel Revere and orders,
then I proceeded to the place where our Men landed, met some of them
coming up & in the whole collected about forty . . . Colonel Revere had
an Opportunity to have given orders to me, or to the Men, before we left
the River & I expected to have received orders from him, but did not."[38]

Following up on a particular anecdote that had been swirling around
Boston, a member of the committee inquired whether Cushing had ever
heard chatter from the general's marquee to the effect that no matter how
long the siege continued Lieutenant Colonel Paul Revere could not be
relied upon with orders. "I heard such conversation," replied Cushing.[39]

Revere glared angrily at his artillery captain but dared not offer a
question to counter his testimony.

On Saturday, September 25, several more sea captains were called to
the witness chair, each providing detailed accounts of the expedition
and opinions as to the causes of its failure. As a postscript to his deposition before the committee, Captain John Williams described the travails of his sailors in hauling the eighteen-pound cannons up the cliffs
of Majabigwaduce and recounted their anger in the apparent absence of
Revere and his artillerymen. "I do not recollect that I Saw a Soldier pull
a Rope, or assist in getting up the Guns," observed Williams indignantly.
"I observed it in the time, & thought we had not the assistance from
the [Artillery] Train I expected."[40] Captain John Cathcart, who also provided assistance with the cannon, joined Williams in his assessment and
swore under oath to its accuracy.[41]

By the start of the following week, the committee had heard from
the militia leaders Samuel McCobb and Jeremiah Hill, who each had
provided compelling accounts of the land assaults on Majabigwaduce,
as well as the unfortunate circumstances of the Rebel retreat. On the
morning of Wednesday, September 29, however, all eyes were fixed on
General Peleg Wadsworth.

A Harvard-educated schoolteacher by trade, Wadsworth was eloquent with the written word, and his deposition flowed with effusive description, in sharp contrast to that of his lower officers. "The Failure of the Expedition under Enquiry," began the general, "seems to me to be owing principally to the Lateness of our Arrival before the Enemy, the Smallness of our Land Forces, & the uniform Backwardness of the Commander of the Fleet."[42]

Wadsworth enumerated a series of unavoidable delays at Nantasket attendant with the initial arrangement of the fleet and the perils of bad weather, but then placed the blame squarely on Paul Revere, who along with some of his men had spent the evening before the departure at home in Boston. "[T]he whole Fleet was obliged to heave to for several hours to wait for the Ordnance Brigg," testified Wadsworth.[43]

After modestly concurring with General Lovell's account of the heroic ground assault upon the heights, Wadsworth focused the balance of his narrative on his efforts to mount a defense after the sorrowful retreat from Majabigwaduce—and on his frustration with Paul Revere.

As the committee listened intently, Wadsworth described returning to the transports after locating an appropriate upriver location to fortify, only to find the ships clustered and ablaze. He testified about his need for Revere's Castle barge in the perilous rescue of the small schooner that had torn away and drifted toward the enemy. Though the schooner contained a crew of imperiled men and provisions, "I was directly opposed by Lieut. Col. Revere who said that I had no right to command either him or the Boat & gave orders to the contrary."[44] "The Reason Lt. Colonel Revere gave for the Boat's not going off to the Schooner," Wadsworth tersely complained, "was that he had all his private baggage at Stake."[45]

Wadsworth testified that, amid Revere's protestations, "He was promised An Arrest as soon as the Army should be collected."[46]

At the conclusion of the general's statement, a member of the committee inquired if he recollected asking Colonel Revere to cut out the embrasures for the Rebel breastworks on the heights.

"I am not positive that I asked him, but had thoughts in my Mind why I had not seen him there at the fixing [of] the Batteries," came the response.

"[Was] Colonel Revere . . . missing on Shore?"

"I saw him but seldom on shore during the first week after our landing."[47]

At that, Paul Revere leapt to his feet and approached the witness. His black artillery boots were scuffed and worn from his travels through the wilderness of Maine, though the limp that he had developed on the journey was now only barely perceptible. With the sprightly deportment of a state's attorney, he began firing questions at Peleg Wadsworth.[48]

"Do you recollect," began Revere with characteristic Yankee enunciation, "my carrying you to a place & showing it as a proper one for getting up the Cannon & cutting a Road?"—the word "proper" sounding more like "propah."

"I remember being on a Bank with Colonel Revere and pitching on a place to get up the Cannon, where we afterward got them up."

"Do You remember sending for me to go to an Island to the Eastward of Hackers Island to find a post to annoy the enemy's Shipping?"

"I Remember you went with me," responded Wadsworth. "I don't recollect sending for you, but don't think it improbable . . ."

Thomas Carnes then rose and approached the general.[49] Sensing an opportunity to attack his nemesis and recalling a statement made by Captain Cushing regarding the distrust that Lovell and Wadsworth harbored for Revere, he offered, "Did you say or hear General Lovell say that if the siege Continued seven years, if it was possible to avoid it he would not order Colonel Revere to take any Command?"

Refusing to engage Carnes in his personal quarrels with Revere, Wadsworth responded, "I have no recollection of the sort, or even that it ever was in my Mind,—if I had said it, 'tis probable it would have left some traces in my mind."

Artemas Ward then impatiently interjected the fundamental question.

"Did you during the siege discover any inattention or backwardness to duty in Colonel Revere? He asked."

As Revere braced for the answer, Wadsworth paused in reflection and tactfully replied, "I did not see him so frequently in Camp as I expected—This was in my mind in the time of it . . ."[50] Wadsworth then described Revere's less-than-enthusiastic record of votes during the various councils of war and how his opinions were always at variance with his own. The inference, of course, was that Revere had consistently voted to end the siege and retreat the army.

Following General Wadsworth's testimony, the commander of the ordnance brig, the *Samuel*, was called to the witness chair. Captain James Brown informed the committee of the great panic and confusion that imbued the fleet as the armed vessels chaotically stormed past the transports in the narrows of the Penobscot River. "[F]inding no assistance," lamented Brown, "I asked Colonel Davis, 'What I should do?'—he answered me, that He did not know what to do!"[51] Brown testified that as the British ships approached in the distance, he was left with no choice but to run the brig ashore and flee into the woods.

Captain Carnes, emboldened by his examination of General Wadsworth and determined to continue the focus on Revere, asked Brown if he recalled when Revere received the billet ordering him to appear before General Lovell to explain his absence from the shore. After providing a confused response to the question, Revere then asked the captain, "How often did I come on board the Ordnance Brig, after our baggage was carried on shore?"[52]

"Very seldom," replied Brown. "[Y]ou was not on board every day & when you came 'twas on particular business to shift yourself or to do something relative to the service—I particularly remember that you several days, sawed off the fuses of the Shells . . . & seemed always anxious to be on shore as soon as possible . . ." Brown then turned to the panel and added, "Colonel Revere refused to stay & drink Coffee & dine when I had asked him."[53]

Thomas Carnes was then called to the witness chair. As Revere watched with piqued indignation, Carnes introduced himself to the panel as commander of the marines aboard the ship *Putnam*, and then he immediately launched his tirade against the artillery commander.

Beginning with the events of July 28 and the assault upon the cliffs of Majabigwaduce, Carnes testified that Revere and his men were to land as a reserve corps and were to keep to the rear as close to the main force as possible.

His Corps landed, to the left, of the Marines. I supposed him to be with them, but did not then see him [until] some time after the Marines was engaged, they kept on the beach, till the troops had got possession of the heights, and did not come to the top of the heights, till some time after the troops had halted . . . Colonel Revere left his men on Shore and went on board the Transport at Breakfast time, and Dinner time, towards evening, he went on board again . . . and for Several days after he could not be found.[54]

Carnes testified as to General Lovell's displeasure over Revere's absence from the lines and recounted the order and personal billet that was issued directing him to encamp on shore with his men. He stated that Revere was seldom present to provide instruction or direction to his artillerymen, and he disparaged his ability as a commander of artillery and his understanding of the cannon under his control. "I thought it impossible that a Colonel of Artillery, should make such bad shot, and know no more about Artillery," said Carnes.[55]

Though infuriated by Carnes's statements, Revere, lacking in any legal training, conducted only a short and ineffective cross-examination of his rival, choosing instead to present his defenses through the testimony of friendly witnesses. He was incensed that Carnes, as the proponent of the charges, had even been permitted to testify and offer evidence in furtherance of his own complaint. Revere clearly felt abused by the process and especially by committee member Francis Dana, who according to Revere, "treated me as though I had been a malefactor, and he State's Attorney; they even admitted Carnes, who was my accuser, to be an evidence against me."[56]

Yet now, when given the opportunity to cross-examine his rival and set the record straight before the committee and his countrymen, Revere faltered. With his mind racing with anger and incredulity, he gathered himself and managed to ask Carnes only whether he had ever seen orders directing the artillerymen to land on July 28 as a corps de reserve.

Perplexed by the question, Carnes replied simply, "Yes."[57]

On the same day, September 29, the committee called another of Revere's enemies, Major William Todd, to offer his sworn statement. Surprisingly circumspect, Todd focused his lengthy deposition primarily on the military maneuvers of General Lovell's men and the maddening difficulties he had encountered with the commodore. "[I]t was easy . . . ," opined Todd, "for our Fleet to have attacked & destroyed the enemy's shipping at any time before the arrival of the enemy's reinforcement."[58]

Without specifying names, but unquestionably referring to Paul Revere, Todd then informed the committee, "Some officers' Conduct in my Opinion very unsoldierlike, Some Commanders of Corps seldom with them."[59] More detailed allegations, specifically directed against Revere, followed. He criticized those under whose care the ordnance brig—perhaps the most important of the transports—rested, including the "Commanding Officer of our Artillery," and scolded that had the stores been properly secured during the retreat, a defensive stand might have been successfully achieved.[60] Todd accused Revere of failing to move upriver with his men to refortify during the retreat despite orders for him to do so, and he reiterated General Lovell's surprise at Revere's inattention to duty and frequent absence from camp. "I heard General Wadsworth say . . . that if the siege continued seven years (if it was possible to avoid it)—he should not ask him to take any Command."[61]

Perhaps the most damning allegations against Revere came from his commissary of ordnance, Gilbert Speakman. Admittedly requested by Thomas Carnes to produce a written statement of "what I know concerning the conduct of Lieutenant Colonel Revere at Penobscot,"[62] Speakman recounted a litany of offenses allegedly committed by the artillery commander.[63]

He informed the committee of how, when ordered to bring some guns onto Nautilus Island after its capture from the British, Revere bristled. "[H]e could not think the General meant for him to go, but believed 'twas a mistake . . ."

Speakman stated that a few days later some of General Lovell's men had asked Revere to borrow his Castle barge but were refused. "He replied he wanted it himself," said Speakman. "[He] said he brought that Barge for his own use & not for the General's."

Speakman testified that General Lovell had openly wondered if Revere, by his continued absence, purposefully was keeping himself "out of the way." He then recounted how Major Todd, at the insistence of the general, had prepared a billet for delivery to Revere demanding that he attend the general's marquee to address the problem and how Revere had scoffed at the issue after meeting with Lovell. "[H]e made a trifling matter of it," said Speakman.

And finally, Speakman described how, upon the first day of retreat up the Penobscot River, Major Todd had delivered the general's order to Revere that he remove the cannons from Nautilus Island and secure them for use in a fortification to hinder the advancing British fleet. According to Speakman, Revere refused the order saying that he had no boat available, though he would later gripe that he simply chose not to risk his men on such a mission. Then, continued Speakman, Revere examined his original orders and stated that since he was mandated by the Massachusetts Council to be under the general's command "during the Penobscot Expedition," and since, for all practical purposes, the expedition had ended, he no longer considered himself bound by the general's orders.

On Friday, October 1, the final day of the hearing, Revere requested that General Lovell be recalled to the witness chair. Though angered and befuddled by the testimony against him, Revere finally had formulated a strategy of defense that focused on clearing his name of the primary charges before the committee.

In a series of questions designed to refresh Lovell's recollection of certain events, Revere attacked the premise that he had somehow purposefully absented himself from the Rebel camp or the danger of battle on Majabigwaduce.[64]

He stood reverently before the general and slowly began, "Did you on the 28th of July, the day you landed on Magabigwaduce, see me, with the Corps I commanded?" asked Revere.

"Yes."

"Do you remember that you ordered me to follow you with my men, and that we followed you up the steep, and kept close to your rear, till you Ordered me to halt? That just after you halted, you Ordered me to git a field piece on Shore; I asked you, if I should take one of my companies to do it, that you answered me yes."

"Yes," replied Lovell, "I remember the whole."

Revere then skillfully took the general back through a succession of mutual dealings on Majabigwaduce in which Lovell had issued orders to gather or reposition certain artillery and equipment, and to which Revere dutifully had complied.

"Was there a day," continued Revere, "from the time we landed on Majabigwaduce, to the day we retreated up the River, but what you saw me at least twice a day?"

Lovell paused in reflection, then replied, "I do not recollect every day but remember I [saw] you often."

No doubt pleased with the response, Revere ventured, "Did you ever send, or Give me an Order Verbally which I did not obey?"

"No," said Lovell, "except on the day after we retreated."

Not wishing to pursue this, Revere quickly changed topics. He removed a small piece of paper from the pocket of his breeches and studied it for a moment.

"Did you on the Evening of the 29th of July send me a Billet . . . to wit, The General is surprised that he had not seen Colonel Revere & desires he would wait upon him immediately?"

"Such a Billet was sent but I cannot recollect the time when," replied Lovell, and then to Revere's satisfaction, he added, "And the Colonel waited upon me immediately & satisfied me that he had been well employed."

Thomas Carnes watched with mounting frustration as the general seemed to bolster Revere's defense. It was now time for him to remind Lovell of certain *other* events that bore upon Revere's actions and character at Majabigwaduce.[65]

Sensing that he had become a mere instrument in a battle of personal invective, however, Lovell clearly had now turned hostile toward Carnes and appeared less willing to assist in his campaign against Revere. As Carnes approached the witness chair, he studied the general, measuring his patience and hoping that the questions would enlighten rather than irritate.

"Do you Remember," began Carnes, ". . . Sending for Colonel Revere several times whilst we Lay on [Majabigwaduce], and Received for Answer he was not to be found?"

"I did once," responded Lovell.

"Do you Remember of Saying, at Several times that you was Surprised of Colonel Revere's Inattention to his Duty?"

"I do not remember it."

"Do you Remember of Saying Let the Siege Continue as Long as it will, you should not Desire, or order Colonel Revere to take any Command?"

Lovell shifted in his chair and appeared angered by the question. "I do not remember saying any such thing."

"Do you Remember," persisted Carnes, "when you sent the orders for some Pieces of Artillery to be carried on [Nautilus] Island, whether You meant for Colonel Revere to go himself or to order some officer to go?"

"I expected he would see it done," tersely replied Lovell.

Recognizing that extensive inquiry could only be counterproductive, Carnes ventured one final question.

"Do you Remember Giving Colonel Revere orders to Retreat up the River with his men, as you was determined to fortify?"

"Yes," responded the general. "He answered [that the] Ordnance Brig was destroyed and there were no Cannon to make a Stand . . ."

Carnes returned to the gallery benches believing that the matter was concluded, but the committee, apparently fascinated by the exchange, was intent on continuing Lovell's examination. Directing him to remain in the witness chair, the panel began asking questions.[66]

"Do you Remember," inquired the committee, ". . . seeing any thing of Colonel Revere after you gave him orders to go up the River with his men till you [saw] him in Boston?"

"I do not," replied Lovell. He paused for a moment and then, with the demeanor of a man who wished to unburden himself, began speaking about Revere's activities after the Rebels won the heights of Majabigwaduce—though he had not been directly asked about the topic.

"I ordered Colonel Revere to land with his Men, with their Muskets.

In about an hour after our landing I ordered him to take one of his Companies and the Cannon on shore from on board the transport."

With Paul Revere listening intently from the gallery, General Lovell's voice seemed to rise with anger.

"I gave no permission to Colonel Revere," he continued, "to go on board the Transport to Dine, Sup, lodge or Breakfast . . . but expected he was on shore with his Men, till the contrary was represented to me, which occasioned my order of the 30th of July to him to encamp with the Corps on Shore with the Army."

In an effort to place on the record that which the committee already knew, one member then asked, "Did you write to the Council to give Colonel Revere a reprimand for his unsoldierlike behavior?"

As Carnes no doubt smiled derisively from the gallery, Lovell replied, "Yes, and I had reference to his disobedience of the order of the 15th of August [to retreat up the river with his men] . . . And his leaving the army without permission."

At once clarifying but also confusing the issue of Revere's behavior on the Penobscot Expedition, the committee closed their examination of General Lovell with one final question.

"When Colonel Revere lodged on board," asked a member of the panel, "did you consider it as a disobedience of orders?"

Lovell reflected for a moment and then, choosing his words cautiously and with precision, responded, "I did not consider it as a disobedience of orders for I had given no orders that he should be on shore, but expected that he & every other officer that had any thing to do with the army, should be on shore."

Artemas Ward had heard enough. After ten days of angry finger-pointing and heated exchanges, of vivid descriptions and mournful narratives, the testimony finally was concluded. On the afternoon of October 1, 1779, he gaveled the hearing closed and adjourned the inquiry into the failure of the Penobscot Expedition.

Chapter 12 "Dearer to Me Than Life"

Even as the committee began deliberating on the volumes of testimonial evidence that it had adduced during its inquiry, petitions from the people of eastern Maine continued to pour into Boston. With the Rebel forces vanquished from Majabigwaduce and with the fishing and lumber trades completely in enemy hands, destitute families looked to the Massachusetts Council for relief. Samuel Burgess, a longtime resident of Lincoln County and one such victim of the British incursion, forwarded his dire remonstration to the government and pleaded for assistance. "Cruel Enemies of these American States," wrote Burgess, "Invaded Penobscot and Destroyed your Petitioner's House and Stripped him and his Family of all that he had in the wide world, so that he and his family are by their merciless cruelty reduced to the utmost distress Poverty and want."[1]

Burgess's appeal was typical of the region, and the suffering was not confined to Maine—nor was it limited to individuals or families. In Boston, the Board of War informed the Massachusetts General Court of the "difficulties and embarrassments inextricable, and without . . . immediate interposition, totally insurmountable" that it found itself in as a result of the "unfortunate Expedition" to Maine.[2] The financial and emotional impact to the region would prove staggering.

Amid this turmoil Paul Revere anxiously prepared his own plea—his closing argument—for presentation to Artemas Ward and his fellow panel members. He had intended to deliver this epistle to the committee prior to its adjournment but found that the sheer breadth of the document detained him past the deadline. Shortly after the inquiry, a rambling letter of defense—nearly three thousand words in length—arrived in the Council Chamber and was added to the mass of evidence to be weighed by the Committee.

"It lays with You in a great measure," Revere's letter began, "from the evidence for and against me, to determine what is more dearer to me than life; my character."[3] He explained that certain "prejudices" against him as expressed to the committee were, in fact, the result of "stories, propagated by designing men to my disadvantage." Accordingly, urged Revere, a little history of his predicament was in order.

Referencing the reduction of the Massachusetts Artillery Train in early 1779 and the resulting resignation of many of its officers, including William Todd, Revere insisted that his assumption of power and rigid manner of authority had created enemies in the regiment. "I accepted the command, (which was by desire of the Council) and did all in my power, to hinder the men from deserting . . . ," wrote Revere. "And because I would not give up my Commission, the same way the other officers did, some of them propagated every falsehood Malice could invent in an underhanded way."[4] Here, according to Revere, was the genesis of the conspiracy.

With Todd named as an integral member of General Lovell's camp on the Penobscot Expedition, Revere pointed out "what a situation I was in, with such an inveterate enemy in the General's Family." He explained to Lovell how "disagreeable" Todd had been to him, and he vowed that he would never exchange words with him on the expedition unless required by duty. This fact, according to Revere, explained why he may not have been seen at the general's camp on Majabigwaduce as often as other officers had been.

Revere insisted that he nonetheless met with the general during the expedition at least twice a day. "He saw me often," wrote Revere. "Yet he never gave me the most distant hint that he thought I omitted or neglected any part of my duty."

Revere's letter then focused on the allegations of William Todd. "I have not the least doubt," wrote Revere, "but . . . Todd procured the [orders and allegations against me]." One by one, Revere addressed the charges leveled by Todd and his surrogates.

"He swears that I did not land [during the assault on the cliffs] in time, and insinuates it was done with design." Though the testimony on this point was contradictory at best, Revere, relying on the statements of several militia officers, baldly concluded, "[T]o his confusion, [this charge] was proved to be false."

That Todd had heard General Wadsworth avow an unwillingness to rely on his artillery commander with orders if the siege had lasted "seven years," Revere directed the committee to Wadsworth's own denial of ever making such a statement.

To the allegation that he was frequently on board the transports "by which [my accusers] would insinuate that I went there to keep out of the way," Revere relied on the testimony of James Brown, captain of the *Samuel*. "I never came on board, but to do something for the Service . . . and when I was on board, I was anxious to git on shore, for fear I should be wanted."

And as to the charge that he had failed to move upriver after the retreat as ordered by General Lovell, Revere pointed to several officers who had informed the committee that he was, in fact, seen as far north as Grant's Mills, twenty miles upriver. "I stayed there, the whole of that day . . . ," insisted Revere, "and did not leave the River till I was assured they would burn the Ships next morning."

Revere then turned to the formal complaint lodged by Thomas Carnes, upon which his arrest by the council had been based. "I expected," wrote Revere, "he would have endeavored to have proved [each charge], one by one; But when he found his witness failed He was suffered to appear as an evidence Himself; I say suffered; for it was the first instance I ever heard of, in Matters of this sort; (in Military affairs), that a man should be accuser and evidence."

Revere queried with a hint of sardonic scorn, "After all, what does he swear to; First that I stayed on the Beach with my men, and did not go up the Steep till the Marines and Militia had got possession of the Heights. 2nd That I carried all my men on board the Transport and that they lodged there. And that the Sailors got my Cannon on Shore."

Each allegation, he insisted, had been disproved by the evidence. As to the first, he stated that General Lovell himself had sworn that Revere was close in the rear of the assault. He denied that he and his men had stayed aboard the transport until ordered on shore, and he directed the committee to his officers' testimony in support. "That the Sailors got my Cannon on Shore is true in part," he wrote. The sailors did haul the eighteen-pound guns on shore, but he insisted that his artillerymen had towed and positioned the twelve-pound howitzer and heavy fieldpiece into place. "You find," wrote Revere, "all my Officers swear they and the men were assisting the whole time."

Revere next turned to Carnes's charge that he had, on several in-stances during the Penobscot Expedition, disobeyed orders. To refute this allegation, Revere reminded the committee of General Lovell's statement that he knew of no such instance other than Revere's refusal to proceed up the river on August 15. "I think it is amply proved," stated Revere, "that I did go up the River, 20 miles . . . If the General did not see me there it was not my fault."

To Carnes's unabashed allegation of "unsoldierlike behavior during the whole expedition to Penobscot, which tends to cowardice,"[5] Revere chose to ignore the testimony of his detractors and simply wrote, "If to obey Orders, and to keep close to my duty is unsoldierlike; I was Guilty. As to Cowardice, During the whole expedition, I was never in any Sharp Action, nor was any of the Artillery; but in what little I was, no one has dared to say I flinched. My Officers all swear, that when ever there was an alarm, I was one of the first in the Battery; I think that's no mark of Cowardice."

Perhaps the most volatile charge against Revere—and one for which he was promised an immediate arrest—was his alleged refusal to release the Castle barge to General Wadsworth for the rescue of the disabled schooner during the upriver retreat.

Wadsworth had testified in detail regarding the event before the com-mittee, and Carnes had included it as a specific allegation in his com-plaint. In his letter of defense, Revere admitted that his personal bag-gage, including his linen, some instruments, and other items of value, had been stored on the barge, and that when Wadsworth demanded its use to rescue the men, he had balked. "I refused at first," confessed Revere, "but afterwards Ordered her to go, and she did go."

On Carnes's final allegation that Revere essentially had abandoned his men during the retreat, he brusquely protested, "The . . . charge is Malicious and false as has been proved by all my Officers," and mentioned nothing further of it.

But Revere wasn't finished. He was determined to address *every* charge and incrimination that had been leveled against him at the hearing. His character and his reputation demanded no less.

He insisted that Wadsworth had contradicted himself by stating that he had not seen Revere as often as he expected, while at other times acknowledging his presence, and he scolded the general for using Revere's record of adverse votes at the various councils of war against him. "I never before now ever heard, that an Officer was called to account for Actions at a Council of War. I believe for the future, that Officers will be careful how they attend Councils," he wrote. He then pointed out that, of the seven councils he had attended, five had produced unanimous votes.

Revere then felt compelled to address why he had slept on board the transport after the Rebel landing on Majabigwaduce. "The reason," wrote Revere, ". . . was merely for convenience. (Those who Judge it was from fear, Judge from their own feelings not mine) . . . [T]he Vessel was handy to the shore and all our Baggage on board, and a boat to fetch and carry us, we could have been to our duty much sooner than if we had lodged in the woods."

At the committee hearing, General Lovell affirmed that after the defeat he had written to the council requesting that Revere be given a "severe reprimand" for leaving the army without orders.[6] "That I came home without his Orders is true," conceded Revere in his letter of defense. "[W]here could I have found either the General or Brigadier [Wadsworth], if it had been necessary to have got Orders?" Then, in an astonishingly legalistic exercise, Revere referred the committee to his orders from the council that required him to obey General Lovell and his superior officers "during the Continuance of the Expedition."

"Surely," continued Revere, "no man will say, that the Expedition was not discontinued, when all the shipping was either taken, or Burnt, [and] the Artillery and Ordnance Stores all destroyed."

With that, Paul Revere concluded his letter and placed his fate in the hands of the committee members.

Chapter 13 Judgment

BY THE EARLY autumn of 1779, the colonies were facing, perhaps, the most difficult period of the Revolutionary War. Even as Massachusetts grappled with the suffering and depredation of the Penobscot Expedition, General Washington languished in the Hudson River Valley while Admiral d'Estaing and General Benjamin Lincoln faced defeat in Savannah.[1] The French had not yet fully committed their land and sea forces to the Rebel cause, and the morale of the colonies seemed to falter.[2]

Although the ongoing economic woes from the defeat at Penobscot had staggered the beleaguered Massachusetts government, the political focus in the state had, by then, shifted to the ratification of a new state constitution. While the committee inquiring into the failure of the expedition pored over the evidence adduced during its hearings, a constitutional convention had convened in Boston, and the arduous process of forming a permanent state government had begun.

Originating in Berkshire County in the western part of Massachusetts and taking hold after the signing of the Declaration of Independence, the campaign for a statewide charter was premised upon the axiom that "the people are the fountain of power."[3]

On February 28, 1778, the first state constitution in the American colonies was submitted for popular vote in Massachusetts. This poorly drafted document provided no Bill of Rights and contained critical flaws with regard to the qualification and payment of representatives. It was roundly criticized—and emphatically rejected by the people of the state.[4] The opposition movement, however, founded on the philosophical teachings of Locke and Montesquieu, would lay the cornerstone for debate of the coming state and federal constitutions. The essence of the popular argument was the recognition of certain rights as God-given and inalienable and the adoption of a practical framework of government to protect those rights.[5] This framework, as articulated by John Adams, contemplated the creation of "an empire of laws, and not of men"—a government balanced with coequal legislative, judicial, and executive branches designed to check and restrain "the efforts in human nature towards tyranny."[6]

By 1779 the respective counties of Massachusetts once again authorized the General Court to convene a constitutional convention. The legislature approved the measure in late spring and directed each town to elect a number of delegates equal to their current legislative representation, to be comprised of freemen over the age of twenty-one regardless of property ownership.[7] The first session of the Constitutional Convention was called for September 1 at the Old Meeting House in Cambridge—just as word of the failed Penobscot Expedition began spreading throughout Boston.

In a "general and free conversation" that lasted much of the day,[8] the convention enacted a set of rules and appointed a committee of thirty-one members assigned the task of drafting a new Massachusetts constitution. John Adams, Samuel Adams, and James Bowdoin were selected as a subcommittee for the undertaking—which, in turn, finally delegated John Adams to compose the actual document. The second session of the convention was scheduled for October 28, giving Adams ample time to complete his draft and circulate it among the other delegates.

With this and other important matters before the General Court, the committee inquiring into the failure of the Penobscot Expedition was anxious to complete its work and put an end to the sorry affair. Indeed, one of its members, Timothy Danielson, the chief justice of the Court of Common Pleas for Hampshire County and an officer in the Continental Army, had been named as a delegate from Brimfield to the Constitutional Convention.[9] It was clearly time for the people of Massachusetts to lay the failures of Penobscot aside.

Scarcely seven days after the last witness gave testimony before the committee of inquiry, General Ward and five other panel members gathered in the Council Chamber, debated the evidence, and issued their report.[10]

In a series of questions asked and then answered, the findings, accompanied by the deposition of each testifying witness, began, "Is it the Opinion of this Committee that they have made sufficient Enquiry into the Causes of the Failure of the late Expedition to Penobscot?"

"Answer. Unanimously, Yes."

Then, in a scathing and caustic attack that would effectively end his military career,[11] the full blame and culpability for the defeat was laid on the shoulders of Commodore Dudley Saltonstall.

"What appears to be the principle Reason of the Failure?" queried the report.

"Answer. Unanimously, Want of Proper Spirit and Energy on the part of the Commodore."

"What in the Opinion of this Committee was the Occasion of the total Destruction of our Fleet?"

"Answer. Principally the Commodore not exerting himself at all at the time of the Retreat in opposing the Enemy's foremost Ships in pursuit."

"Does it appear that the Commodore discouraged any Enterprises or offensive Measures on the part of our Fleet?"

"Answer. Unanimously, Yes, and though he always had a Majority of his Naval Council against offensive Operations which Majority was mostly made up of the Commanders of the private Armed Vessels yet he repeatedly said it was [a] Matter of favor that he called any Councils and when he had taken their Advice he should follow his own Opinion."

If it was the objective of the committee to allocate financial responsibility for the expedition to the Continental Congress by laying blame for its failure upon a Continental officer, its members were as concise and clear as a fact-finding body could be. Dudley Saltonstall had, in the considered and unequivocal opinion of the committee, caused the failure of the Penobscot Expedition.

As thoroughly as the committee condemned the commodore, however, it absolved Generals Lovell and Wadsworth as well as the naval commanders from the State of Massachusetts of any blame for the loss.

"Was General Lovell culpable in not Storming the Enemy's principal Fort?" posed the committee.

"Answer. Unanimously, No."

"Does it appear that General Lovell throughout the expedition and the Retreat acted with proper Courage and Spirit?"

"Answer. Unanimously, Yes, and it is the Opinion of the Committee had he been furnished with all the Men ordered for the Service or been properly supported by the Commodore he would probably have reduced the Enemy."

"What was the Conduct of Brigadier Wadsworth during his Command?"

"Answer. Brigadier Wadsworth (the Second in Command) throughout the whole Expedition, during the Retreat & after, until ordered to return to Boston, conducted [himself] with great Activity, Courage, Coolness and Prudence."

In a parting shot of anger, the report concluded that the number of men detached for service at Penobscot was deficient by nearly a third, and the committee resolved that any brigadier or officer found to be at blame for this "shameful neglect" be punished in accordance with the Militia Act.

As to Lieutenant Colonel Paul Revere, though the committee had heard hours of testimony and pored over hundreds of pages of documentary evidence concerning his behavior on the Penobscot Expedition—and despite enduring a formal complaint, an order for his arrest, a probing and humiliating inquiry, and the scorn of his countrymen—the report mentioned not a word, not a breath, of him. Though the people of Massachusetts may now have considered the sorry chapter of the Penobscot Expedition closed, to Paul Revere the matter had just begun.

Chapter 14 *Monument of Disgrace*

FOLLOWING THE Penobscot inquiry, the committee ordered that a copy if its final report be immediately dispatched to Congress sitting in Philadelphia "that they may take such order thereon, as to them may seem most conducive to public Justice."[1] It also directed that, as soon as the court-martial proceedings against Dudley Saltonstall were concluded, the report was to be published in one of the Boston newspapers. Paul Revere, however, would receive news of the findings well before Congress or the public at large.

Prior to the announcement of the committee's findings, Revere had received assurances that he would be exonerated of the charges against him. In private conversations among his friends in the legislature, he had been informed that it was the council's opinion that Carnes had not proved his allegations. Even Timothy Danielson had said, according to Revere, that there was not "the shadow of a crime" against him. And yet, Revere complained bitterly upon reading the findings that "the Committee in their report have not mentioned me."[2]

On October 8, the day after the report was issued, Revere drafted and forwarded a petition not only to the council but to the entire Massachusetts House of Representatives complaining that his character had been greatly abused by the many false reports and rumors propagated against him and that, although he had endured the humiliation of complaint, arrest, and inquiry, the committee "have neither condemned, or acquitted him." Accordingly, he requested that the committee reconvene to consider his case exclusively—or as an alternative, that a court-martial be appointed for his immediate trial according to Continental regulations.[3] On October 12, Revere again petitioned the council and specifically requested that a court-martial be convened to hear the charges against him. Concerned that several of his "chief evidences" were heading to sea, Revere requested that quick action be taken on his behalf.

With the assistance of several friends in the Assembly, Revere received near-instant results. The matter was immediately submitted back to the committee of inquiry; and though the legislature had refused to initiate a full military court-martial, summonses were forwarded yet again to several sea captains and sailors of the Penobscot Expedition ordering their appearance on the second Thursday of the next legislative session "to give evidence of what they know respecting the Conduct of Lieutenant Colonel Paul Revere during the aforesaid expedition."[4]

Revere had made an extraordinary demand on the Massachusetts legislature. It had spent countless hours in investigating and inquiring into the expedition, and the committee had issued its findings after careful deliberation. The work of government and the massive problems faced by the province required the full attention of those in the legislature, yet Paul Revere once again demanded that the clearing of his reputation become a priority of the people. Despite the daunting task in Massachusetts of conceiving the first state constitution and the continuing travails of a country torn by revolution, it appeared that the cheerless memory of the Penobscot Expedition would linger a little longer.

Paul Revere had, through the years, kept a very detailed ledger book of day-to-day business matters, but he is not known to have ever maintained a personal diary or journal. When the committee appointed by the General Court reconvened on November 11 in the east lobby of the Massachusetts State House, however, Revere submitted such a diary to the members and swore to its truthfulness as his formal deposition under oath.

The diary, which began with the arrival of the fleet at Townsend on July 21 and concluded with the discovery of his artillerymen at Fort Western on August 19, appears to be a sanitized litany of orders followed, councils of war attended, and events witnessed.[5] It offers no hint of controversy or dissatisfaction surrounding his actions at Majabigwaduce, nor does it provide any basis for accusation. Unsurprisingly, Revere's diary stands as a chronicle of a steadfast and reliable officer on the Penobscot Expedition. What is not entirely clear, however, is whether its entries were recorded contemporaneous to the events described or if they were created later in specific preparation for the coming inquest.[6] In either case, the members of the committee accepted Revere's "deposition" without known comment or further inquiry of its author.

While each of the several witnesses compelled by the committee had received summonses on October 19 to attend the November hearing and to testify as to what they knew, the committee only provided Revere himself with formal notice of the proceedings the day before they were to take place and simply "requested" that he attend.[7] Clearly, the committee had no intention of formally examining the accused. The sworn witnesses, however, would provide compelling evidence—both for and against Revere.

Of the surviving records from the November 11 hearing, it is known that Revere examined Captain Alexander Holmes of the *Charming Sally*,[8] who had not appeared or offered any statement during the initial committee hearings. When asked whether he had, in fact, seen Revere with his men on July 28 and 29 "busily employed in getting up the Cannon" after the Rebels had gained the heights, Holmes replied that he had.

"Did you see me active, as active to promote the service, as any other officer during the expedition?" asked Revere.

"Yes."

Thomas Wait Foster, the gunner aboard the *Warren*, who also had not appeared at the earlier hearings, testified about the repeated difficulties experienced by the marines in getting artillery supplies and equipment from Revere after the taking of Nautilus Island.[9] "Captain Furlong applied to Captain Saltonstall for Shot . . . Furlong said he had applied several times to Colonel Revere, but could not get Shot that were suitable, all the Shot he had received were too small." Foster testified that he was called on to deliver cartridges, sponges, and worms to the Rebel guns on Majabigwaduce from the *Warren's* own much-needed stock because Revere had not supplied them when requested.

Despite Foster's apparent condemnation of the artillery commander, however, he stated that he never encountered "any backwardness" in

Revere during the expedition. "[H]e ever appeared to me to be busy in endeavoring to find out the strength of [the] enemy."

With the additional testimony of its new witnesses together with the various statements compiled in the prior hearings, the committee then closed the proceedings. It would now reconsider the evidence as it related solely to Paul Revere and, as requested in the petition, render an opinion as to his conduct alone during the Penobscot Expedition.

Prior to the start of the initial committee hearings on September 22, the Massachusetts Council had forwarded an appeal to John Jay, president of the Continental Congress, informing him of the dire financial situation the state found itself in as a result of the failed expedition. The petition also boldly requested the authority to withhold six million dollars of Continental tax receipts to defer the attendant expenses of the mission.[10]

On November 16, Elbridge Gerry, James Lovell, and Judge Samuel Holton, all members of the Massachusetts delegation to the Second Continental Congress, drafted a letter to the state legislature warning its members of the lukewarm federal response to their petition for economic aid. The Penobscot Expedition, it had been argued during congressional debates, was exclusively a *state-run* venture and its failure, cautioned the delegates, will not, without opposition, be accepted as a Continental liability.[11]

The battle over economic responsibility for the defeat at Penobscot clearly would be an ongoing affair, but the question of *military* responsibility, the Massachusetts Council hoped, would finally be settled on the committee's rendered opinion on Paul Revere.

The distressing news from Congress would take several days to reach Boston, but as Gerry, Lovell, and Holton dispatched their letter from Philadelphia, Artemas Ward and his reconvened committee considered the evidence both for and against their obstinate artillery commander and formulated their decision.

The committee delivered the final report, also in question-and-answer format, to the Massachusetts Council on November 16; and several days later, John Hancock, speaker of the house, concurred with the opinion.

1. Was Lieutenant Colonel Paul Revere culpable for any of his conduct during his stay at Bagaduce, or while he was in, or upon the River Penobscot?

   Answer: Yes.

2. What part of Lieutenant Colonel Paul Revere's Conduct was culpable?

   Answer: In disputing the orders of Brigadier General Wadsworth respecting the Boat; & in saying the Brigadier had no right to command him or the boat.

3. Was Lieutenant Colonel Paul Revere's conduct justifiable in leaving the River Penobscot, and repairing to Boston, with his Men, without particular orders from his Superior Officer?

   Answer: No, not wholly justifiable.[12]

In the meteorological parlance of the day, the winter of 1779–80 would be spoken of by the people of Boston as the last "old-fashion winter."[13] The snows, blinding and deep, began in November, and by January the town had found itself entombed, its roads navigable only by snowshoe or child's sled. The temperature had dropped so bitterly low that the ice accumulated on fragile rooftops without a trace of thaw, and Boston Harbor itself froze solid almost to Nantasket. Not since 1717 had inclement weather driven everyday industry to such a thorough standstill.[14]

While the snow and cold effectively postponed the third session of the Massachusetts Constitutional Convention until late January, it could not prevent the people of Boston from deriding Paul Revere with a torrent of gossip. Word of the committee's adverse ruling had inflamed an already negative public sentiment, and feelings began to run high against the town's artillery commander.

Though the committee had distilled the multiple allegations against Revere into two simple findings of culpability—refusing use of the Castle barge to General Wadsworth and leaving the Penobscot without orders—Revere still remained outraged by the pall of doubt cast on his character. In the weeks following the decision, he braved the bitter temperatures of Boston and badgered his friends in the legislature and Board of War for the appointment of a court-martial to rehear and formally determine the charges against him. On January 4, 1780, however, a committee comprised of Samuel Adams, Timothy Danielson, and Noah Goodman—all members of the Constitutional Convention—voted unanimously to deny Revere's demands.[15]

There was, perhaps, a sense among Revere's contemporaries that he had gotten exactly what he deserved.[16] Unsatisfied because the committee had neither acquitted nor condemned him, he had refused to let the matter rest. He had insisted on a new inquiry, one specifically focused on him, believing that once a full and fair hearing was convened, he would, of course, be acquitted on every count. Now, with Revere having received the inquest that he wanted, though the committee had decided against him, it was said that he ought to "pocket the chagrin and humiliation"[17] and put the Penobscot Expedition behind him.

But Revere was not a man to put away his pride—especially in matters of character and reputation. He fully believed that he had been falsely accused, and it was not within him to let others have the final word regarding his personal or professional integrity.

On January 17, 1780, Revere once again took quill to paper and, in a flourish of obdurate frustration, reproved the Massachusetts Council for its impolitic refusal to grant him a court-martial. "I must once more beg your Honors indulgence on a matter that so [d]early affects me . . . ," began Revere.

> It is more than four months since I was arrested by your Honors, and Ordered to give up the command of the Castle . . . Twice I have petitioned your Honors and once the House of Representatives for a Court Martial but have not obtained one. I believe that neither the Annals of America, or Old England, can furnish an Instance (except in despotic Reigns) where an Officer was put under an arrest, and he petitioned for a Trial, (although the Arrest was taken off) that it was not granted.[18]

Manifestly recognizing that his place in history was at stake, Revere continued his impassioned plea:

> The complaint upon which my arrest was founded, [is] amongst your Honors' papers and there will remain an everlasting monument of my disgrace if I do not prove they are false. Is there any other legal way to prove them false, than by a Court Martial? Have not I a Right to demand one? . . . It is indifferent to me who are the members of the Court, provided they are not my personal Enemies, and are honest Men.[19]

And again Revere lamented the damage to his reputation as a result of the persistent rumors circulating about him. "It is reported through the State, that I have been broke and cashiered (I have heard of it more than once) and lay under every disgrace that the malice of my enemies can invent, and it will remain so till the Facts are published."[20]

"I would once more Pray your Honors that you grant me a [trial] by a Court Martial," begged Revere.

As part of his petition, Revere also requested that the Council deliver his back rations of food and pay, which had been withheld since the end of the Penobscot Expedition. "I have been maintaining a Family of Twelve ever since, out of the remains of what I have earned by twenty years hard labor . . . and am now brought to almost my last shilling," he wrote.[21] He signed the letter, "Your Suffering Humble Servant, Paul Revere."[22]

Four days later, the council issued an order granting Revere all of his back and future rations.[23] It completely ignored, however, his ardent plea for a court-martial.

Chapter 15 The Court-Martial of Paul Revere

AS REVERE CONTINUED his personal crusade for vindication, the American Revolution neared its fifth year. In Morristown, New Jersey, General Washington and his depleted army endured their second harsh winter at the strategic enclave. "The situation of the Army with respect to supplies, is beyond description, alarming," wrote Washington to Joseph Reed, governor of Pennsylvania. "We have never experienced a like extremity at any period of the war."[1]

While Revere still could not persuade the Massachusetts Council to convene a court-martial to hear his case, Benedict Arnold finally would receive his own. From December 19 through January 26, Arnold would be tried in Morristown for the misappropriation of government property and the illegal transaction of goods, and he would receive a reprimand from Washington after a mixed verdict from the appointed panel.[2] It was a punishment that would portend Arnold's infamous act of treason—his plot to turn the fort at West Point over to the British.

In Boston, the General Court still wrestled with the Continental Congress in an effort to shift the economic burdens of the Penobscot Expedition "to the Continent in general."[3] On February 9, Jeremiah Powell again dispatched to Philadelphia and argued, perhaps with a trace of duplicity, that the expedition had been undertaken from the start with the expectation that Congress would fund the mission.[4] Powell pointed out that the fisheries and timber grounds of the eastern shores were of vast importance to North America as a whole and that it was "just and reasonable" for the country to bear the expense of its protection. "We are persuaded," concluded Powell, "that no Exertions of yours will be wanting upon this occasion."[5]

Angered by the Council's refusal to grant him a court-martial, but undeterred and nearly obsessive, Paul Revere filed yet another petition with the General Court on March 9. He protested that for the last six months he had been "suffering all . . . [the] Indignity which his Enemies, who he conceives make it a personal affair, are pleased to impose upon him," and he once again begged the legislators "to take his Case under Consideration and Order a Court Martial to try his conduct."[6]

A week later, John Hancock ordered a legislative committee, fortuitously chaired by Revere's friend and former customer Joseph Greenleaf, to "report what is proper to be done" on Revere's renewed petition.[7] As a member of the North Caucus and Boston's Committee of Correspondence since 1772, Greenleaf had close dealings with Revere, and the two had developed a friendship. In early 1775, Greenleaf, while working with Isaiah Thomas on the start-up *Royal American Magazine*, had employed Revere to create political cartoons and engravings for the publication and their relationship expanded. Whether as a result of political influence, fair and deliberative adherence to law, or sheer and utter exasperation, on March 18, 1780, to the astonishment of many including, no doubt, Paul Revere himself, the Massachusetts Council voted to grant Revere his court-martial.[8] A combination of assiduous conviction and unrelenting perseverance finally had given him the opportunity to clear his name. To the people of Boston, however, Revere's court-martial would represent yet another sad chapter in the ruinous Penobscot debacle that the Castle Island artillery commander simply refused to let die.

Under the Massachusetts Militia Act, which governed and regulated the state-operated militia regiments during the Revolutionary War, a court-martial consisting of "a majority of the field officers of the same brigade" was appointed to try any "field officer" (which included Revere) accused of a misdemeanor or breach of duty in violation of the act.[9] Though the task of appointing the actual court-martial was, according to a strict reading of the law, reserved for the brigadier of the charged party, General Wadsworth, Revere's brigadier general, had been sent back to Maine in defense of the region; thus, this legal oversight apparently was ignored in deference to pragmatism. The court-martial, ordered by the Massachusetts Council, would be conducted in Wadsworth's absence.

In the coming weeks the council agreed on the details and particulars of the proceedings, and it designated the members of the tribunal. The council ordered the court-martial of Paul Revere to take place on April 18 at the County Courthouse on Queen Street in Boston, before an array of eleven militia officers, with William Tudor as judge advocate and Edward Proctor as president.[10]

A merchant and importer of West Indian goods, Proctor was widely recognized as a prominent citizen of Boston and an ardent Patriot. He was an officer in the local militia unit and, as a devoted servant to the cause of liberty, was known as "prompt, efficient, and thoroughly loyal."[11] Edward Proctor was also, perhaps, the worst choice that could have been made as president of Revere's court-martial.

As early as 1765, Proctor is known to have been a customer of Revere's goldsmith shop and, as sword bearer in the Grand Lodge of Ancient Masons, was a Masonic brother to Revere.[12] As the seeds of rebellion began germinating in the taverns and meetinghouses of Boston, the two men were closely affiliated in the North Caucus and as fellow Sons of Liberty. They worked on town committees together, and Proctor was known to have joined Revere as an active participant of the Boston Tea Party.[13] It is fairly evident that the two men were, at a minimum, close acquaintances and more likely intimate friends.

One may speculate that the council's perplexing choice of Edward Proctor to preside over the court-martial may have been designed to avoid even the slightest hint of bias against Revere in the event of an adverse ruling. Given that Revere evidently seized on the slightest hint of conspiracy against him, perhaps the council wished to preclude any possibility of further petitions and appeals. Whatever the reason, Proctor was having none of it.

On April 15, two days after his appointment, he wrote to the council and begged leave to decline the position. "[N]ot only on Account of the intimacy that has long subsisted between us," explained Proctor, "but as Colonel Revere is an Officer of the Train of Artillery, I cannot think myself a competent Judge (it being out of my line) . . . for these & many other Reasons that might be Offered—your Petitioner has no doubt your honor's will excuse him from the Above mentioned Service."[14]

On April 17, the day before Revere's court-martial was to assemble, the council summarily denied Proctor's petition for recusal. The original order appointing the tribunal directed Proctor to summon Paul Revere and such other witnesses as he may deem necessary and, at the conclusion of the proceedings, to deliver a copy of the decision to the council. Proctor, a man of intense loyalty, elected to completely ignore the order and refused to convene the inquest. As Revere would later muse, "[F]or reasons best known to himself, he never called them together."[15]

Once again frustrated and confounded by the political doings of those thought to be his friends, Revere found himself ignored and seemingly powerless to clear his name. Though he had envisaged the charges against him to be an "everlasting monument of . . . disgrace," it seemed that the people of Boston had lost interest. Talk of the Penobscot Expedition had begun to fade, and Revere's unrelenting ruminations and political prodding had become an unwelcome reminder of the entire sorry escapade. Forbes would write of the time, "[N]o one cared whether Paul Revere went up or down a river and in what or whose boat; whether on a certain night he slept on shore or on a transport."[16]

And now Revere faced another problem: the three-year interval during which the artillery regiment was raised was set to expire in early May. Though his personal military commission as an officer in the state militia would remain unaffected, the expiration of his regiment would effectively end his military career—and potentially render any court-martial proceeding moot. "I was left without a trial," he wrote.[17]

The Massachusetts Constitution, drafted by John Adams and debated by the various towns and villages throughout the winter and spring of 1780, was placed before the people on June 5 and, article by article, approved by a two-thirds majority. On June 15 the Constitutional Convention affirmed the ratifying vote and authorized the first election of a governor and new General Court in the state. "This great business," wrote Samuel Adams to his cousin John Adams on July 10, 1780, "was carried through with much good Humor among the people . . . Never was a good Constitution more wanted than at this Juncture."[18]

Meanwhile in Philadelphia, James Lovell, one of the Massachusetts delegates to the Continental Congress, informed the council that the question of financial responsibility for the Penobscot Expedition had been left "undecided." He lamented whether it was even proper for them to have so strenuously argued the point in view of "the then apparent Temper of Congress" against the measure.[19] The message was clear; for the time being, Massachusetts would have to deal with the economic consequences of the disaster on its own. Through its tax measures and with resort to whatever remained in its public treasury, Massachusetts would, for the time being, be left to its own devices to rebuild its navy, to satisfy the many claims for loss of vessels and property, and to respond to the stream of petitions for economic assistance from the inhabitants of the eastern country. On February 26, 1780, Abigail Adams wrote to her "dearest friend" John Adams, who was by then on a diplomatic mission to Paris, enclosing a list of taxes to be paid. "In April a much larger [tax] is to be collected to pay Penobscot score," she added.[20]

As obsessed as he was over his own reputation, Paul Revere was far from oblivious to the momentous events and tribulations that pervaded his town and state. As angered and frustrated as he remained over his inability to obtain what he perceived as justice, it was clear that he had no choice but to quietly suspend his personal battles while political events unfolded around him.

"I thought it best to go to my business again," Revere wrote to a cousin regarding the expiration of his engagement with the artillery regiment. "I am in middling circumstances and very well off for a tradesman."[21] With the financial burdens created by his lengthy military service, Revere returned his attentions to the goldsmith and engraving trades. He began dealing with imported goods; and his merchant accounts indicate, at the time, a willingness to accept payment for services with such merchandise as "indigo, silk handkerchiefs, plated spoons" and other exotic goods.[22] Though Revere no doubt thought himself shabbily treated by those in government, in 1780 the Massachusetts legislature entrusted the task of engraving a new state seal, upon ratification of the new constitution, to none other than Paul Revere. And as was the norm with Revere's prior requisitions for payment, the state also thought this one high and reduced it by a third.[23]

By January of 1781, however, with newly elected Governor John Hancock settling into his post, Revere's thoughts again turned to Penobscot. On the twenty-second he crafted yet another impassioned plea to the General Court explaining that on six separate occasions since 1779 he had filed petitions for a trial by court-martial, but none had ever taken place. In a tone of near-hopelessness, he requested that his case be taken under consideration and that a court-martial "or a number of Officers, three, five, seven, or any number the Honorable Court may see proper . . ." be appointed to inquire into his conduct during the Penobscot Expedition—". . . that the truth may appear and be published to the World."[24] Notwithstanding the expiration, in May of 1780, of the time for which the artillery regiment had been raised, Revere still pleaded for a forum—*any* forum—to hear his case. His engagement with the military may have expired, but as far as he was concerned, the cloud of controversy regarding his service remained. As a still-commissioned soldier, a court-martial was preferable, but any body of qualified officers to hear his case was apparently acceptable to Revere.

Though the Massachusetts Council had once before found ample evidence to rule against him, and despite a record of questionable conduct on the Penobscot Expedition supported by the testimony of multiple witnesses, Revere refused to accept even the possibility of his guilt. "I am not conscious of the least failure of duty," he would write.[25] With his military service apparently at an end and his business endeavors reemerging, Paul Revere placed his trust in the newly formed government and clung to the hope of evenhanded justice.

But again Revere's efforts met with frustration. His petition was all but ignored—referred to a committee and marked by the clerk "ordered to lie till next Sessions."[26] Clearly dissatisfied with this result, Revere began inquiring of the committee to which the matter had been sent, and he was informed by its chairman that a petition for court-martial should be submitted directly to the governor.[27]

Meanwhile, Major General Benjamin Lincoln, home from the disastrous southern campaigns of the Continental Army and reeling from inquiries into his own conduct regarding the fall of Charleston,[28] apparently sympathized with Revere's plight and offered to intercede on his behalf. "About that time the honorable Major General Lincoln offered me his service to mention the affair to the Governor," Revere wrote. "A few days after he sent me word, that he had made application to the Governor, and that he would appoint [a court-martial] upon my application."[29]

Cheered by the news and anxious to finally clear his name, Revere petitioned Hancock on March 1, 1781, and, for the eighth time since the Penobscot Expedition, requested the convening of a court-martial into his conduct. On the twentieth, Hancock sent word to Revere that he would get his wish. "I received his Excellency's promise that he would appoint one," Revere later wrote.[30]

As the weeks passed, Revere anxiously waited for his court-martial to be summoned, but antonishingly the promise again proved to be an empty one. "I heard no more of the matter," he would write.[31]

🔖 His campaign effectively on hold, Revere returned his attention to business and reacquainted himself, through a series of letters, with extended family in St. Foy (Quebec City) and on the Isle of Guernsey, off the coast of Brittany.

In October of 1781, Revere informed his second cousin, Mathias Rivoire, of his "situation in life" and of his previous military service. "Before this reaches you," wrote Revere, "you will have heard of the victory gained over the British Army by the Allied Armies [at Yorktown] commanded by the brave General Washington."[32] Though the actual surrender of General Cornwallis would not occur for several weeks, Revere expressed his hope that the campaign would result in peace in the colonies.

To his cousin on the Isle of Guernsey, John Rivoire, who with his strong imperialist leanings expressed grave doubts about the Franco-American alliance and disparaged the colonial uprising against Great Britain, Revere responded, revealing in passionate terms his characteristic and still adamant political zeal. "You do not use all the candor which

I am sure you are master of, else you have not looked into the merits of the quarrel," he lectured.

> [The British] covenanted with the first settlers of this country, that we should enjoy "all the Liberties of free natural born subjects of Great Britain." They were not contented to have all the benefit of our trade, in short to have all our earnings, but they wanted to make us hewers of wood, & drawers of water. Their Parliament have declared "that they have a right to tax us & Legislate for us, in all cases whatever"—now certainly if they have a right to take one shilling from us without our consent, they have a right to all we possess; for it is the birthright of an Englishman, not be taxed without the consent of himself, or Representative.[33]

Notwithstanding the continuing frustrations suffered by the workings of his own government in Boston, Revere's personal convictions regarding the cause of liberty and the tyranny of England remained unshakable. In stark contrast to Benedict Arnold, who had likewise suffered perceived indignities at the hands of Congress and the Continental Army and who consequently had plotted with the British to turn over control of the fort at West Point, Revere had remained true to the cause. For all of his frantic self-importance, his loyalty to country had not faltered.

In the first week of January 1782, as all hope of personal vindication seemed to fade, "a friend" assured Revere that if he once again applied to the governor, a court-martial would in fact be appointed. As directed, Revere promptly renewed his petition and on the sixth again requested Governor Hancock to convene the hearing.

Perhaps John Hancock had, by now, gained a clear understanding of the tenacious and resolute constitution of Paul Revere. Though he had been criticized, ridiculed, and ultimately ignored, he had refused, for right or for wrong, to retreat from a matter of principle and a question of character. Undeniably fixated on his perceived standing in the community and angrily driven to clear his reputation, Revere repeatedly had sought scrutiny into his own conduct, and though the results had not yet been to his liking, he demanded the opportunity for further inquiry. After nearly three years of relentless pursuit, Hancock could no longer deny Revere his court-martial.

On Tuesday, February 19, 1782, a general court-martial was convened in Boston "by virtue of the Orders of his Excellency John Hancock, Esq. Governor & Commander in chief of the Commonwealth of Massachusetts, for the Trial of Lieutenant Colonel Paul Revere of the Corp of Artillery late belonging to this State, touching his Behavior as an Officer when retreating from [Majabigwaduce]."[34]

Brigadier General Warham Parks, an aide to Benjamin Lincoln during the battle of Stillwater—but otherwise having no disqualifying connection to Paul Revere (as had Edward Proctor, the president of Revere's first appointed court-martial)—had been appointed by the governor as president of the court-martial and presided over a panel of twelve other legal and military minds. John Ashley Jr., Seth Cushing, Seth Washburn, Gideon Burt, Ebenezer Battle, Charles Cushing, Joseph Webb, Lieutenant Colonel John May, Major Captain Edward Farmer, Ebenezer Mattoon, Joseph Bradley Varnum, and Thompson J. Skinner all had extensive military experience in various Massachusetts Militia regiments and possessed at least some working knowledge of the artillery regiment and its functions.

The court previously had been provided with the detailed depositions from the 1779 committee of inquiry, and several witnesses had been summoned and now appeared at the county courthouse, amid the Atlantic winter chill, to testify of what they knew.

The judge advocate, Joshua Thomas, a Continental officer and soon to be president of the Plymouth County Bar,[35] was charged with the responsibility of advising the members of the court-martial and presenting the evidence against the defendant in accordance with applicable law. The November 16, 1779, committee report already had distilled the myriad charges and allegations against Revere to two remaining triable counts. The proceedings, therefore, would be narrow in scope and limited only to the issues in question.

General Parks called the hearing to order and administered an oath of duty and allegiance to the members of the court. Joshua Thomas then rose and firmly delivered the formal charges against Lieutenant Colonel Paul Revere.

"For his refusing to deliver a certain Boat to the Order of General Wadsworth . . . upon the Retreat up Penobscot River from [Majabigwaduce]."

"For his Leaving Penobscot River without Orders from his Commanding Officer."[36]

In light of the extensive witness statements already available to the court as a result of the earlier council inquiries, Thomas felt it unnecessary to produce any live witnesses at Revere's court-martial. The already established record would speak for itself.

In support of the first indictment, Thomas recited the damning allegations from General Wadsworth's original deposition regarding Revere's refusal to allow the use of the Castle barge in the rescue of the floundering schooner. "[T]hat upon the Retreat of the Army up Penobscot River," began Thomas, "a small schooner having on Board the greatest Part of the Provisions, was then in the Strength of the Tide, drifting down on the Enemy,—that it was in vain that a Number of Boats were ordered to tow her across the Stream, and with much Difficulty that a Boat was got off to take out her Crew,—that in endeavoring this, he was directly opposed by Lieutenant Colonel Revere, who said, that he (the General) had no Right to command either him or the Boat, and gave orders to the contrary."[37]

The members of the court listened intently to the allegations narrated by the judge advocate, and the tension in the courtroom no doubt escalated while the accused quietly contained his mounting unease.

"The General further deposes," continued Thomas, "that the Reason Lieutenant Colonel Revere assigned for refusing the Boat was, that he had all his private Baggage at Stake, & asked who would thank him for loosing that, in attempting to save the Schooner to the State?"[38]

Following the hearing Revere would make light of Wadsworth's charge, saying that whether it was true or false it presented little consequence to his honor.[39] The people at large, he premised, would place no

significance on the allegation since it had not affected the overall success or failure of the expedition. In reality, Revere could not help but to
have been embarrassed by the implication that he had placed his personal business and property ahead of the mission to which he had been
charged. The allegation itself was damning on its face and his enemies
would take notice. "[T]hat this Colonel did refuse General Wadsworth
a certain boat is clearly demonstrated," William Todd would later write.
"The truth of the affair is, that Lieut. Colonel Revere had his Baggage on
the boat . . . he exclaimed against the maneuver, and said his baggage was
more to him than all the vessels, and that if he left it the State would give
him no recompence."[40]

Regarding the second charge against Revere, Joshua Thomas relied
solely on the prior statements of Artillery Captain Perez Cushing and
asserted before the court "that upon the Retreat up Penobscot River,
Colonel Revere to whose Corps he belonged, left him on the Bank of the
River, promising to return in a few Minutes,—that he continued there
with about forty men he had collected, expecting the Return of Colonel
Revere . . . but saw Nothing of [him], until he got to Kenneheck River."[41]

Scanning Cushing's deposition, Thomas distilled the salient allegations and concluded his indictment of the accused. "[T]hat Colonel
Revere had an Opportunity of giving Orders to . . . [Cushing] and the
Men before he & they left Penobscot River, if he had inclined to, but did
not."[42]

With that, Judge Advocate Thomas rested his case.

Called to offer his defense, Paul Revere gathered his thoughts and
ambled toward the witness stand. Revere was now forty-eight years old,
and his straight brown hair showed signs of graying. His bulbous face
had grown worn from fatigue, but his eyes still burned with the passion
of absolute resolve. Revere turned toward the panel of judges, raised his
artisan-worn hand before Warham Parks, and swore to tell nothing but
the truth in the matter before the court.

Revere began his defense with an uncharacteristic admission. He confessed that, in fact, he *had* refused to deliver the Castle barge to General
Wadsworth on his order to do so. He stated, however, that his refusal had

been issued impulsively and without thought or the intention to violate orders. Upon "immediately recollecting that General Wadsworth was his Superior Officer," stated Revere, he insisted that the barge was delivered without further delay.[43] "[W]hether this could be called 'a sudden refusal' or one dictated by reflection," wrote William Todd, "I will not myself determine. I think it answers for itself."[44]

On the question of leaving Penobscot River without orders, Revere testified that during the retreat from Majabigwaduce the entire army was in a state of confusion and that he departed in the company of other officers on the same orders to leave the river as had been delivered to the whole.[45] "I might as well have been charged with leaving that river without orders from the Council or the General Court," later complained Revere. "When the whole army was routed and dispersed, when no place of rendezvous was appointed, the militia scattered and twenty four hours advanced on their way with the principal part of my men through the woods to Kennebeck River, the ships and transports on fire, and the officers and men setting off for their respective homes, I could not conceive myself bound to wait there till I received orders to change my situation."[46]

Revere offered no evidence as to his retreat from Majabigwaduce other than his own testimony on the issue, but he called three witnesses who all swore to his "good Conduct . . . in general, [and] that he was Judicious, calm, vigilant, and attentive to the Object of the Expedition."[47] Captain Amos Lincoln, Revere's son-in-law, joined fellow artillerymen Lieutenants Nicholas Phillips and Andrew McIntyer, who loyally testified on behalf of their commanding officer.

Having no further witnesses, the defense was then closed, and the court-martial of Lieutenant Colonel Paul Revere was adjourned.

Though the court, on mature deliberation, issued its findings in Revere's case fairly quickly (even the judgment in the month-long court-martial of Benedict Arnold was issued within four days of submitting the case),[48] "[i]ndisposition & some little matters of business" prevented Joshua Thomas from immediately providing a transcribed copy of the proceedings and judgment to the governor.[49] With humble apologies for the delay, Thomas finally delivered the findings of the court to John Hancock on February 28. The furnished order, which derived from a true copy of the minutes, described the formal charges against Revere as well as the evidence adduced during the hearing and then formulated its detailed conclusions.

> The Court find[s] the first Charge against Lieutenant Colonel Paul Revere to be supported (to wit) his refusing to deliver a certain Boat to the Order of General Wadsworth when upon the Retreat up Penobscot River from [Majabigwaduce]; but the Court taking into Consideration the Suddenness of the Refusal, and more especially, that the same boat was in fact employed by Lieutenant Colonel Revere to effect the Purpose ordered by the General, as appears by the General's Deposition, are of Opinion that Lieutenant Colonel Revere be acquitted of this Charge.

> On the Second Charge, the Court considering, that the whole Army was in great Confusion, and so scattered and dispersed, that no regular Orders were or could be given, are of the Opinion, that Lieutenant Colonel Revere be acquitted with equal Honor as the other Officers in the same expedition.[50]

Governor John Hancock pondered the findings for a moment and, perhaps, reflected on the service Paul Revere had rendered to his country and even the selfless warning he had provided to Hancock himself on the evening of April 18, 1775. Revere had been a dedicated asset to the American cause of liberty, and though his military service might be questioned, his allegiance to country never was. The disastrous Penobscot Expedition would tarnish the man for a time, but Revere was determined to never let it define him.

John Hancock dipped his quill into the vessel of ink and began writing on the bottom margin of Joshua Thomas's findings.

"I approve of the opinion of the Court Martial as stated in the foregoing Report—John Hancock."[51]

E*pilogue*

The court-martial had not quite provided the unqualified exoneration for which Revere had hoped. Though he had been acquitted on both charges, the ruling confirmed that in fact he had refused the barge to General Wadsworth and that he did leave the Penobscot without direct orders to do so. Moreover, an acquittal "with equal honor as the other Officers in the same expedition" seemed, in light of the circumstances, a rather empty victory. Nevertheless, Revere was resignedly satisfied with the court's judgment, and he accepted it as a complete and absolute vindication of his actions on the Penobscot Expedition. As far as he was concerned, the matter was now concluded.

Others, however, begged to differ.

On March 14, excerpts from the decision of the court-martial appeared in newspapers throughout the region, and it finally appeared that Revere had received the public recognition of innocence that he had sought. Several days later, however, an open letter appeared in the *Boston Gazette* that would shatter his short-lived gratification and, once again, thrust the ugly Penobscot debacle—and Paul Revere's role in it—back into the public eye.

Under the pseudonym of "Veritas," the letter writer resurrected every unwelcome allegation against Revere—from delaying the outset of the expedition, to sleeping on board the transports, to disobeying General Wadsworth's orders—and scourged the members of the court-martial for acquitting Revere of the charges. "[T]hat this is satisfactory to the people at large," wrote Veritas, "is a doubt with me."[1] And taking great exception to the court's finding of equivalence between Revere and the other officers, Veritas angrily protested, "For this Lieut. Co. *Paul Revere* to be ranked as acting with equal courage as other Officers on the expedition when several fell bravely advancing . . . when numbers on that expedition either for courage or conduct . . . stand without blot or censure—to have such a man ranked on the same footing, is what, in private opinion, the world may determine."[2]

Revere's response to the "Veritas" letter was swift and predictably bellicose. In a tedious and irate diatribe that splashed across two separate issues of the *Boston Gazette* for all to see, Revere snapped back with characteristic fury. Describing himself as "greatly abused" by the published letter, he immediately revealed the "infamous author of the infamous remarks," apparently "justly ashamed of his true name and character," to be none other than William Todd.[3] He then lambasted his attacker.

"From motives of revenge . . . ," claimed Revere, "this man has been aiming at my ruin, in a series of the most wicked and unmanly attacks upon my reputation . . . I'm sure the justice of my country would have . . . [shielded] my character from every dishonorable imputation, had not he, like an assassin stabbed it in the dark."[4]

With vitriolic intransigence, Revere tediously addressed each of the charges upon which he was tried and reiterated his defenses to every one. He restated verbatim excerpts of both sets of findings of the committee of inquiry, and he described in detail every procedural step—date by date—that had led him to acquittal. As to the allegation that he had left the Penobscot without orders, Revere sardonically scolded, "[P]erhaps Mr. Todd, under such circumstances, would have seized the opportunity of raising a monument on the . . . merit of maintaining an undisputed post on the banks of the Penobscot River."[5] And with regard to Thomas Carnes's original complaint of September 6, 1779, Revere levied his suspicion that Carnes had, in fact, been hired to lodge it.

On April 4, Carnes himself joined the fray. In a caustic letter to the publisher of the *Continental Journal* (that would also appear in the *Boston Gazette* four days later), he took angry exception to the claim that somehow he had been hired to issue his complaint. "That I was desired to do it is true," wrote Carnes, "had I not been, the duty I owe my country demanded it."[6] He again accused Revere of delaying the fleet at Nantasket, eating and lodging on the transports, and generally absenting himself during the expedition when needed. And he stated that, at some point after he filed his complaint, Revere had called at his home "to require satisfaction." Not above a violent encounter, Revere had been known in the past to resort to fisticuffs when he felt ill-treated.[7] "I am of the opinion," wrote Carnes, "fighting is not a science, that gentlemen, no more than myself is fond of."[8]

The war of words quickly escalated. Responding to Revere's acerbic rejoinder in the *Boston Gazette*, William Todd, in a letter that appeared in the same paper on April 8, revealed himself as "Veritas" and furthered his attack on Revere. "That I ever aspersed Lt. Col. Revere's character, I deny. If I said anything of him, it was the *truth*—if the *truth* aspersed his character, so let it be," wrote Todd.[9]

Revere refused to let the matter die, and he refused to let others have the last word on the subject of his character. Three days after Carnes's letter appeared in the Boston newspapers, the *Continental Journal* published a responsive barb authored by Revere. Noting that Carnes had echoed many of the same allegations previously asserted by Todd, he reiterated his claim of conspiracy. "I am confirmed in my opinion," he wrote, "that . . . [Carnes] was originally hired as a tool, to father a number of falsehoods which a man who had any reputation to lose would be afraid to utter."[10]

Then, in an attempt to close the entire indecorous affair with Carnes, Revere ended his missive with a parting shot. "I shall take no further notice of what has been or may be published by any person under the signature of T. J. Carnes, from the same motives that I do not stop to reason with every puppy that barks at me in the street."[11]

But Revere was not done with William Todd. "I am sorry to trouble you or the public again in taking the least notice of Mr. Todd's exhibitions . . . ," wrote Revere in a letter to the publisher of the *Boston Gazette* that appeared in the paper on April 15, "but, as I have been publicly abused, I think myself entitled to a candid hearing, and claim it as my right."[12]

Todd had accused Revere of absenting himself from the regiment during the expedition and of busying himself with menial and insignificant chores that should have been left to noncommissioned officers, such as fixing artillery fuses and culling cannon shot, "to avoid the perils of an engagement." Revere, once again, felt compelled to defend his honor against the charge, mockingly writing, "[P]erhaps so great a man as Mr. Todd might have thought it below his dignity to stoop to so degrading a piece of military duty as to give a pattern for a case of grape shott (which is all that I did) . . . I have known a greater General than I believe Mr. Todd will ever be, literally stoop to lay a dirty sod upon a breastwork, while a number of common soldiers were engaged in the same dirty employment; no one thought it his duty, perhaps if Mr. Todd had been present he would have disputed his right."[13]

Revere closed his letter—indeed his entire dialogue on the matter— with a final appeal to his community:

> I now call upon the impartial public to determine how a single article, advanced with so much confidence and plausibility, is supported by the smallest degree of evidence, if a man's reputation is to be blasted because an *envious, disappointed, malicious man* has the hardiness to publish a parcel of the most abominable falsehoods against him; and when called upon, has not the least colour of evidence to support them, it is hardly worth a man's while to endeavour to acquit himself in the public opinion. But I flatter myself the case is otherwise, and that the resentment and contempt of my country will fall on the man who, by such artifices, has attempted to deceive them, and not on the intended victim of his malice.[14]

In an incendiary exclamation point to the affair, Thomas Carnes published one further letter in the *Continental Journal* in response to what he called Revere's "scurrilous language" against him. "I should be very sorry," wrote Carnes, "to put my character on a footing with Paul Revere, who the world knows to be a coward."[15]

But the public would have the final word. In a letter from "A Customer" printed in the *Boston Gazette* on April 15, the following lines of verse appeared regarding Paul Revere:

> If his deeds would but shine, as he wishes to tell,
> It would please us to read, but we know the man well.[16]

As Paul Revere battled with his enemies in the columns of Boston's newspapers, trouble continued to brew in Maine. After the American defeat at Majabigwaduce, Tories and British Loyalists joined with British soldiers to plunder the villages on the shores of Penobscot Bay. Long-simmering political rancor in the region came to a boil, and the area was thrust into a state of perpetual crisis and hardship. In an effort to stabilize the situation, General Peleg Wadsworth, who had been exonerated with glowing accolades by the committee of inquiry in 1779, was returned to the region in an effort to restore order.

With the regional timber and fishing industries in British hands and the local inhabitants "entirely exposed to the fury of the Enemy,"[17] Massachusetts soon contemplated yet another attempt to remove the British from Majabigwaduce. When the idea found its way to Morristown, however, the response was less than enthusiastic. "I have attentively considered the application . . . on the Subject of an Expedition against the Enemy at Penobscot," wrote General Washington to the Massachusetts Council on April 17, 1780. "It appears to be of great Importance in several points of view that they be dislodged — but circumstanced as we are I do not see how the attempt can be made with any prospect of Success."[18]

Without the hope of another determined attack upon British positions on Majabigwaduce, General Wadsworth was left to command and secure the region with the limited tools of martial law and common sense. He set up his headquarters in Thomaston and immediately issued a proclamation in Lincoln County and throughout the coastal islands forbidding any assistance or aid to the enemy, upon the penalty of execution.[19] As the months unfolded, however, Wadsworth found himself unable to raise any troops to defend the area or to gain a foothold against the British, and by 1781 he requested a discharge from his duties and prepared to leave the area.

On the night of February 18, General McLean, recognizing the weakness of the Rebel force in Thomaston, dispatched a company of twenty-five men from Majabigwaduce to storm Wadsworth's headquarters. After a fierce battle in which he was wounded in the arm, Wadsworth was captured and ultimately imprisoned at Fort George. Though treated well by McLean, after several months in captivity Wadsworth received word that he was most likely to be sent to England to face trial and execution.[20] In the late night of June 18, Peleg Wadsworth cut a hole through the ceiling of his prison cell and daringly escaped from Majabigwaduce.

He made his way back to Massachusetts, where he reunited with his family and remained until the end of the war. Eventually settling in Maine, Wadsworth would enter into business and, in 1792, be elected as a member of Congress from the Cumberland District, where he served until 1807.[21]

Fort George, the problematic objective of the Penobscot Expedition, would remain in British hands throughout the Revolution. "When the war ended," wrote historian Charles Bracelen Flood, "a British officer waited impatiently for some American representative to appear and claim . . . [the fort]. Day after day he waited; no American bothered to come to this place for which forty ships and an army had once been lost. Finally the British officer burnt the barracks that had been built inside the earth walls of Fort George and sailed to Canada."[22] It would be the last British stronghold ceded by the king's forces after the war.

In 1778, Elizabeth Wadsworth, the general's wife, gave birth to the couple's third child, a girl whom they named Zilpah. In a family history of the Wadsworths in America published in 1883, the following is written of Zilpah Wadsworth: "In her character of rare excellence was combined all that exalts and ennobles the heart of a Christian lady. She also possessed intellectual qualities of a very high order. One fact alone would well cause her name to be spoken with reverence in every civilized land beneath the sun: *she was the mother of Henry Wadsworth Longfellow.*"[23]

Little is know of the fate of William Todd and Thomas Carnes following Revere's court-martial. Todd, a Leicester, Massachusetts, native, would resettle in Keene, New Hampshire, where he owned the Ralston Tavern and later became the town postmaster.[24] He would live in the town at least until 1803 and, interestingly, become active in local Freemasonry, rising to the title of master of the Rising Sun Lodge.[25]

Thomas Carnes would serve as a captain of the Massachusetts Marines until 1781. He appears to have experienced some problems in his personal life following his military service, as on June 14, 1783, the following advertisement appeared in the *Boston Evening Post*:

> The impartial Public will be pleased to take notice, That the certain Woman by the name of MIME CARNES, wife of THOMAS JENNER CARNES, and published by him in the paper of last Monday, as a runaway — is a poor, unfortunate, distressed female, who, being seduced by the false promises of the above-named Thomas J. Carnes, has been over persuaded to abandon her parents, her friends and her country, and become his wife, depending upon him only for her protection, support and happiness, but who, after having repeatedly suffered every species of cruelty and insult that villainly and infidelity to her bed could suggest, and inhumanity could inflict, has been obliged, in regard to her own personal safety, and to obtain the common necessaries of her existence, to seek for this shelter which he denied to her, from one of his own relations.[26]

The same notice would appear in the Boston newspapers *Continental Journal* and *Independent Ledger* on June 12 and June 16, 1783. He married again on March 22, 1798, to Elizabeth Fennecy of Boston, presumably forming a more compatible union. The *Register of Members of the Massachusetts Society of the Sons of the American Revolution* indicates that Carnes "died in Maine after 1802."[27]

Upon his return home from the Penobscot Expedition, General Solomon Lovell resumed his position as commander in chief of the Suffolk County Militia. In April of 1780 the people of Weymouth, Massachusetts, chose Lovell to join a committee to report on the new state constitution. He was instructed to vote for its adoption with several amendments. Lovell remained active in town and state politics, serving as a selectman from March of 1781 through 1787 and as a representative in the General Court from May 1781 until 1783. His involvement in the disastrous failure of the Penobscot Expedition did not seem to lower his standing among his countrymen. Gilbert Nash, Lovell's primary biographer, would write, "Esteemed and honored in his town, where most familiarly known, respected and trusted in the counsels of the State, which he for many years served faithfully and well, his name has been handed down through the generations, as that of one of whom the town may well be proud, one to whom the young may look with respect and veneration, whose example it were safe to follow, and upon whom all may look as a high-minded and worthy citizen."[28] Lovell died on September 9, 1801, at the age of sixty-nine.

On June 29, 1793, fourteen years after the Penobscot Expedition began, Congress finally would award Massachusetts $1,248,000 as the state's share for losses suffered during the war.[29] With the American victory over Great Britain and the ratification of the new federal constitution, thoughts turned away from the humiliating defeat at Penobscot, and soon the fiasco would be all but forgotten.

Paul Revere slowly would consign Penobscot and its gloomy aftermath to the unchangeable past. He rededicated himself to business and, in a show of camaraderie with the only other officer of the expedition to face a court-martial, Revere purchased shares in the privateer *Minerva*—commanded in 1781 by none other than Dudley Saltonstall. The venture proved successful, and Saltsonstall would, in fact, distinguish himself with the capture of the British vessel *Hannah* and her cargo worth eighty thousand pounds.[30]

As the war came to a close, Revere had intended to enter the world of trade, but with the bulk of his money lent to government, he returned to his goldsmith shop and, in partnership with his son Paul Jr., continued to serve the people of Boston with his artistic craft.

Finally advancing into the mercantile ranks, he opened a hardware shop in 1783 on Essex Street opposite the site of the old Liberty Tree, where he sold various domestic and imported goods as well as his own assortment of personally fashioned jewelry, teapots, buckles, medallions, and candlesticks.[31]

Revere was focused on business after the war, but his political passions clearly had not ebbed. During the fiery public debate on the ratification of the United States Constitution in early 1788, Revere was decidedly in favor. Samuel Adams, however, whose vote as a member of the Massachusetts delegation would be critical to the effort, was wavering. Amid the turmoil, a group of local artisans and mechanics led by Revere held a meeting at the Green Dragon, and several resolutions were unanimously passed in favor of ratification. The crowd of men then marched to Adams's home and presented him with their resolves. Forty-five years after the fact, in a speech delivered to a crowd in Pittsburgh, Daniel Webster would relay Revere's pivotal and dramatic exchange with Adams:[32]

> "Mr. Revere, how many mechanics were there in the Green Dragon when these Resolutions were passed?" asked Adams.
> "More, sir, than the Green Dragon could hold."
> "And where were the rest, Mr. Revere?"
> "In the streets, sir."
> "And how many were in the streets?"
> "More sir! than there are stars in the sky."

On February 6, 1788, the Massachusetts Convention voted narrowly to ratify the United States Constitution. Samuel Adams would vote in favor.

With the establishment of a firm and stable federal government and with his hardware shop struggling to remain profitable, Revere attempted, in the late 1780s and early 1790s, to secure a public position through the influence of his friend Congressman Fisher Ames. A post, perhaps in the National Mint Revere thought, would be appropriate given his experience as an engraver. Even Ames, however, had to be cautious about Revere's chances. "I am no stranger to your services and zeal on the side of liberty," wrote Ames in April of 1789, "and in my mind that sort of merit will greatly support the claims of the candidate who can plead it. The number of expectants however will be considerable, and may have merit and powerful patronage."[33] Though his efforts to acquire an appointment with the federal government would indeed fail, Revere would be chosen to serve locally as president of the board of health in Boston and even as county coroner.[34]

In the early 1790s, however, Revere's entrepreneurial efforts finally would blossom. He discontinued the hardware business and, together with his son, established a bell and cannon foundry on Foster Street, now Causeway Street, in the north part of Boston. Through the years, he would cast no fewer than sixty church bells, some of which are still hung in New England steeples, including in the Old South Meetinghouse on Washington Street in Boston, and he would even supply the copper bolts and fittings for the U.S.S. *Constitution—Old Ironsides*, as she would come to be known—upon her construction in 1798.[35]

Encouraged by his success in the copper trade, Revere would purchase an old iron mill in Canton, Massachusetts, and in 1801 convert the site into a thriving sheet-copper-rolling mill. He would be asked to supply the copper sheets for the dome of the Massachusetts State House in 1802; and a year later, when the U.S.S. *Constitution* required replating, Revere was entrusted to supply the sheets of copper for the task. His copper-rolling mill was an enterprise that would ultimately allow Paul Revere to retire in 1811, a wealthy man.[36]

Throughout his advancing years, Revere continued his active service in many civic and fraternal organizations. At the age of sixty he was elected grand master of the Massachusetts Grand Lodge, and he would become an organizing member of the Massachusetts Charitable Mechanic Association. Through the years he would involve himself in such associations as the Boston Library, the Boston Humane Society, and the Massachusetts Charitable Fire Society.[37]

In 1787, as his entrepreneurial and civic interests expanded, Paul Revere began referring to himself in business and in official documents as "Esquire."[38] No longer confined to the role of mere goldsmith, he had advanced at last to the coveted status of "gentleman."

Revere would assume many titles during his life: Patriot, Freemason, artisan, mechanic, dentist, entrepreneur; but the title he preferred—the one that he carried throughout his days—was Lieutenant Colonel Paul Revere.

Revere died on May 10, 1818, at the age of eighty-four. One obituary appearing in the *New-England Galaxy & Masonic Magazine* included the following tribute:

During his protracted life, his activity in business and benevolence, the vigour of his mind, and strength of his constitution were unabated. He was one of the earliest and most indefatigable Patriots and Soldiers of the Revolution, and has filled with fidelity, ability and usefulness, many important situations in the military and civil service of his country, and at the head of valued and beneficent Institutions. Seldom has the tomb closed upon a life so honourable and useful.[39]

Boston plainly had forgiven Paul Revere for his transgressions. This man of contrasts undeniably had earned the respect of his countrymen and found his place in the local history of Boston. But his lifelong achievements did not immediately propel him to enduring fame, and over time, the memory of Revere's creditable service to the ideal of freedom began to fade.

Through the gifted quill of Henry Wadsworth Longfellow, however, Paul Revere would ultimately find immortality. While strolling past the Old North Church and Copp's Hill Burying Ground in the North End of Boston on April 5, 1860, with his friend Senator George Sumner, Longfellow immediately was struck by the history of the area and the relevance of that history to the Union cause in antebellum America.[40] He would find in the streets of Old Boston a mythical rallying cry that would inspire a nation. *Paul Revere's Ride*, published in the *Atlantic Monthly* in January 1861, would awaken patriotic fervor on the eve of the Civil War[41] — in much the same way that Revere's ride itself had served as its own clarion call to arms eighty-six years earlier. Though Longfellow would sacrifice historical accuracy for patriotic imagery, he would, in the process, transform Revere into a national icon.

A hurry of hoofs in a village street,
A shape in the moonlight, a bulk in the dark,
And beneath, from the pebbles, in passing, a spark
Struck out by a steed flying fearless and fleet;
That was all! And yet, through the gloom and the light,
The fate of a nation was riding that night;
And the spark struck out by that steed, in his flight,
Kindled the land into flame with its heat.

Longfellow's fictionalized account, set in poetic verse, would replace much of what we know to be true about Paul Revere—and the distasteful memory of his role in the Penobscot Expedition would be, perhaps, the first victim of revised history.

"A cry of defiance, and not of fear," wrote Longfellow of Revere's courageous trek.

> A voice in the darkness, a knock at the door,
> And a word that shall echo forevermore!
> For, borne on the night-wind of the Past,
> Through all our history, to the last,
> In the hour of darkness and peril and need,
> The people will waken and listen to hear
> The hurrying hoof-beats of that steed,
> And the midnight message of Paul Revere.[42]

The enchanting image of a Patriot astride Deacon Larkin's elegant mare, spreading the midnight alarm through the farms and villages of Middlesex County, endures even today and reminds us of the everlasting legend, but not necessarily the man.

Acknowledgments

Norman Mailer once wrote, "Writing books is the closest men ever come to childbearing." While the point may be exaggerated, it is undeniable that nonfiction only comes to life through an enormous and necessarily collaborative effort. The idea for *The Court-Martial of Paul Revere* found its genesis in a 1977 law review article of the same name written by attorney Frederick Grant Jr. Mr. Grant graciously shared his recollections on the topic and pointed me in the right direction to begin my research. I am grateful for his advice and encouragement on the idea for the book. Likewise, I am indebted to various authors, such as George Buker, Bernard Cornwell, and Charles Bracelen Flood, who have enlightened me with their various histories of the Penobscot Expedition and Paul Revere's intriguing role in it.

A special thank-you to Patrick Leehey, research director of the Paul Revere House, for opening up his files to me and for agreeing to read the manuscript in advance. Our discussions and correspondence on the nuances of Paul Revere's personality and military career were helpful in drawing an accurate depiction of his postride travails.

For assistance in accessing the many valuable resources at the Massachusetts Archives, I am grateful to Jennifer Fauxsmith, reference supervisor and archivist; and for guidance and direction with the collections of the Massachusetts Historical Society, Betsy Boyle was, as always, extremely helpful.

I am grateful for the kindness and assistance of the people of Castine, Maine, most notably Dr. Lynn Parsons, who provided valuable suggestions for improving the manuscript, as well as Paige Lilly, curator of the Castine Historical Society, who allowed me access to the society's files and historical images. Castine is a lovely town with a storied history, and I found its people warm and welcoming.

I also wish to thank my good friend Laura Knott for reading the manuscript in advance and for providing insight and accuracy to the historical backdrop of the story.

For assistance with photo images at the Massachusetts Archives, I extend a note of appreciation to Carolyn McPherson, who produced exceptional archival reproductions under difficult conditions.

Finally, I thank my agent, John Rudolph, editor, Stephen Hull, and copy-editor, Elizabeth Forsaith, each of whom provided encouragement, enthusiasm, and much hard work in bringing *The Court-Martial of Paul Revere* to life.

Note on Sources

As a result of its dreadful outcome, the Penobscot Expedition became one of the most closely examined events of the Revolutionary War, and its detailed history survives today. The conduct of Paul Revere—and to a lesser extent, his court-martial—is found within this history and reveals itself through the personal accounts or "depositions" of nearly every officer involved in the expedition. These original statements are housed in the Massachusetts Archives, vol. 145, and have been restated in various volumes of the *Documentary History of the State of Maine: The Baxter Manuscripts*. I have relied heavily on these primary sources for the details of the story spoken in the words of its participants. Though every quote in this book is derived from actual documented statements, I have on occasion, for the sake of readability, corrected some of the more obvious spelling, punctuation, and grammatical errors, which often and understandably found their way into the word-for-word transcribed accounts.

Treatment of the Penobscot Expedition and Paul Revere's ensuing tribulations in the various Revere biographies has been sparse. Esther Forbes devoted about eight pages to the topic in her 1942 Pulitzer Prize–winning *Paul Revere and the World He Lived In* and benignly entitled the chapter "Confusion on the Penobscot." The late nineteenth-century and early twentieth-century books by Elbridge Henry Goss, *The Life of Colonel Paul Revere*, and Charles Ferris Gettemy, *The True Story of Paul Revere: His Midnight Ride, His Arrest and Court-Martial, His Useful Public Services*, provide much more in-depth accounts of Revere's role at Penobscot and rely heavily on the existing primary sources found in the Massachusetts Archives. Jayne Triber's excellent biography, *A True Republican: The Life of Paul Revere*, explores some of Revere's problematic relationships and how they culminated in 1779, but devotes only passing reference to his court-martial. Each of these works, however, proved invaluable in recreating Paul Revere and his place in history.

Several fine books have delved into the Penobscot Expedition and explored the role that Paul Revere played. Most notably, Charles Bracelen Flood's book, *Rise, and Fight Again*, offers a wonderfully detailed rendering of the story and affords a harsh but accurate glimpse into Revere's less-than-exemplary conduct on the expedition. Similarly, Bernard Cornwell's 2012 work, *The Fort*, provides a fictional though historically accurate account of Penobscot and Revere's troubled role. Perhaps the most comprehensive book on the subject is George Buker's *The Penobscot Expedition*, which remains the most authoritative secondary source on the subject.

Notes

PROLOGUE

1. William W. Wheildon, *Siege and Evacuation of Boston and Charlestown, with a Brief Account of Pre-Revolutionary Public Buildings* (Boston: Lee and Shepard, 1876), 41.

2. Ibid., 42.

3. Ibid., 49–50.

4. Edward Rowe Snow, *The Islands of Boston Harbor* (Carlisle, Mass.: Commonwealth Editions, 1935, 1971, 2003), 62–64.

5. Wheildon, *Siege and Evacuation*, 50.

6. Ibid., 51.

7. Jayne E. Triber, *A True Republican: The Life of Paul Revere* (Amherst: University of Massachusetts Press, 1998), 121.

8. Ibid., 112. For the appointment of Gridley and Burbeck to complete the works at Castle Island, see *The Acts and Resolves, Public and Private, of the Province of Massachusetts Bay*, vol. 20, 1777–1778, chap. 989 (Boston: Wright and Potter, 1918), 381–382.

9. Snow, *The Islands*, 64.

10. Charles Ferris Gettemy, *The True Story of Paul Revere: His Midnight Ride, His Arrest and Court-Martial, His Useful Public Services* (Boston: Little, Brown, 1905), 3.

11. Susan Wilson, *Boston Sites and Insights: An Essential Guide to Historic Landmarks In and Around Boston* (Boston: Beacon Press, 2004), 313.

12. Ibid.; Museum of Fine Arts Boston, *Paul Revere's Boston: 1735–1818* (Meriden, Conn.: Meriden Gravure, 1975), 141 n. 191.

13. Triber, *A True Republican*, 124. Several sources indicate that Revere was ordered to the repair and restoration work on Castle Island by George Washington himself. See, e.g., Esther Forbes, *Paul Revere and the World He Lived In* (Boston: Houghton Mifflin, 1942), 317; Elbridge Henry Goss, *The Life of Colonel Paul Revere*, 2 vols. (Boston: Joseph George Cupples, 1891), 1:278. These sources also indicate that Revere employed a newly designed gun carriage that he specifically invented for the damaged cannon; but in November of 1776, Richard Gridley signed a certificate stating that the true inventor of the device was an Amherst

doctor by the name of Preserved Clap. See New England Historic Genealogical Society, *New England Historical and Genealogical Register*, vol. 8 (London: Samuel G. Drake, 1859), 378.

14. Goss, *The Life*, 1:278.

15. Forbes, *Paul Revere*, 320.

16. Gettemy, *The True Story*, xiv.

17. Goss, *The Life*, 1:280, quoting letter from John Lamb to Paul Revere, April 5, 1777; Joel J. Miller, *The Revolutionary Paul Revere* (Nashville, Tenn.: Thomas Nelson, 2010), 218.

18. Forbes, *Paul Revere*, 319.

19. Gettemy, *The True Story*, xv.

20. Chester B. Kevitt, *General Solomon Lovell and the Penobscot Expedition* (Weymouth, Mass.: Weymouth Historical Commission, 1976), 1.

21. Roger F. Duncan, *Coastal Maine: A Maritime History* (New York: W. W. Norton, 1992), 214–215; Navy Historical Center, *The Penobscot Expedition Archaeological Project: Field Investigations 2000 and 2001, Final Report* (Washington Navy Yard, D.C.: Navy Historical Center, 2003), 20.

22. George E. Buker, *The Penobscot Expedition: Commodore Saltonstall and the Massachusetts Conspiracy of 1779* (Annapolis: Naval Institute Press, 2002), 1; Castine Historical Society, *The Penobscot Expedition 1779*.

23. William D. Williamson, *The History of the State of Maine: From Its First Discovery, A.D. 1602, to the Separation, A.D. 1820, Inclusive* (Hallowell, Maine: Galzier, Masters and Smith, 1839), 468–469.

24. Goss, *The Life*, 2:325–326.

25. Buker, *The Penobscot Expedition*, 45; Williamson, *The History of the State of Maine*, 474.

26. Williamson, *The History of the State of Maine*, 476.

27. "Complaint of T. J. Carnes," in Joseph Williamson, "The Conduct of Paul Revere in the Penobscot Expedition" in *Collections and Proceedings of the Maine Historical Society*, quarterly pt., no. 4 (Portland, Maine: Brown Thurston, October 1892), 381.

1. "THE PRIDE OF NEW ENGLAND"

1. Richard Frothingham, *History of the Siege of Boston, and of the Battles of Lexington, Concord, and Bunker Hill* (Boston: Little, Brown, 1903), 19, quoting the letter of a physician, November 8, 1774.

2. Ibid., 19.

3. Ibid., 21. I also rely on David Hackett Fischer, *Paul Revere's Ride* (New York:

Oxford University Press, 1994), 10, and Miller, *The Revolutionary*, 6, for descriptions of colonial Boston.

4. For a detailed examination of Revere's ancestry, see Patrick M. Leehey, "Reconstructing Paul Revere: An Overview of His Ancestry, Life, and Work," in *Paul Revere—Artisan, Businessman, and Patriot: The Man Behind the Myth*, ed. Nina Zannieri, Patrick M. Leehey, et al. (Boston: Paul Revere Memorial Association, 1988), 15–24.

5. Goss, *The Life*, 1:267, quoting the letter from John Rivoire to Paul Revere, January 12, 1775.

6. See Triber, *A True Republican*, 10–15, for a good discussion of class differences in colonial Boston.

7. Anne Duncan-Page, *The Religious Culture of the Huguenots, 1660–1750* (Farnham, U.K.: Ashgate, 2006), 102.

8. Miller, *The Revolutionary*, 21.

9. Ibid., 23–25; Triber, *A True Republican*, 20.

10. William B. Weedon, *Economic and Social History of New England 1620–1789* (Boston: Houghton, Mifflin, 1899), 86.

11. Miller, *The Revolutionary*, 28.

12. Goss, *The Life*, 1:19–20.

13. Triber, *A True Republican*, 25; Gettemy, *The True Story*, 4.

14. Gilbert Nash, *The Original Journal of General Solomon Lovell, Kept During the Penobscot Expedition, 1779: With a Sketch of His Life* (Weymouth, Mass.: Weymouth Historical Society, 1881), 31–34; see also Miller, *The Revolutionary*, 268 n. 16.

15. See Forbes, *Paul Revere*, 485–490, for a detailed genealogical record of the Revere family.

16. A detailed account of Revere's customers and business orders is found in *Waste Book and Memoranda*, Revere Family Papers, Massachusetts Historical Society, Boston, vol. 1 (1761–83), roll 5.

17. Ibid. Also see Deborah A. Federhen, "From Artisan to Entrepreneur: Paul Revere's Silver Shop Operation," in *Paul Revere—Artisan, Businessman, and Patriot: The Man Behind the Myth*, ed. Nina Zannieri, Patrick M. Leehey, et al. (Boston: Paul Revere Memorial Association, 1988), 91 n. 28.

18. *Boston Gazette and the Country Journal*, September 19, 1768, quoted in Gettemy, *The True Story*, 6.

19. *Boston Gazette and the Country Journal*, July 30, 1770, quoted in Gettemy, *The True Story*, 7–8.

20. See Edith J. Steblecki, "Fraternity, Philanthropy, and Revolution: Paul Re-

vere and Freemasonry," in *Paul Revere—Artisan, Businessman, and Patriot: The Man Behind the Myth*, ed. Nina Zannieri, Patrick M. Leehey, et al. (Boston: Paul Revere Memorial Association, 1988), 117–147, for a detailed examination of Revere's Masonic activities.

21. Triber, *A True Republican*, 30.

22. Steblecki, "Fraternity, Philanthropy, and Revolution," 117.

23. Triber, *A True Republican*, 35.

24. Goss, *The Life*, 2:667.

25. For a detailed examination of the Navigation Acts, see Charles McLean Andrews, *The American Nation: A History of Colonial Self-Government 1652–1689* (New York: Harper and Brothers Publishers, 1904) 3–22; see also Edmund S. Morgan, *The Birth of the Republic, 1763–89* (Chicago: University of Chicago Press, 1992), 9–11.

26. Morgan, *The Birth of the Republic*, 10.

27. Josiah Quincy, *Reports of Cases Argued and Adjudged in the Superior Court of Judicature of the Province of Massachusetts Bay Between 1761 and 1772* (Boston: Little, Brown, 1865), 395–540.

28. Triber, *A True Republican*, 32.

29. Albert Bushnell Hart and Edward Channing, eds., *James Otis's Speech on the Writs of Assistance, 1761*, American History Leaflets Colonial and Constitutional, no. 33 (New York: Parker P. Simmons, 1906), 13.

30. Ibid., 17.

31. Ibid., 13.

32. Triber, *A True Republican*, 39.

33. John Ferling, *A Leap in the Dark: The Struggle to Create the American Republic* (New York: Oxford University Press, 2003), 30–31.

34. Gordon S. Wood, *The American Revolution: A History* (New York: Modern Library, 2002), 27–28; George Elliott Howard, *The American Nation: A History*, vol. 8: *Preliminaries of the Revolution, 1763–1775* (New York: Harper and Brothers, 1906), 102–120.

35. Triber, *A True Republican*, 39.

36. Howard, *The American Nation*, 110.

37. Ibid., 112; Morgan, *The Birth of the Republic*, 18–19; Edmund S. Morgan, *The Challenge of the American Revolution* (New York: W. W. Norton, 1976), 15.

38. William Tudor, *The Life of James Otis of Massachusetts* (Boston: Wells and Lilly, 1823), 122.

39. John K. Alexander, *Samuel Adams: America's Revolutionary Politician* (Lanham, Md.: Rowman and Littlefield, 2002), 20; Howard, *The American Nation*, 110.

2. "MESSENGER OF THE REVOLUTION"

1. Miller, *The Revolutionary*, 71.

2. Wood, *The American Revolution*, 27.

3. Howard, *The American Nation*, 136.

4. Bernard Bailyn, *The Ideological Origins of the American Revolution* (Cambridge: Belknap Press of Harvard University, 1967), 101.

5. Triber, *A True Republican*, 41.

6. Howard, *The American Nation*, 140.

7. Justin Winsor, ed., *The Memorial History of Boston* (Boston: Ticknor, 1881), 18 n. 2.

8. Ibid., 144.

9. Wood, *The American Revolution*, 28.

10. D. W. Meinig, *The Shaping of America: A Geographical Perspective on 500 Years of History*, vol. 1 (New Haven: Yale University Press, 1986), 306; Winsor, *The Memorial History of Boston*, 155.

11. Triber, *A True Republican*, 41.

12. Howard, *The American Nation*, 150; see also Merrill Jensen, *The Founding of a Nation: A History of the American Revolution, 1763–1776* (New York: Oxford University Press, 1968; Indianapolis: Hackett, 2004), 130.

13. Frank Moore, *Songs and Ballads of the American Revolution* (New York: D. Appleton, 1855), 20.

14. Howard, *The American Nation*, 151.

15. Miller, *The Revolutionary*, 78.

16. Thomas Hutchinson, *The History of the Province of Massachusetts Bay from 1749 to 1774* (London: John Murray, 1828), 124.

17. Miller, *The Revolutionary*, 74.

18. Triber, *A True Republican*, 47–48.

19. Gettemy, *The True Story*, 10; Goss, *The Life*, 31–33.

20. Triber, *A True Republican*, 49.

21. Ibid., 50.

22. Forbes, *Paul Revere*, 116.

23. Gettemy, *The True Story*, 12.

24. Howard, *The American Nation*, 172–173.

25. Frothingham, *History of the Siege of Boston*, 29.

26. Benj. F. Stevens, "Some of the Old Inns and Taverns of Boston," *The Bostonian* 2 (April–September 1895): 24.

27. Sometimes referred to as the "North End Caucus."

28. Morgan, *Birth of the Republic*, 34.

29. Wood, *The American Revolution*, 32.

30. Ibid.

31. Ferling, *A Leap in the Dark*, 67.

32. Howard, *The American Nation*, 187.

33. Winsor, *The Memorial History*, 23; see also Ferling, *A Leap in the Dark*, 67–68.

34. Howard, *The American Nation*, 189.

35. Ibid., 190.

36. Ibid.

37. Edward D. Collins, *Committees of Correspondence of the American Revolution* (Washington, D.C.: American Historical Association, 1901; Government Printing Office, 1902), 245.

38. Triber, *A True Republican*, 64.

39. Ibid. Museum of Fine Arts, *Paul Revere's Boston*, 118. The Museum of Fine Arts in Boston acquired the Liberty Bowl in 1949. At the time, it was referred to as America's "'third most cherished historical treasure' after the Declaration of Independence and the Constitution." Ibid.

40. Forbes, *Paul Revere*, 134–135.

41. Ellen Chase, *The Beginnings of the American Revolution, Based on Contemporary Letters Diaries and other Documents*, vol. 1 (New York: Baker and Taylor, 1910), 99.

42. Harry Alonzo Cushing, ed., *The Writings of Samuel Adams*, vol. 2, 1770–1773 (New York: G. P. Putnam's Sons, 1906), 242.

43. Howard, *The American Nation*, 195.

44. Winsor, *The Memorial History*, 23.

45. Howard, *The American Nation*, 196.

46. Ibid., 197.

47. Bailyn, *The Ideological Origins*, 114.

48. Gettemy, *The True Story*, 30–31.

49. Howard, *The American Nation*, 202.

50. Miller, *The Revolutionary*, 103.

51. Triber, *A True Republican*, 70–71.

52. Winsor, *The Memorial History*, 30, quoting Rev. S. Cooper to Governor Thomas Pownall, January 1, 1770.

53. Triber, *A True Republican*, 74, quoting *Boston Gazette*, February 26, 1770.

54. Ibid., 220 n. 4.

55. *A Short Narrative of the Horrid Massacre in Boston* (Boston: Town of Boston, 1770; John Doggett Jr., 1849), 6.

56. C. James Taylor, ed., *Founding Families: Digital Editions of the Papers of the Winthrops and the Adamses* (Boston: Massachusetts Historical Society, 2007). http://www.masshist.org/ff/.

57. Winsor, *The Memorial History*, 31.

58. Ibid.

59. Ibid., 32.

60. Ibid., 40–41.

61. Triber, *A True Republican*, 78.

62. Winsor, *The Memorial History*, 36.

63. Goss, *The Life*, 1:73–74.

64. Ibid., 71.

65. Gettemy, *The True Story*, 22.

66. Paul Leicester, "Some Pelham-Copley Letters," *Atlantic Monthly* 71, no. 46 (April 1893), 500; Gettemy, *The True Story*, 23–24.

67. Patrick Leehey, research director of the Paul Revere House, states in a private e-mail to the author of January 13, 2014, "It has been suggested that Pelham and Revere planned to collaborate and something went wrong."

68. Winsor, *The Memorial History*, 41.

69. Triber, *A True Republican*, 85, quoting *Boston Gazette*, March 11, 1771.

70. *Boston Gazette*, March 11, 1771.

71. Triber, *A True Republican*, 85.

72. *Boston Gazette*, March 11, 1771.

73. Wood, *The American Revolution*, 36.

74. Winsor, *The Memorial History*, 42, quoting Adams's resolution of November 2, 1772, before the town meeting.

75. Forbes, *Paul Revere*, 185.

76. Winsor, *The Memorial History*, 44.

77. Miller, *The Revolutionary*, 162; Goss, *The Life*, app. C, 641.

78. Winsor, *The Memorial History*, 45.

79. Martha J. Lamb, ed., *Magazine of American History with Notes and Queries* 15, no. 1 (January 1886), 6.

80. Goss, *The Life*, 1:120.

81. Ibid.

82. Richard Frothingham, *The Life and Times of Joseph Warren* (Boston: Little, Brown, 1865), 275.

83. Ibid., 268–269.

84. Ibid., 269; Winsor, *The Memorial History*, 45.

85. Winsor, *The Memorial History*, 49.

86. Frothingham, *The Life and Times*, 278.

87. Samuel B. Griffith, *The War for American Independence: From 1760 to the Surrender at Yorktown in 1781* (Champaign: University of Illinois Press, 2002), 86.

88. Frothingham, *The Life and Times*, 279.

89. Ibid., 280–281.

90. Forbes, *Paul Revere*, 197.

91. Ibid., 201.

92. Goss, *The Life*, 1:131.

93. Boston Committee of Correspondence to the New York Sons of Liberty, December 17, 1773; Goss, *The Life*, 1:131.

94. Lamb, *Magazine of American History*, 3.

95. Winsor, *The Memorial History*, 52 n. 2.

96. Ferling, *A Leap in the Dark*, 107.

97. Winsor, *The Memorial History*, 53, quoting Lord George Germain's comments during debate.

98. Ibid., 52–53.

99. Gettemy, *The True Story*, 55.

100. Ibid., 56.

101. Fischer, *Paul Revere's Ride*, 31.

102. Ibid., 36–41.

103. Winsor, *The Memorial History*, 56.

104. Lamb, *Magazine of American History*, 4.

105. Goss, *The Life*, 1:159–162.

106. Lamb, *Magazine of American History*, 4, quoting Paul Revere to John Lamb, September 4, 1774.

107. Revere to Belknap.

108. Winsor, *The Memorial History*, 66.

3. "LISTEN, MY CHILDREN . . ."

1. Triber, *A True Republican*, 102, quoting extract of a letter from Lord Dartmouth to General Gage, London, April 15, 1775, American Archives, 4.2.336.

2. William D. D. Gordon, *The History of the Rise, Progress, and Establishment of the Independence of the United States of America* (New York: Printed by Samuel Campbell for John Woods, 1801), 309.

3. Jonas Clarke, *Opening of the War of the Revolution 19th of April 1775: A Brief Narrative of the Principal Transactions of that Day* (Lexington, Mass.: Lexington Historical Society, 1901), 1–2; Gettemy, *The True Story*, 104, quoting Jonas Clarke, *A Sermon, Preached at Lexington, April 19, 1776. To Commemorate the Murder, Bloodshed, and Commencement of Hostilities, Between Great Britain and America, in That Town, by a Brigade of Troops of George III, under Command of Lieutenant-Colonel Smith, on the Nineteenth of April, 17, 1775. To Which Is Added a Brief Narrative of the Principal Transactions of That Day* (Boston: Powars and Willis, 1776).

4. Forbes, *Paul Revere*, 247.

5. Museum of Fine Arts, *Paul Revere's Boston*, 130.

6. See Nathaniel Philbrick, *Bunker Hill: A City, a Siege, a Revolution* (New York: Viking, 2013), 66–69.

7. Forbes, *Paul Revere*, 248.

8. Paul Revere to Jeremy Belknap, circa 1798, *Collections of the Massachusetts Historical Society*, 1st ser., vol. 5 (1798). Revere prepared three separate accounts of his activities of April 18 and 19, 1775, all of which are currently housed at the Massachusetts Historical Society in Boston. The first two accounts were composed of a draft and "fair copy" of a deposition probably given at the request of the Massachusetts Provincial Congress. The congress had collected a series of sworn statements in an effort to prove that the English troops were first to fire at Lexington on April 19, 1775, and Revere's deposition was one such statement (though he does not offer a clear opinion on which side fired first). The third and most detailed account of Revere's activities is contained in a letter dated January 1, 1798, written to Jeremy Belknap, the corresponding secretary of the Massachusetts Historical Society. The letter contains some interesting notations in the hand of Revere, including a written request at the end of the document that he be named simply "A Son of Liberty of the year 1775," apparently wishing to remain anonymous. Belknap seems to have ignored Revere's request. See also Fischer, *Paul Revere's Ride*, 328–329.

9. Fischer, *Paul Revere's Ride*, 93.

10. Ibid., 85.

11. Extract from Lord Dartmouth to General Gage, London, April 15, 1775, *American Archives*, 4.2.336.

12. Forbes, *Paul Revere*, 253.

13. Fischer, *Paul Revere's Ride*, 95, quoting from Jeremy Belknap, *Journal of My Tour to the Camp and the Observations I Made There* (Boston: Massachusetts Historical Society, 1798), 77–86.

14. On the controversy surrounding the identity of Warren's informant, see Fischer, *Paul Revere's Ride*, 387 n.14; also see Miller, *The Revolutionary*, 283 n. 12. Nathaniel Philbrick points out that Margaret Gage did not leave Boston until later that summer and that her husband soon joined her. Philbrick, *Bunker Hill*, 117.

15. Revere to Belknap.

16. Forbes, *Paul Revere*, 254.

17. Fischer, *Paul Revere's Ride*, 388–389 n. 29, makes the case that Pulling assisted Newman in his trek to the top of the church steeple and with the lighting of the lanterns. Most other historians conclude that it was Newman alone with Pulling and, perhaps, Revere's neighbor Thomas Barnard keeping watch.

Fischer points to the physical difficulty of one person carrying both lanterns up the full flight of stairs, lighting them with flint sticks at the top, and displaying them from the window.

18. Forbes, *Paul Revere*, 55.

19. Goss, *The Life*, 1:190.

20. Ibid. A Revere descendent insists, "The story is authentic . . ." Patrick Leehey, research director of the Paul Revere House, suggests in an e-mail to the author of December 27, 2013, that Revere may have concocted the stories of the family dog and the girlfriend's undergarments to amuse his grandchildren.

21. Revere to Belknap.

22. Ibid.

23. Fischer, *Paul Revere's Ride*, 389 n. 38; Ferling, *A Leap in the Dark*, 129.

24. Forbes, *Paul Revere*, 257.

25. Revere to Belknap.

26. Ibid.

27. Ibid. *Paul Revere's Deposition, Fair Copy, Circa 1775*, Massachusetts Historical Society.

28. See Abner Cheney Goodell Jr., *The Trial and Execution for Petit Treason of Mark and Phillis, Slaves of Capt. John Codman* (Cambridge, Mass.: John Wilson and Son, 1883).

29. Revere to Belknap.

30. *Paul Revere's Deposition, Fair Copy.*

31. Revere to Belknap.

32. Clark, *A Brief Narrative*, 1–2.

33. Affidavit of William Munroe, March 7, 1825, from Elias Phinney, *History of the Battle at Lexington, on the Morning of the 19th April, 1775* (Boston: Phelps and Farnham, 1825), 33.

34. Ibid.

35. Phinney, *History of the Battle*, 17, emphasis added by Forbes, *Paul Revere*, 261.

36. The actual number of British troops was somewhere between 600 and 900 and was comprised not of a full brigade but of light infantry and grenadiers. See Fischer, *Paul Revere's Ride*, 313.

37. Clark, *A Brief Narrative*, 3.

38. Forbes, *Paul Revere*, 261.

39. Affidavit of William Munroe.

40. Ellen Chase, *The Beginnings of the American Revolution, Based on Contemporary Letters, Diaries, and Other Documents*, vol. 2 (New York: Baker and Taylor, 1910), 347.

41. Revere to Belknap.

42. Ibid.

43. *Paul Revere's Deposition, Draft, Circa 1775.*

44. Ibid.

45. Henry W. Holland, *William Dawes and His Ride with Paul Revere* (Boston: John Wilson and Son, 1878), 37.

46. Fischer, *Paul Revere's Ride*, 131–132.

47. Frothingham, *History of the Siege of Boston*, 60.

48. All dialogue between Revere and his captors is derived from *Paul Revere's Deposition, Fair Copy, Circa 1775; Paul Revere's Deposition, Draft, Circa 1775*; and Revere to Belknap.

49. Frothingham, *History of the Siege of Boston*, 44, quoting the letter of a British officer.

50. See Fischer, *Paul Revere's Ride*, 138–148.

51. Phinney, *History of the Battle*, 18.

52. Clark, *A Brief Narrative*, 4.

53. Elizabeth Clark to Lucy Ware Allen, April 19, 1841, Lexington Historical Society, *Proceedings* 4 (1905–1910), quoted in Fischer, *Paul Revere's Ride*, 176.

54. Forbes, *Paul Revere*, 265.

55. *Paul Revere's Deposition, Fair Copy, Circa 1775.*

56. Frothingham, *History of the Siege of Boston*, 61.

57. Revere to Belknap.

58. Forbes, *Paul Revere*, 266.

59. Frothingham, *History of the Siege of Boston*, 61.

60. *Paul Revere's Deposition, Fair Copy, Circa 1775.*

61. Clark, *A Brief Narrative*, 6.

62. *Paul Revere's Deposition, Fair Copy, Circa 1775.*

63. Letter from Boston to a Gentleman in New York, April 19, 1775, in *American Archives*, 4.2.359.

64. Forbes, *Paul Revere*, 268.

4. SEEDS OF DISCONTENT

1. Forbes, *Paul Revere*, 274.

2. Revere to Belknap.

3. Goss, *The Life*, 1:263, quoting Paul Revere to Rachel Revere and Paul Revere Jr., May 2, 1775.

4. Gettemy, *The True Story*, 121.

5. Benson John Lossing, ed., *Harpers Encyclopedia of United States History* (Harper and Brothers Publishers, 1902), 464. Patrick Leehey, research director

of the Paul Revere House, points out in an e-mail to the author of January 13, 2014, that while Revere is often credited with printing this "pasteboard currency" it is questionable whether he actually did so.

6. Forbes, *Paul Revere*, 289.

7. Goss, *The Life*, 1:280, quoting John Lamb to Paul Revere, April 5, 1777; Miller, *The Revolutionary*, 218.

8. Harry Alonzo Cushing, ed., *The Writings of Samuel Adams*, vol. 3, 1773–1777 (New York: G. P. Putnam's Sons, 1907), 394; Miller, *The Revolutionary*, 218.

9. Forbes, *Paul Revere*, 319.

10. On the process of selection of Continental officers and Revere's bitter disappointment at being overlooked see Triber, *A True Republican*, 112–122. In *The Diary of John Rowe: A Boston Merchant, 1764–1779, a Paper Read by Edward L. Pierce before the Massachusetts Historical Society on March 14, 1895* (Cambridge, Mass.: John Wilson and Son, 1895), Pierce makes the following personal observation: "The private dinners at which Rowe was host or guest bring before us the principal citizens of Boston at that time. One misses altogether, in the repeated list of names, Paul Revere, not then ranking with people of social consideration . . ." (p. 31).

11. Ibid.

12. Triber, *A True Republican*, 114.

13. See *King v. Parker, et al*, 9 Cushing 71 (1851).

14. Robert Freke Gould, *A Library of Freemasonry* (New York: John C. Yorston Publishing, 1906), 322. Triber, *A True Republican*, 90.

15. Ibid.

16. Goss, *The Life*, 1:268, quoting John Rivoire to Paul Revere, January 12, 1775.

17. Goss, *The Life*, 1:280, quoting John Lamb to Paul Revere, April 5, 1777.

18. Gettemy, *The True Story*, 152.

19. William Russell and James Kimball, *Orderly Book of the Regiment of Artillery Raised for the Defence of the Town of Boston in 1776*, Essex Institute Historical Collections, vol. 13 (Salem, Mass.: Salem Press, 1876), 243.

20. Ibid., 123.

21. Ibid., 240.

22. Forbes, *Paul Revere*, 334.

23. Russell and Kimball, *Orderly Book*, 13:245; Goss, *The Life*, 288.

24. Russell and Kimball, *Orderly Book*, 13:246.

25. Ibid., 248.

26. Goss, *The Life*, 1:291; Forbes, *Paul Revere*, 337.

27. Russell and Kimball, *Orderly Book*, 14:60.

28. Forbes, *Paul Revere*, 341.

29. General Heath to Paul Revere, March 1, 1778, in Massachusetts Archives, vol. 174, 410.

30. Paul Revere to Rachel Walker Revere, August 1778, in *Proceedings of the Massachusetts Historical Society, 1873–1875* (Cambridge, Mass.: John Wilson and Son, 1875), 251.

31. Russell and Kimball, *Orderly Book*, 14:204.

32. Paul Revere to Rachel Walker Revere, August 1778.

33. Russell and Kimball, *Orderly Book*, 14:198–199.

34. Lt. Col. Paul Revere to Massachusetts Council, March 27, 1779, in Massachusetts Archives, vol. 175, 211.

35. Forbes, *Paul Revere*, 347.

36. Triber, *A True Republican*, 133–134.

37. "Defence of Col. Paul Revere," in James Phinney Baxter, *Documentary History of the State of Maine, The Baxter Manuscripts*, vol. 17 (Portland, Maine: Lefavor-Tower, 1913), 216.

5. NEW IRELAND

1. George Augustus Wheeler, "William Hutchings' Narrative of the Siege, and Other Reminiscences," in *History of Castine, Penobscot, and Brooksville, Maine* (Bangor, Maine: Burr and Robinson, 1875), 327.

2. Ibid., 322.

3. Samuel Francis Batchelder, *The Life and Surprising Adventures of John Nutting Cambridge Loyalist and His Strange Connection with the Penobscot Expedition of 1779* (Cambridge, Mass.: Cambridge Historical Society, 1912), 75.

4. James S. Leamon, *Revolution Downeast: The War for American Independence in Maine* (Amherst: University of Massachusetts Press, 1993), 104–105.

5. Henry I. Shaw Jr., "Penobscot Assault—1779," *Military Affairs* 17, no. 2 (Society for Military History, Summer 1953): 83.

6. Batchelder, *The Life and Surprising Adventures*, 74.

7. Ibid. Brig.-Gen. Francis McLean to Sir Henry Clinton, March 6, 1779, in *Report on American Manuscripts in the Royal Institution of Great Britain*, vol. 1 (London: Mackie, 1904), 393.

8. Batchelder, *The Life and Surprising Adventures*, 75.

9. Lord George Germain to Gen. Sir Henry Clinton, September 2, 1778, in *Report on American Manuscripts*, 284.

10. Gen. Sir Henry Clinton to Brig.-General Francis McLean, February 11, 1779, in *Report on American Manuscripts*, 1:381.

11. Ibid.

12. John Calef, "The Journal of the Siege of Penobscot," *Magazine of History*

with Notes and Queries, extra issue no. 11 (New York: William Abbatt, 1910): 12; Charles Bracelen Flood, *Rise, and Fight Again: Perilous Times Along the Road to Independence* (New York: Dodd, Mead, 1976), 157.

13. Calef, "The Journal of the Siege," 12; Flood, *Rise, and Fight Again*, 157.

14. Calef, "The Journal of the Siege," 12; Flood, *Rise, and Fight Again*, 157.

15. Calef, "The Journal of the Siege," 12.

16. Flood, *Rise, and Fight Again*, 157.

17. Henry Mowat, "A Relation of the Services in which Captain Henry Mowat of the Royal Navy Was Engaged in America, from 1759 to the End of the American War in 1783," *Magazine of History with Notes and Queries*, extra issue no. 11 (New York: William Abbatt, 1910): 337.

18. George E. Buker, *The Penobscot Expedition: Commodore Saltonstall and the Massachusetts Conspiracy of 1779* (Annapolis: Naval Institute Press, 2002), 1; Castine Historical Society, *The Penobscot Expedition 1779*.

19. Flood, *Rise, and Fight Again*, 158.

20. For descriptions of Majabigwaduce, see Flood, *Rise, and Fight Again*, 158–159; Mowat, *A Relation*, 337; and Buker, *The Penobscot Expedition*, 9.

21. Mowat, *A Relation*, 337.

22. Batchelder, *The Life and Surprising Adventures*, 75.

23. Mowat, *A Relation*, 337; Brig.-General Francis McLean to Gen. Sir Henry Clinton, June 26, 1779, in *Report on American Manuscripts*, 1:458.

24. Batchelder, *The Life and Surprising Adventures*, 79.

25. Mowat, *A Relation*, 337.

26. Flood, *Rise, and Fight Again*, 158; Percy Groves, *History of the 91st Princess Louise's Argyllshire Highlanders* (Edinburgh and London: W. and A. K. Johnston, 1894), 3; Brig.-General Francis McLean to Gen. Sir Henry Clinton, May 28, 1779, in *Report on American Manuscripts*, 1:440.

27. Brig.-General Francis McLean to Gen. Sir Henry Clinton, March 6, 1779, in *Report on American Manuscripts*, 1:393.

28. Brig.-Gen. Francis McLean to Sir Henry Clinton, June 26, 1779, in *Report on American Manuscripts*, 1:460.

29. Samuel Adams Drake, *Nooks and Corners of the New England Coast* (New York: Harper and Brothers, 1875), 68.

30. *Collections and Proceedings of the Maine Historical Society*, 2nd ser., vol. 1 (Portland: Maine Historical Society, 1890), 73.

31. Ibid., for a description of Mowat's exploits in Falmouth, Maine; Flood, *Rise, and Fight Again*, 156; Kevitt, *General Solomon Lovell*, 173; Buker, *The Penobscot Expedition*, 6. On February 24, 1898, Dr. Charles E. Banks read a notification of the 1798 death of Henry Mowat before the Maine Historical Society. Banks

noted that the words "universally lamented" appeared on Mowat's gravestone. Banks then added, "I assume the members will agree with me that the words 'except by the people of Falmouth, Maine' were inadvertently omitted, for I believe it will be generally agreed that they had no special reason to grieve over the news of his death . . . I presume that it will be a satisfaction to some to be assured that this gentleman is safely underground, with a heavy stone on top of him." *Collections and Proceedings of the Maine Historical Society*, 2d ser., vol. 9, (Portland: Maine Historical Society, 1898), 308–309.

32. Brig.-Gen. Francis McLean to Captain Andrew Barkley, June 25, 1779, in *Report on American Manuscripts*, 1:456.

33. Mowat, *A Relation*, 360.

34. Brig.-Gen. Francis McLean to Sir Henry Clinton, June 26, 1779, in *Report on American Manuscripts*, 1:458.

35. Mowat, *A Relation*, 362–363.

36. Buker, *The Penobscot Expedition*, 7.

37. Brig.-Gen. Francis McLean to Sir Henry Clinton, June 26, 1779, in *Report on American Manuscripts*, 1:460.

38. Captain H. Mowat to General Sir Henry Clinton, June 27, 1779, in *Report on American Manuscripts*, 1:462.

39. Brig.-Gen. Francis McLean to Sir Henry Clinton, June 26, 1779, in *Report on American Manuscripts*, 1:458.

40. Ibid.

41. "Proclamation of June 15, 1779," *Magazine of History with Notes and Queries*, extra issue no. 11 (New York: William Abbatt, 1910): 322–323.

42. Ibid., 324.

43. Flood, *Rise, and Fight Again*, 161.

44. "Proclamation of June 15, 1779," *Magazine of History*, 324.

45. In the Letter from David Perham, Giving Colonel Brewer's Account of the Expedition against Penobscot, in 1779 (Wheeler, *History of Castine*, 328–329), Brewer recalled some years after the fact that the landing had "struck the inhabitants with terror—especially the women and children."

46. Ibid., 329.

47. Wheeler, *History of Castine*, 40.

48. Buker, *The Penobscot Expedition*, 9.

49. Leamon, *Revolution Downeast*, 106–107.

50. Williamson, *The History of the State of Maine*, 375.

51. John Murray to the Massachusetts Council, June 18, 1779, in James Phinney Baxter, *Documentary History of the State of Maine: The Baxter Manuscripts*, vol. 16 (Portland, Maine: Lefavor-Tower, 1910), 290.

52. Ibid., 292 (emphasis added).

53. *William Hutchings' Narrative*, 323.

6. CAPTIVATE, KILL, OR DESTROY

1. Flood, *Rise, and Fight Again*, 167.

2. Paul Revere to Rachel Walker Revere, August 1778, in *Proceedings of the Massachusetts Historical Society, 1873–1875* (Cambridge, Mass.: John Wilson and Son, 1875), 252.

3. Letter of Chas. Cushing, Brigr, June 19, 1779, in Baxter, *Documentary History*, 16:295–296.

4. Committee Opinion, June 24, 1779, in Baxter, *Documentary History*, 16:305.

5. Ibid.

6. Council Letter, June 25, 1779, in Baxter, *Documentary History*, 16:308.

7. James Thacher, *A Military Journal during the American Revolutionary War from 1775 to 1783* (Boston: Cottons and Barnard, 1827), 166. See also Buker, *The Penobscot Expedition*, 23–24.

8. Buker, *The Penobscot Expedition*, 24.

9. Gardner Weld Allen, "State Navies and Privateers in the Revolution," *Proceedings of the Massachusetts Historical Society*, vol. 46 (Cambridge, Mass.: John Wilson and Son, Oct. 1912–June 1913), 184.

10. Letter from the Council Chamber, June 30, 1779, in Baxter, *Documentary History*, 16:316; Buker, *The Penobscot Expedition*, 29.

11. Letter from the Council Chamber, June 30, 1779, in Baxter, *Documentary History*, 16:317–318.

12. Letter from Navy Board Eastern Department, June 30, 1779, in Baxter, *Documentary History*, 16:316.

13. John Tracey to the Massachusetts Council and House of Representatives, June 23, 1779, in Baxter, *Documentary History*, 16:308–309.

14. Order of Council, June 30, 1779, in Baxter, *Documentary History*, 16:316–317.

15. Thomas Cushing to the Massachusetts Council, in Baxter, *Documentary History*, 16:376.

16. Order of Council, July 2, 1779, in Baxter, *Documentary History*, 16:319–320.

17. Charles Oscar Paullin, *The Navy of the American Revolution* (Chicago: University of Chicago, 1906), 349–350.

18. Ibid., 349.

19. Nash, *The Original Journal*, 57.

20. Ibid., 52.

21. "Journal of the Committee Who Built the Ships *Providence* and *Warren*

for the United States in 1776," *Magazine of History with Notes and Queries* 8, no. 5 (New York: William Abbatt, 1908): 249.

22. Buker, *The Penobscot Expedition*, 23.

23. Resolution of the Massachusetts Council, July 3, 1779, in Baxter, *Documentary History*, 16:323.

24. *Warrant of the Massachusetts Council*, in Kevitt, *General Solomon Lovell*, 68.

25. Buker, *The Penobscot Expedition*, 25.

26. Statement of Ajdt. Genl. Hill Sworn, September 29, 1779, in Baxter, *Documentary History*, 17:263. See also Buker, *The Penobscot Expedition*, 25.

27. Paul Revere to William Heath, October 24, 1779, in *Collections of the Massachusetts Historical Society*, 7th ser., vol. 4 (1894), 324.

28. The visual of Captain Saltonstall sauntering the deck of the *Warren* angry about privateers is derived from Bernard Cornwell, *The Fort: A Novel of the Revolutionary War* (New York: Harper, 2010), 20–22. Though a fictional account, Cornwell makes the accurate point that privateering was adverse to the captain's current interests as a Continental Naval officer.

29. William James Morgan, *Captains to the Northward: The New England Captains in the Continental Navy* (Barre, Mass.: Barre Gazette, 1959), 25; Flood, *Rise, and Fight Again*, 163.

30. Louis Arthur Norton, *Captains Contentious: The Dysfunctional Sons of the Brine* (Columbia: University of South Carolina Press, 2009), 73.

31. Flood, *Rise, and Fight Again*, 163.

32. Massachusetts Council to Dudley Saltonstall, July 1779, in Kevitt, *General Solomon Lovell*, 67.

33. Orders to Brigadier General Lovell from the Council Chamber, July 2, 1779, in Baxter, *Documentary History*, vol. 16, 321.

34. For biographical information, see Kevitt, *General Solomon Lovell*, 151–165; and Nash, *The Original Journal*, 24–51.

35. Flood, *Rise, and Fight Again*, 163; Kevitt, *General Solomon Lovell*, 153.

36. Account of Thomas Philbrook, in Benjamin Cowell, *Spirit of '76 in Rhode Island: Or Sketches of the Efforts of the Government and People in the War of the Revolution* (Boston: A. J. Wright, 1850), 317.

37. Orders to Brigadier General Lovell from the Council Chamber, July 2, 1779, in Baxter, *Documentary History*, vol. 16, 321; Orders to Dudley Saltonstall Esq. from Navy Board Eastern Department, July 13, 1779, in Baxter, *Documentary History*, vol. 16, 355.

38. William Frost, Esq. to War Office, July 7, 1779, in Baxter, *Documentary History*, vol. 16, 330.

39. Defence of Col. Paul Revere, in Baxter, *Documentary History*, vol. 17, 216.

40. Ibid.

41. Ibid., 216–217.

42. Seth Loring to William Heath, July 7, 1779, in *Collections of the Massachusetts Historical Society*, 7th ser., vol. 4 (1894).

7. THE PENOBSCOT EXPEDITION

1. Brig.-General Francis McLean to Sir Henry Clinton, June 26, 1779, in *Report on American Manuscripts*, 1:460.

2. Letter of James McCobb, Esq., June 30, 1779, in Baxter, *Documentary History*, 16:317.

3. William Vernon and J. Warren to Jeremiah Powell, July 7, 1779, in Baxter, *Documentary History*, 16:329.

4. Navy Board to Marine Committee of the Continental Congress, July 14, 1779, in United States Navy Board Eastern District, *Letter Book*, quoted in Flood, *Rise, and Fight Again*, 165; Buker, *The Penobscot Expedition*, 24.

5. Baxter, *Documentary History*, 16:365.

6. Williamson, *The History of the State of Maine*, 470.

7. Orders to Lieut. Col. Paul Revere from the Council Chamber, July 8, 1779, in Baxter, *Documentary History*, 16:391; Orders to Brigadeer Lovell from the Council Chamber, July 12, 1779, in Baxter, *Documentary History*, 16:353–354.

8. For descriptions of Fort George, see Batchelder, *The Life and Surprising Adventures*, 79, and Williamson, *The History of the State of Maine*, 469.

9. Nash, *The Original Journal*, 55.

10. Ibid., 96.

11. Statement of Ajdt. Genl. Hill Sworn, September 29, 1779, in Baxter, *Documentary History*, 17:263.

12. Paul Revere to William Heath, October 24, 1779, in *Collections of the Massachusetts Historical Society*, 7th ser., vol. 4 (1894), 324.

13. Account of Thomas Philbrook, in Cowell, *Spirit of '76*, 316.

14. Paul Revere to William Heath, October 24, 1779, 320.

15. For biographical information about Peleg Wadsworth, see Williamson, *The History of the State of Maine*, 471; Flood, *Rise, and Fight Again*, 167–168; William Richard Cutter, *New England Families Genealogical and Memorial*, vol. 2 (New York: Lewis Historical Publishing, 1913), 735.

16. Wheeler, "William Hutchings' Narrative," 324.

17. Council Chamber to Brig. General Lovell, July 23, 1779; in Baxter, *Documentary History*, 16:393.

18. Calef, "The Journal of the Siege," 17.

19. Deposition of Col. Paul Revere, in Baxter, *Documentary History*, 17:201; Goss, *The Life*, 2:364.

20. Flood, *Rise, and Fight Again*, 173.

21. Letter from David Perham, Giving Colonel Brewer's Account of the Expedition against Penobscot, in 1779, in Wheeler, *History of Castine*, 329.

22. Testimony of Capt. Philip Brown, in Baxter, *Documentary History*, 17:287.

23. Orders of General Lovell, July 24, 1779, in Baxter, *Documentary History*, 17:394.

24. Testimony of Capt. Philip Brown, in Baxter, *Documentary History*, 17:288.

25. Calef, "The Journal of the Siege," 18.

26. Paul Revere to William Heath, October 24, 1779, 320.

27. Letter from David Perham, Giving Colonel Brewer's Account of the Expedition against Penobscot, in 1779, in Wheeler, *History of Castine*, 330–331.

28. Ibid.

29. Flood, *Rise, and Fight Again*, 176.

30. Nash, *The Original Journal*, 98.

31. Statement of Gilbert W. Speakman, in Baxter, *Documentary History*, 17:321; Flood, *Rise, and Fight Again*, 177.

32. Testimony of Thomas Wait Foster, Baxter, *Documentary History*, 17:433.

33. Ibid.

34. Petition, July 27, 1779, in Baxter, *Documentary History*, 16:400.

35. Minutes of Council of War Held on the *Warren*, July 27, 1779, in Baxter, *Documentary History*, 16:401.

36. Peleg Wadsworth to William D. Williamson, January 1, 1828, in *Collections and Proceedings of the Maine Historical Society*, 2nd ser., vol. 10 (Portland: Maine Historical Society, 1899), 70.

37. Paul Revere to William Heath, October 24, 1779, 321.

38. Peleg Wadsworth to William D. Williamson, January 1, 1828, in *Collections and Proceedings of the Maine Historical Society*, 2d ser., vol. 10, (Portland: Maine Historical Society, 1899), 73.

39. Nathan Goold, "Colonel Jonathan Mitchell's Cumberland County Regiment, Majabigwaduce Expedition, 1779," read before the Maine Historical Society, October 27, 1898, in *Collections and Proceedings of the Maine Historical Society*, 2d ser., vol. 10 (Portland: Maine Historical Society 1899), 145 n. 1; Flood, *Rise, and Fight Again*, 182.

40. Goold, "Colonel Jonathan Mitchell's Cumberland County Regiment," 62.

41. Deposition of Col. Paul Revere, Baxter, in *Documentary History*, 17:202.

42. James Carrick Moore, *The Life of Lieutenant-General Sir John Moore, K.B.*, vol. 1 (London: John Murray, 1833), 22.

43. Deposition of Col. Paul Revere, Baxter, in *Documentary History*, 17:203.

44. Letter from David Perham, Giving Colonel Brewer's Account of the Expedition against Penobscot, in 1779, in Wheeler, *History of Castine*, 332.

45. Wheeler, "William Hutchings' Narrative," 323.

46. Account of Thomas Philbrook, in Cowell, *Spirit of '76*, 319.

47. Nash, *The Original Journal*, 99.

48. For example, Peleg Wadsworth set the number at one hundred; Peleg Wadsworth to William D. Williamson, January 1, 1828, in *Collections and Proceedings of the Maine Historical Society*, 2nd ser., vol. 10 (Portland: Maine Historical Society, 1899), 73. Thomas Philbrook states that forty were killed and twenty wounded in Cowell, *Spirit of '76*, 318; while Paul Revere states that "we lost about 35 killed and wounded." Gardner W. Allen, *A Naval History of the American Revolution* (Boston: Houghton, Mifflin, 1913), 426. General Lovell set the loss at fourteen killed and twenty wounded; Nash, *The Original Journal*, 99.

49. Paul Revere to William Heath, October 24, 1779, 321.

50. Allen, *A Naval History*, 423.

8. "WHAT'S BECOME OF COLONEL REVERE?"

1. Testimony of Thomas Wait Foster, in Baxter, *Documentary History*, 16:433; Flood, *Rise, and Fight Again*, 190.

2. Testimony of Thomas Wait Foster, in Baxter, *Documentary History*, 16:433.

3. Buker, *The Penobscot Expedition*, 47.

4. Calef, "The Journal of the Siege," 20.

5. George Augustus Wheeler, "Calef's Journal of the Siege," in *History of Castine, Penobscot, and Brookville, Maine: Including the Ancient Settlement of Pentagöet* (Bangor, Maine: Burr and Robinson, 1875), 295.

6. "Journal Found on Board the *Hunter*, Continental Ship, of Eighteen Guns," in *The Historical Magazine, and Notes and Queries Concerning the Antiquities, History and Biography of America*, vol. 8 (New York: John G. Shea, February 1864), 52.

7. S. Lovell B G to Commodore Saltonstall, August 6, 1779, in Baxter, *Documentary History*, 16:429.

8. Testimony of Capt. Carnes, in Baxter, *Documentary History*, 17:282.

9. Henry Whittemore, *The Heroes of the American Revolution and Their Descendants* (Brooklyn, N.Y.: Heroes of the Revolution, 1897; supp. to sect. 1, 1898), 31.

10. Testimony of Capt. Carnes, in Baxter, *Documentary History*, 17:282; Flood, *Rise, and Fight Again*, 186.

11. Mr. Thomas Jenner Carnes's Declaration, *Boston Gazette and the Country Journal*, April 8, 1782.

12. Testimony of Capt. Carnes, in Baxter, *Documentary History*, 17:282.

13. Daily Orders of July 28, 1779, in Baxter, *Documentary History*, 16:402.

14. William Todd to Messieurs Edes, *Boston Gazette and the Country Journal*, April 8, 1782.

15. Testimony of Capt. Carnes, in Baxter, *Documentary History*, 17:282.

16. Statement of Major Todd, in Baxter, *Documentary History*, 17:301.

17. Statement of Gilbert W. Speakman, in Baxter, *Documentary History*, 17:322.

18. S. Lovell Br. Gen. to Hon. J. Powell, July 28, 1779, in Baxter, *Documentary History*, 16:403.

19. Proclamation of Solomon Lovell, Esq., in Baxter, *Documentary History*, 16:404–407.

20. Statement of Capt. Williams, in Baxter, *Documentary History*, 17:226.

21. Minutes of Council of War, July 29, 1779, in Baxter, *Documentary History*, 16:409.

22. Daily Orders of July 30, 1779, in Baxter, *Documentary History*, 16:410–411.

23. Ibid., 411.

24. Statement of Gilbert W. Speakman, in Baxter, *Documentary History*, 17:323–324.

25. Ibid., 322.

26. Wheeler, "William Hutchings' Narrative," 323

27. Letter of General McLean to Lord George Germain, August 26, 1779, in John E. Cayford, *The Penobscot Expedition Being an Account of the Largest American Naval Engagement of the Revolutionary War* (Orrington, Maine: C and H Publishing, 1976), 74.

28. Calef, "The Journal of the Siege," 22.

29. Ibid; Nash, *The Original Journal*, 67; Letter of General McLean to Lord George Germain, August 26, 1779, in Cayford, *The Penobscot Expedition*, 74.

30. Testimony of Capt. Carnes, in Baxter, *Documentary History*, 17:283.

31. Ibid.

32. Moore, *The Life of Lieutenant-General Sir John Moore*, 1:25.

33. Flood, *Rise, and Fight Again*, 173.

34. Testimony of Capt. Philip Brown, in Baxter, *Documentary History*, 17:288.

35. Flood, *Rise, and Fight Again*, 193–194.

36. Sergeant Lawrence's Journal, in Wheeler, *History of Castine*, 316.

37. Paul Revere to William Heath, 322.

38. Flood, *Rise, and Fight Again*, 197.

39. S. Lovell, Br. Gen. to Hon. Jeremiah Powell, President of the Council, August 1, 1779, in Baxter, *Documentary History*, 16:417.

40. *The Washington Historical Quarterly* 2 (Seattle: Washington University State Historical Society, October 1907 to July 1908), 105.

41. Gen. Washington to the President of Council, August 3, 1779, in Baxter, *Documentary History*, 16:424.

42. Nash, *The Original Journal*, 101.

43. Statement of Gilbert W. Speakman, in Baxter, *Documentary History*, 17:321–322.

44. Defence of Col. Paul Revere, in Baxter, *Documentary History*, 17:222.

45. Questions Asked by the Committee to General Wadsworth, in Baxter, *Documentary History*, 17:279.

46. William Todd to Messieurs Edes, *Boston Gazette and the Country Journal*, April 8, 1782.

47. General Lovell to Commodore Saltonstall, in Baxter, *Documentary History*, 16:427.

48. Statement of Capt. Williams, in Baxter, *Documentary History*, 17:227.

49. Ibid., 230.

50. Proceedings of a Council of War, August 6, 1779, in Baxter, *Documentary History*, 16:431.

51. Ibid.

52. Paul Revere to William Heath, October 24, 1779, 322. For the content of the council of war see Proceedings of a Council of War Held on Board the Brig *Hazard* off Magabagaduce, August 7, 1779, in Baxter, *Documentary History*, 16:432–434.

53. Shaw, *Penobscot Assault*, 93, quoting Sergeant Lawrence's Journal.

54. Calef, "The Journal of the Siege," 22.

55. Account of Thomas Philbrook, in Cowell, *Spirit of '76*, 319.

56. Council Chamber to General Gates, August 8, 1779, in Baxter, *Documentary History*, 16:436.

57. Flood, *Rise, and Fight Again*, 204.

58. Account of Thomas Philbrook, in Cowell, *Spirit of '76*, 319.

59. Nash, *The Original Journal*, 70.

60. Buker, *The Penobscot Expedition*, 68.

61. At a Council of War held on board the *Warren* off Magabagaduce, August 10, 1779, in Baxter, *Documentary History*, 16:445–446.

62. Samuel Adams to Hon. Jeremiah Powell, Pres., August 10, 1779, in Baxter, *Documentary History*, 16:446.

63. Jeremiah Powell to Brig. Gen. Solo Lovell, August 11, 1779, in Baxter, *Documentary History*, 16:448.

64. Nash, *The Original Journal*, 103.

65. Deposition of Col. Paul Revere, in Baxter, *Documentary History*, 17:205.

66. Nash, *The Original Journal*, 104.

67. Proceedings of a Council of War held at Head Quarters Magabagaduce, August 11, 1779, in Baxter, *Documentary History*, 16:453.

68. Navy Board Eastern Department to Commodore Saltonstall, August 12, 1779, in Baxter, *Documentary History*, 16:455.

69. Henry Jackson to Hon. Jere. Powell, August 11, 1779, in Baxter, *Documentary History*, 16:449; see also Thacher, *A Military Journal*, 167.

70. Thacher, *A Military Journal*, 168.

9. "THIS TERRIBLE DAY"

1. "Journal Found on Board the Hunter, Continental Ship, of Eighteen Guns," *Historical Magazine, and Notes and Queries Concerning the Antiquities, History and Biography of America*, vol. 8 (New York: John G. Shea, February 1864), 54.

2. Paul Revere to William Heath, October 24, 1779, 323.

3. "A True Relation of the Facts Concerning the Penobscot Expedition," in Baxter, *Documentary History*, 17:259.

4. Daily Orders, Head Quarters Majabigwaduce, August 12, 1779, in Baxter, *Documentary History*, 16:453.

5 Capt. Hallet's Statement, in Baxter, *Documentary History*, 17:234.

6. Calef, "The Journal of the Siege," 19

7. Saltonstall to Lovell, in Baxter, *Documentary History*, 16:461.

8. General Lovell to the Council, August 13, 1779, in Kevitt, *General Solomon Lovell*, 108.

9. Nash, *The Original Journal*, 105.

10. John Campbell, *Lives of the British Admirals: Containing an Accurate Naval History from the Earliest Periods*, vol. 5 (London: C. J. Barrington, Strand, and J. Harris, 1817), 497.

11. Sir George Collier to General Sir Henry Clinton, August 24, 1779, in *Report on American Manuscripts in the Royal Institution of Great Britain*, vol. 2 (Dublin: John Falconer, 1906), 18.

12. Flood, *Rise, and Fight Again*, 196.

13. Sir George Collier to General Sir Henry Clinton, August 19, 1779, in *Report on American Manuscripts*, vol. 2, 12.

14. Brig. Gen. Francis McLean to Sir Henry Clinton, August 23, 1779, in *Report on American Manuscripts*, vol. 2, 16.

15. Minutes of a Council of War, August 14, 1779, in Baxter, *Documentary History*, 16:470; Captain Hallet's Statement, in Baxter, *Documentary History*, 17:234.

16. Statement of John Cathcart, in Baxter, *Documentary History*, 17:245.

17. Deposition of Titus Salter, in Baxter, *Documentary History*, 17:214.

18. General Lovell to the Council, September 3, 1779, in Baxter, *Documentary History*, 17:77.

19. Statement of Gilbert W. Speakman, in Baxter, *Documentary History*, 17:322.

20. Ibid.

21. Sir George Collier to General Sir Henry Clinton, August 19, 1779, in *Report on American Manuscripts*, 2:12.

22. Statement of Major Todd, in Baxter, *Documentary History*, 17:297.

23. Ibid.

24. Ibid.; see also Flood, *Rise, and Fight Again*, 221.

25. Sir George Collier to General Sir Henry Clinton, August 19, 1779, in *Report on American Manuscripts*, 2:12.

26. Ibid.

27. Ibid., 13.

28. Testimony of Lieut. George Little, in Baxter, *Documentary History*, 17:238.

29. Deposition of Titus Salter, in Baxter, *Documentary History*, 17:214.

30. Flood, *Rise, and Fight Again*, 223.

31. Testimony of Joshua Davis, in Baxter, *Documentary History*, 17:314.

32. General Lovell to the Council, September 3, 1779, in Baxter, *Documentary History*, 17:77.

33. Deposition of Col. Paul Revere, in Baxter, *Documentary History*, 17:206.

34. Peleg Wadsworth Brig. General to the President of the Council, August 19, 1779, in Baxter, *Documentary History*, 17:29.

35. For a description of Wadsworth's movements, see Statement of General Wadsworth, in Baxter, *Documentary History*, 17:274–275; Flood, *Rise, and Fight Again*, 225–227; Testimony of Waterman Thomas, in Baxter, *Documentary History*, 17:308.

36. Peleg Wadsworth to William D. Williamson, in *Collections and Proceedings*, 10:71.

37. Statement of General Wadsworth, in Baxter, *Documentary History*, 17:276.

38. Ibid., 275.

39. See Ibid., 275–276, for Wadsworth's account of the exchange between him and Revere.

40. Buker, *The Penobscot Expedition*, 88; Flood, *Rise, and Fight Again*, 228.

41. Deposition of Col. Paul Revere, in Baxter, *Documentary History*, 17:207.

42. Deposition of Capt. Cushing, in Baxter, *Documentary History*, 17:210.

43. Peleg Wadsworth to William D. Williamson, January 1, 1828, in *Collections and Proceedings*, 10:70.

44. Nash, *The Original Journal*, 105.

45. Deposition of Col. Paul Revere, in Baxter, *Documentary History*, 17:207.

46. Testimony of Lieut. George Little, in Baxter, *Documentary History*, 17:238; Testimony of Waterman Thomas, in Baxter, *Documentary History*, 17:309.

47. Deposition of Col. Paul Revere, in Baxter, *Documentary History*, 17:207.

48. Testimony of Waterman Thomas, in Baxter, *Documentary History*, 17:309.

49. For accounts of the perils, rescue, and chase of the *Samuel*, see Testimony of Lieut. George Little, in Baxter, *Documentary History*, 17:238–240; Testimony of Waterman Thomas, in Baxter, *Documentary History*, 17:309–310; and Flood, *Rise, and Fight Again*, 232–233.

50. Testimony of Lieut. George Little, in Baxter, *Documentary History*, 17:240.

51. For accounts of the confrontation between George Little and Saltonstall, see Testimony of Lieut. George Little, in Baxter, *Documentary History*, 17:240–241; Testimony of Waterman Thomas, in Baxter, *Documentary History*, 17:310; and Flood, *Rise, and Fight Again*, 234.

52. Testimony of Lieut. George Little, in Baxter, *Documentary History*, 17:241.

53. Statement of Major Todd, in Baxter, *Documentary History*, 17:297; see also Testimony of Waterman Thomas, in Baxter, *Documentary History*, 17:311.

54. Deposition of Col. Revere, in Baxter, *Documentary History*, 17:207.

55. Statement of Capt. Williams, in Baxter, *Documentary History*,17:228.

56. Testimony of Capt. Phillip Brown, in Baxter, *Documentary History*, 17:288; Flood, *Rise, and Fight Again*, 238.

57. Ibid., 236.

58. Testimony of Waterman Thomas, in Baxter, *Documentary History*, 17:311.

59. Testimony of Capt. Philip Brown, in Baxter, *Documentary History*, 17:291.

60. Ibid.

61. Statement of John Cathcart, in Baxter, *Documentary History*, 17:246.

10. OUTRAGE AND ALLEGATIONS

1. Brig. Gen. Francis McLean to Sir Henry Clinton, August 23, 1779, in *Report on American Manuscripts*, 2:16.

2. Account of Thomas Philbrook, in Cowell, *Spirit of '76*, 320.

3. Paul Revere to Rachel Walker Revere, August 1778, in *Proceedings of the Massachusetts Historical Society, 1873–1875* (Cambridge, Mass.: John Wilson and Son, 1875), 252.

4. Peleg Wadsworth Brig. General to the President of the Council, August 19, 1779, in Baxter, *Documentary History*, 17:30.

5. Ibid.

6. Statement of General Wadsworth, in Baxter, *Documentary History*, 17:277.

7. Report of J. H. Allen, September 10, 1779, in Baxter, *Documentary History*, 17:106.

8. Letter from General Lovell, August 28, 1779, in Baxter, *Documentary History*, 17:61–63.

9. Ibid., 62.

10. General Lovell to the Council, September 3, 1779, in Baxter, *Documentary History*, 17:78.

11. Account of Thomas Philbrook, in Cowell, *Spirit of '76*, 320–321.

12. Statement of Lieut. Phillips, Baxter, in *Documentary History*, 17:344.

13. Sergeant Lawrence's Journal, in Wheeler, *History of Castine*, 320.

14. Calef, "The Journal of the Siege," 31.

15. Sir George Collier to General Sir Henry Clinton, August 24, 1779, in *Report on American Manuscripts*, 2:18–19.

16. "*Proclamation* of August 23, 1779," *Scots Magazine* 41 (Edinburgh: A. Murray and J. Cochran, September 1779), 497.

17. Buker, *The Penobscot Expedition*, 100–101.

18. Ibid., 104.

19. Petition of Inhabitants of Lincoln, in Baxter, *Documentary History*, 17:335.

20. Ibid., 334.

21. Ibid., 335.

22. John Murray to the Honorable Jeremiah Powell, August 21, 1779, in Baxter, *Documentary History*, 17:44.

23. Flood writes, "That was to be the last order he was allowed to give to American soldiers in a field operation." Flood, *Rise, and Fight Again*, 241.

24. Buker, *The Penobscot Expedition*, 102.

25. John Murray to the Hon. Jeremiah Powell, August 21, 1779, in Baxter, *Documentary History*, 17:43.

26. Committee of Georgetown to Massachusetts Council, August 26, 1779, in Baxter, *Documentary History*, 17:50.

27. Defence of Col. Paul Revere, in Baxter, *Documentary History*, 17:217.

28. Gettemy, *The True Story*, xxvii.

29. President of Council to Brig. General Lovell, August 19, 1779, in Baxter, *Documentary History*, 17:33–34.

30. Order to Brigadier General Lovell, August 19, 1779, in Baxter, *Documentary History*, 17:33.

31. A Proclamation of the Massachusetts Council, August 19, 1779, in Baxter, *Documentary History*, 17:25–26.

32. Powell to Jay, September 2, 1779, in Baxter, *Documentary History*, 17:72.

33. Peleg Wadsworth Br. Gl. to the President of the Council, in Baxter, *Documentary History*, 17:28.

34. Ibid., 28–29.

35. H. Jackson to Honorable Jeremiah Powell, Esq., August 22, 1779, in Baxter, *Documentary History*, 17:46.

36. Williamson, *The History of the State of Maine*, 476.

37. Abigail Adams to James Lovell, December 13, 1779, in *Founding Families: Digital Editions of the Papers of the Winthrops and the Adamses*, ed. C. James Taylor (Boston: Massachusetts Historical Society, 2007). http://www.masshist.org/ff/.

38. Goss, *The Life*, 2:328; Massachusetts Archives, vol. 145, 201.

39. Williamson, *The History of the State of Maine*, 476.

40. State of Massachusetts Bay to His Excellency John Jay, September 21, 1997, in Baxter, *Documentary History*, 17:158.

41. Committee of Safety for Falmouth to Honorable Jeremiah Powell, August 30, 1779, in Baxter, *Documentary History*, 17:67.

42. Penobscot Indians to Committee, in Baxter, *Documentary History*, 17:119.

43. Council to Colonel Thomas Crafts, August 26, 1779, in Baxter, *Documentary History*, 17:51.

44. Defence of Col. Paul Revere, in Baxter, *Documentary History*, 17:217.

45. Paul Revere to William Heath, October 24, 1779, 325.

46. Ibid.; Triber, *A True Republican*, 138.

47. Paul Revere to William Heath, October 24, 1779, 325.

48. Ibid.

49. Major John Rice to Gen. Horatio Gates, September 2, 1779, in Gates Papers, New York Historical Society, quoted in Flood, *Rise, and Fight Again*, 245.

50. Paul Revere to William Heath, October 24, 1779, 324.

51. Gen. Lovell to Massachusetts Council, August 28, 1779, in Baxter, *Documentary History*, 17:61.

52. General Lovell to the Council, September 4, 1779, in Baxter, *Documentary History*, 17:86.

53. Gen. Lovell to Massachusetts Council, August 29, 1779, in Baxter, *Documentary History*, 17:65.

54. Ibid.

55. Israel Keith to William Heath, September 26, 1779, in *Collections of the Massachusetts Historical Society*, 7th ser., vol. 4 (1894), 318. Keith wrote, "Nothing is more natural than for an old soldier to despise men in civil life who have never smelled powder and whom he looks upon as cowards."

56. Powell to Jay, September 2, 1779, in Baxter, *Documentary History*, 17:71.

57. Ibid., 72.

58. Paul Revere to William Heath, October 24, 1779, 325.

59. Whittemore, *The Heroes of the American Revolution*, supp. to sect. 1, 31.

60. See chapter 8.

61. Messieurs Edes, *Boston Gazette and the Country Journal*, March 25, 1782.

62. Paul Revere to William Heath, October 24, 1779, 324.

63. Paul Revere to Council, Massachusetts Archives, vol. 201, 272; Gettemy, *The True Story*, 199.

64. Complaint of T. J. Carnes, in Baxter, *Documentary History*, 17:87–88; Complaint of T. J. Carnes, in *Collections and Proceedings of the Maine Historical Society*, quar. pt., no. 4, 381.

65. Order of Council, September 6, 1779, in Baxter, *Documentary History*, 17:86–87.

11. "GREAT AND UNIVERSAL UNEASINESS"

1. *Independent Chronicle*, September 9, 1779, 3; Flood, *Rise, and Fight Again*, 246.

2. Resolutions in House in re Penobscot Expedition, in Baxter, *Documentary History*, 17:99–100.

3. Israel Keith to William Heath, September 26, 1779, in *Collections of the Massachusetts Historical Society*, 7th ser., vol. 4 (1894), 318.

4. John Vance Cheney, "Revolutionary Letters: Third Paper: Major-General Artemas Ward and Others," *Scribner's Monthly* 11, no. 5 (March 1876): 712.

5. Israel Keith to William Heath, 318.

6. Messieurs Edes, *Boston Gazette and the Country Journal*, March 25, 1782.

7. Paul Revere to William Heath, October 24, 1779, 326.

8. Resolve of Council, in Baxter, *Documentary History*, 17:166–167.

9. Cheney, "Revolutionary Letters," 716.

10. See Buker, *The Penobscot Expedition*, 114–135.

11. See The Court Martial in re Capt. Saltonstall, in Baxter, *Documentary History*, 17:155–156, for the procedural history of the case against Saltonstall.

12. Nash, *The Original Journal*, 82.

13. Williamson, *The History of the State of Maine*, 478.

14. Abram English Brown, *Faneuil Hall and Faneuil Hall Market* (Boston: Lee and Shepard, 1900), 139.

15. Fischer, *Paul Revere's Ride*, 4–5.

16. See Herbert L. Osgood, *The American Colonies in the Seventeenth Century*, vol. 1 (New York: Macmillan, 1904), 187, for the use of depositions in legal proceedings and the sparse use of lawyers.

17. Orders to Brigadier General Lovell from the Council Chamber, July 2, 1779, in Baxter, *Documentary History*, 16:320–321.

18. For the full content of Lovell's testimony, see General Lovell's Defence, in Baxter, *Documentary History*, 17:185–187, 190–192.

19. Ibid., 186.

20. Ibid., 187.

21. Ibid., 186.

22. Ibid., 191.

23. Examination of Nathan Brown, in Baxter, *Documentary History*, 17:188–189.

24. For the full content of Carnes's testimony, see The Examination of Captain John Carnes Commander of the Ship Hector, in Baxter, *Documentary History*, 17:189–190.

25. Deposition of Titus Salter, in Baxter, *Documentary History*, 17:215.

26. Statement of Capt. Williams, in Baxter, *Documentary History*, 17:230.

27. Capt. Hallet's Statement, in Baxter, *Documentary History*, 17:235.

28. Ibid., 236.

29. Testimony of Lieut. George Little, in Baxter, *Documentary History*, 17:243.

30. Statement of John Cathcart, in Baxter, *Documentary History*, 17:246.

31. Testimony of Joshua Davis, in Baxter, *Documentary History*, 17:316.

32. Mr. Thomas Jenner Carnes's Declaration, *Boston Gazette and the Country Journal*, April 8, 1782.

33. Deposition of Ph. Marett, Ship Sky Rocket, in Baxter, *Documentary History*, 17:268.

34. Deposition of J Whipple, in Baxter, *Documentary History*, 17:271.

35. Statement of Andrew McIntyer, in Baxter, *Documentary History*, 17:305–306.

36. Ibid., 305.

37. Deposition of Capt. Cushing, in Baxter, *Documentary History*, 17:211.

38. Deposition of Capt. Cushing, in Baxter, *Documentary History*, 17:210–211.

39. Ibid.

40. Statement of Capt. Williams, in Baxter, *Documentary History*, 17:230.

41. Ibid.

42. Statement of General Wadsworth, in Baxter, *Documentary History*, 17:272.

43. Ibid., 273.

44. Ibid., 275.

45. Ibid., 275–276.

46. Ibid., 275.

47. Ibid., 278.

48. Ibid., for Revere's exchange with Wadsworth.

49. Ibid., 279, for Carnes' exchange with Wadsworth.

50. Ibid.

51. Testimony of James Brown, in Baxter, *Documentary History*, 17:280.

52. Ibid., 281.

53. Ibid.

54. Testimony of Capt. Carnes, in Baxter, *Documentary History*, 17:282.

55. Ibid., 283.

56. Paul Revere to William Heath, October 24, 1779, 326.

57. Testimony of Capt. Carnes, in Baxter, *Documentary History*, 17:283.

58. Statement of Major Todd, in Baxter, *Documentary History*, 17:300.

59. Ibid., 295.

60. Ibid., 298.

61. Ibid., 301.

62. Statement of Gilbert W. Speakman, in Baxter, *Documentary History*, 17:321.

63. Ibid., 321–323, for Speakman's allegations.

64. See Questions to General Lovell by Col. Revere, in Baxter, *Documentary History*, 17:319–321.

65. See Answers by General Lovell, in Baxter, *Documentary History*, 17:339.

66. See Questions Asked by the Committee, in Baxter, *Documentary History*, 17:340.

12. "DEARER TO ME THAN LIFE"

1. Petition of Samuel Burgess, in Baxter, *Documentary History*, 17:350.

2. Representation of the Board of War, in Baxter, *Documentary History*, 17:351–352.

3. For reference to all quotes, see Defence of Col. Paul Revere, in Baxter, *Documentary History*, 17:215–224.

4. Ibid., 215.

5. Complaint of T. J. Carnes, in Baxter, *Documentary History*, 17:88; Complaint of T. J. Carnes, in *Collections and Proceedings of the Maine Historical Society*, quar. pt., no. 4, 381.

6. See Questions Asked by the Committee, in Baxter, *Documentary History*, 17:340; Letter from Gen. Lovell, August 29, 1779, in Baxter, *Documentary History*, 17:65.

13. JUDGMENT

1. Society for the Diffusion of Useful Knowledge, *A History of the American Revolution* (Columbus, Ohio: Isaac N. Whiting, 1824), 140–147.

2. Samuel Eliot Morison, *A History of the Constitution of Massachusetts* (Wright and Potter, 1917), 19.

3. See Memorial to the General Court from the Town of Pittsfield, May 29, 1776, quoted in Morison, *A History*, 14.

4. Reverend William Gordon, the chaplain of the Massachusetts House of Representatives, attacked the 1778 Constitution in a series of articles that ap-

peared in the *Independent Chronicle* and which resulted in Reverend Gordon's dismissal from the General Court. "The Constitution, gentlemen," he wrote, "is submitted to your consideration—but how? In the lump—take or reject the whole—no alteration is proposed. Neither is it preceded or accompanied with a declaration of rights." Cornelius Dalton, *Leading the Way: A History of the Massachusetts General Court 1629–1980* (Boston: Office of the Massachusetts Secretary of State, 1984), 51. Twenty-seven-year-old lawyer Theophilus Parson, in his pamphlet the *Essex Result*, eloquently set out the "true principles of government" as based on the political philosophies of John Locke and argued for the inclusion of certain natural and inalienable rights that must be set forth in a Bill of Rights. See Morison, *A History*, 16.

5. Morison, *A History*, 16.

6. Dalton, *Leading the Way*, 56.

7. Morison, *A History*, 19.

8. Ibid., 20.

9. Ibid.

10. For the entire report, see *The Acts and Resolves of the Province of the Massachusetts Bay*, 1779–1780, vol. 21, chap. 459 (Boston: Wright and Potter, 1922), 216–217; see also Report of Committee on Expedition, in Baxter, *Documentary History*, 17:358–360.

11. William D. Williamson writes, "Upon this report the General Court adjudged, "*that Commodore Saltonstall be incompetent ever after, to hold a commission in the service of the State . . .*" Williamson, *The History of the State of Maine*, 478.

14. MONUMENT OF DISGRACE

1. *The Acts and Resolves of the Province of the Massachusetts Bay*, 1779–1780, vol. 21, chap. 459 (Boston: Wright and Potter, 1922), 218.

2. Paul Revere to William Heath, October 24, 1779, 326.

3. Petition of Col. Revere, in Baxter, *Documentary History*, 17:375.

4. Order of Committee of General Court, in Baxter, *Documentary History*, 17:396.

5. For the full text of Revere's diary, see Deposition of Col. Paul Revere, in Baxter, *Documentary History*, 17:201–207.

6. Bernard Cornwell states in his "Historical Note" to *The Fort*, "I have no proof that this 'diary' was manufactured for the inquiry, but it seems very likely." Cornwell, *The Fort*, 463.

7. Notice of General Court to Col. Revere, in Baxter, *Documentary History*, 17:431.

8. Questions Asked at Investigation, in Baxter, *Documentary History*, 17:431.

9. See Testimony of Thomas Wait Foster, in Baxter, *Documentary History*, 17:433, for all dialogue.

10. To His Excellency John Jay, September 21, 1779, in Baxter, *Documentary History*, 17:158–159.

11. Letter Transmitting Resolution of Congress, in Baxter, *Documentary History*, 17:445.

12. Report of Committee in re Col. Revere, in Baxter, *Documentary History*, 17:447–448.

13. Morison, *A History*, 20.

14. Ibid.; see also *The American Almanac and Repository of Useful Knowledge for the Year 1836* (Boston: Charles Bowen, 1835).

15. Report of Committee, January 4, 1780, in James Phinney Baxter, *Documentary History of the State of Maine: The Baxter Manuscripts*, vol. 18 (Portland, Maine: Lefavor-Tower, 1914), 50.

16. See Gettemy, *The True Story*, 210.

17. Ibid.

18. Petition of Col Revere, in Baxter, *Documentary History*, 18:67–68.

19. Ibid., 68.

20. Ibid., 68.

21. Ibid.

22. Ibid.

23. Order of Council, January 21, 1780, in Baxter, *Documentary History*, 18:85.

15. THE COURT-MARTIAL OF PAUL REVERE

1. George Washington to Joseph Reed, December 16, 1779, in William S. Baker, *Itinerary of General Washington from June 15, 1775 to December 23, 1783* (Philadelphia: J. B. Lippincott, 1892), 169.

2. Charles Burr Todd, *The Real Benedict Arnold* (New York: A. S. Barnes, 1903), 196.

3. Representation of Council to the U.S. Congress Relative to Losses by Penobscot Expedition, in Baxter, *Documentary History*, 18:91.

4. Ibid., 89–91.

5. Ibid., 91.

6. Paul Revere to the Council and General Court, in Baxter, *Documentary History*, 18:135.

7. Order dated March 16, 1780, in Baxter, *Documentary History*, 18:135.

8. Resolve of Council in the Case of Col. Revere, in Baxter, *Documentary History*, 18:140.

9. "The Militia Act: Together with the Rules and Regulations for the Militia,"

chap. 10, sect. 14 of *An Act for Forming and Regulating the Militia within the Colony of the Massachusetts Bay, in New England*, in *Province Laws of 1776* (Boston: J. Gill, 1776); see also Frederick Grant Jr., "The Court-Martial of Paul Revere," *Boston Bar Journal* 21, no. 5 (May 1977): 8–9.

10. Order for Court Martial in Case of Col. Revere, in Baxter, *Documentary History*, 18:210.

11. Oliver Ayer Roberts, *History of The Military Company of the Massachusetts Now Called the Ancient and Honorable Artillery Company of Massachusetts: 1637–1888* (Boston: Alfred Mudge and Son, 1897), 85.

12. Triber, *A True Republican*, 40, 67.

13. Ibid., 95.

14. Edward Proctor's Application, in Baxter, *Documentary History*, 18:218.

15. Messieurs Edes, *Boston Gazette and the Country Journal*, March 25, 1782.

16. Forbes, *Paul Revere*, 364.

17. Messieurs Edes, *Boston Gazette and the Country Journal*, March 25, 1782.

18. C. James Taylor, ed., *Founding Families: Digital Editions of the Papers of the Winthrops and the Adamses* (Boston: Massachusetts Historical Society, 2007). http://www.masshist.org/ff/.

19. Letter from Honorable James Lovell, Esq., April 17, 1780, in Baxter, *Documentary History*, 18:220–221.

20. Abigail Adams to John Adams, February 26, 1780, in Taylor, *Founding Families*.

21. Paul Revere to Mathias Rivoire, October 6, 1781, in Gettemy, *The True Story*, 219.

22. Triber, *A True Republican*, 141.

23. Gettemy, *The True Story*, 237.

24. Petition of Paul Revere, in James Phinney Baxter, *Documentary History of the State of Maine: The Baxter Manuscripts*, vol. 19 (Portland, Maine: Lefavor-Tower, 1914), 97–98.

25. Messieurs Edes, *Boston Gazette and the Country Journal*, March 25, 1782.

26. Goss, *The Life*, 2:387.

27. Messieurs Edes, *Boston Gazette and the Country Journal*, March 25, 1782.

28. Jared Sparks, *The Library of American Biography*, vol. 13 (Boston: Charles C. Little and James Brown, 1847), 356–360.

29. Messieurs Edes, *Boston Gazette and the Country Journal*, March 25, 1782.

30. Ibid.

31. Ibid.

32. Paul Revere to Mathias Rivoire, October 6, 1781, in Gettemy, *The True Story*, 220.

33. Paul Revere to John Rivoire, July 1, 1782, in Gettemy, *The True Story*, 227–228.

34. Proceedings of Court Martial in Case of Paul Revere, in Baxter, *Documentary History*, 19:428.

35. Frank A. Gardner, "Colonel Theophilus Cotton's Regiment," *Massachusetts Magazine* 3, no. 2 (April 1910): 105.

36. Proceedings of Court Martial in Case of Paul Revere, in Baxter, *Documentary History*, 19:428.

37. Ibid., 428–429.

38. Ibid., 429.

39. Messieurs Edes, *Boston Gazette and the Country Journal*, March 25, 1782.

40. Messieurs Printers, *Boston Gazette and the Country Journal*, March 18, 1782.

41. Proceedings of Court Martial in Case of Paul Revere, in Baxter, *Documentary History*, 19:429.

42. Ibid.

43. Ibid.

44. Messieurs Printers, *Boston Gazette and the Country Journal*, March 18, 1782.

45. Proceedings of Court Martial in Case of Paul Revere, in Baxter, *Documentary History*, 19:429.

46. Messieurs Edes, *Boston Gazette and the Country Journal*, March 25, 1782.

47. Proceedings of Court Martial in Case of Paul Revere, in Baxter, *Documentary History*, 19:429.

48. Isaac N. Arnold, *The Life of Benedict Arnold: His Patriotism and His Treason* (Chicago: Jansen, McClurg, 1880), 257.

49. Joshua Thomas to Governor, in Baxter, *Documentary History*, 19:427–428.

50. Proceedings of Court Martial in Case of Paul Revere, in Baxter, *Documentary History*, 19:430.

51. Ibid.

EPILOGUE

1. Messieurs Printers, *Boston Gazette and the Country Journal*, March 18, 1782.

2. Ibid.

3. Messieurs Edes, *Boston Gazette and the Country Journal*, March 25, 1782.

4. Ibid.

5. Ibid.

6. Mr. Gill, *Continental Journal and Weekly Advertiser*, April 4, 1782; "Mr. Thomas Jenner Carnes's Declaration," *Boston Gazette and the Country Journal*, April 8, 1782.

7. See, for example, his dispute with Thomas Fosdick, in Goss, *The Life*, 2:667.

8. Mr. Gill, *Continental Journal and Weekly Advertiser*, April 4, 1782; "Mr. Thomas Jenner Carnes's Declaration," *Boston Gazette and the Country Journal*, April 8, 1782.

9. Messieurs Edes, *Boston Gazette and the Country Journal*, April 8, 1782.

10. Mr. Gill, *Continental Journal and Weekly Advertiser*, April 11, 1782.

11. Ibid.

12. Messieurs Edes, *Boston Gazette and the Country Journal*, April 15, 1782.

13. Ibid.

14. Ibid.

15. Mr. Gill, *Continental Journal and Weekly Advertiser*, April 18, 1782.

16. Messieurs Edes, *Boston Gazette and the Country Journal*, April 15, 1782.

17. Report of William Lithgow Junior, October 15, 1779, in Baxter, *Documentary History*, 17:387.

18. James Lovell Enclosing Letter of George Washington to Massachusetts Council, April 21, 1780, in Baxter, *Documentary History*, 18:228.

19. See A Proclamation, in Baxter, *Documentary History*, 18:222–224.

20. Horace Andrew Wadsworth, *Two Hundred and Fifty Years of the Wadsworth Family in America* (Lawrence, Mass.: Eagle Steam, 1883), 44–45.

21. Ibid., 45.

22. Flood, *Rise, and Fight Again*, 250.

23. Wadsworth, *Two Hundred and Fifty Years*, 49.

24. Simon Goodell Griffin, *The History of Keene, New Hampshire* (Keene, N.H.: Sentinel, 1904), 294.

25. Ibid., 546.

26. Advertisement, *Boston Evening-Post and the General Advertiser*, June 14, 1783.

27. Massachusetts Society of the Sons of the American Revolution, *Register of Members* (Springfield, Mass.: F. A. Bassette, 1916), 118.

28. Nash, *The Original Journal*, 89–90.

29. Kevitt, *General Solomon Lovell*, 21.

30. Forbes, *Paul Revere*, 360.

31. Gettemy, *The True Story*, 244; Leehey, *Reconstructing Paul Revere*, 30.

32. Gettemy, *The True Story*, 241–242; Peter Harvey, *Reminiscences and Anecdotes of Daniel Webster* (Boston: Little, Brown, 1878), 382.

33. Fisher Ames to Paul Revere, April 26, 1789, quoted in Goss, *The Life*, 2:460.

34. Leehey, *Reconstructing Paul Revere*, 31.

35. Ibid.; Gettemy, *The True Story*, 244.

36. Leehey, *Reconstructing Paul Revere*, 31.

37. Steblecki, *Fraternity, Philanthropy, and Revolution*, 132–135.

38. Federhen, *From Artisan to Entrepreneur*, 84.

39. Deaths, *New-England Galaxy*, May 15, 1818.

40. Fischer, *Paul Revere's Ride*, 331–332.

41. Ibid., 331.

42. Henry Wadsworth Longfellow, *Tales of a Wayside Inn* (Boston: Ticknor and Fields, 1863), 20.

Selected Bibliography

An Act for Forming and Regulating the Militia within the Colony of the Massachusetts Bay, in New England. Chap. 10, sect. 14. *Province Laws of 1776.* Boston: J. Gill, 1776.

The Acts and Resolves of the Province of the Massachusetts Bay, 1779–1780. Vol. 21. Boston: Wright and Potter, 1922.

The Acts and Resolves Public and Private of the Province of Massachusetts Bay, 1777–1778. Vol. 20. Boston: Wright and Potter, 1918.

Alexander, John K. *Samuel Adams: America's Revolutionary Politician.* Lanham, Md.: Rowman and Littlefield, 2002.

Allen, Gardner W. *A Naval History of the American Revolution.* Boston: Houghton Mifflin, 1913.

Allen, Gardner Weld. "State Navies and Privateers in the Revolution." In *Proceedings of the Massachusetts Historical Society.* 3d ser., vol. 46. Cambridge, Mass.: John Wilson and Son, October 1912–June 1913.

The American Almanac and Repository of Useful Knowledge for the Year 1836. Boston: Charles Bowen, 1835.

Andrews, Charles McLean. *The American Nation: A History of Colonial Self-Government 1652–1689.* New York: Harper and Brothers, 1904.

Arnold, Isaac N. *The Life of Benedict Arnold: His Patriotism and His Treason.* Chicago: Jansen, McClurg, 1880.

Baker, William S. *Itinerary of General Washington from June 15, 1775 to December 23, 1783.* Philadelphia: J. B. Lippincott, 1892.

Batchelder, Samuel Francis. *The Life and Surprising Adventures of John Nutting Cambridge Loyalist and His Strange Connection with the Penobscot Expedition of 1779.* Cambridge, Mass.: Cambridge Historical Society, 1912.

Baxter, James Phinney. *Documentary History of the State of Maine: The Baxter Manuscripts.* Vol. 16. Portland, Maine: Lefavor-Tower, 1910.

Baxter, James Phinney. *Documentary History of the State of Maine: The Baxter Manuscripts.* Vol. 17. Portland, Maine: Lefavor-Tower, 1913.

Baxter, James Phinney. *Documentary History of the State of Maine: The Baxter Manuscripts* Vol. 18. Portland, Maine: Lefavor-Tower, 1914.

Baxter, James Phinney. *Documentary History of the State of Maine: The Baxter Manuscripts.* Vol. 19. Portland, Maine: Lefavor-Tower, 1914.

Boston Evening-Post and the General Advertiser, June 14, 1783.

Boston Gazette and the Country Journal, September 19, 1768.

Boston Gazette and the Country Journal, July 30, 1770.

Boston Gazette and the Country Journal, March 11, 1771.

Boston Gazette and the Country Journal, March 18, 1782.

Boston Gazette and the Country Journal, March 25, 1782.

Boston Gazette and the Country Journal, April 8, 1782.

Boston Gazette and the Country Journal, April 15, 1782.

The Bostonian. Vol. 2. Boston: Bostonian Publishing, April–September 1895.

Brown, Abram English. *Faneuil Hall and Faneuil Hall Market.* Boston: Lee and Shepard, 1900.

Buker, George E. *The Penobscot Expedition: Commodore Saltonstall and the Massachusetts Conspiracy of 1779.* Annapolis: Naval Institute Press, 2002.

Calef, John. "The Journal of the Siege of Penobscot." *Magazine of History with Notes and Queries.* Extra issue no. 11. New York: William Abbatt, 1910.

Campbell, John. *Lives of the British Admirals: Containing an Accurate Naval History from the Earliest Periods.* Vol. 5. London: C. J. Barrington, Strand, and J. Harris, 1817.

Cayford, John E. *The Penobscot Expedition: Being an Account of the Largest American Naval Engagement of the Revolutionary War.* Orrington, Maine: C and H Publishing, 1976.

Chase, Ellen. *The Beginnings of the American Revolution, Based on Contemporary Letters, Diaries, and Other Documents.* Vols. 1–2. New York: Baker and Taylor, 1910.

Cheney, John Vance. "Revolutionary Letters: Third Paper: Major-General Artemas Ward and Others." *Scribner's Monthly* 11, no. 5 (March 1876): 712–720.

Clarke, Jonas. *Opening of the War of the Revolution 19th of April 1775: A Brief Narrative of the Principal Transactions of that Day.* Lexington, Mass.: Lexington Historical Society, 1901.

Collections and Proceedings of the Maine Historical Society. 2d ser., vol. 1. Portland: Maine Historical Society, 1890.

Collections and Proceedings of the Maine Historical Society. Quarterly pt., no. 4. Portland, Maine: Brown Thurston, October 1892.

Collections and Proceedings of the Maine Historical Society. 2d ser., vol. 9. Portland: Maine Historical Society 1898.

Collections and Proceedings of the Maine Historical Society. 2d ser., vol. 10. Portland: Maine Historical Society, 1899.

Collections of the Massachusetts Historical Society. 1st ser., vol. 5. Boston: Massachusetts Historical Society, 1798.

Collections of the Massachusetts Historical Society. 7th ser., vol. 4. Boston: Massachusetts Historical Society, 1894.

Collins, Edward D., *Committees of Correspondence of the American Revolution.* Washington, D.C.: American Historical Association, 1901; Government Printing Office, 1902.

Continental Journal and Weekly Advertiser, April 4–18, 1782.

Cornwell, Bernard. *The Fort: A Novel of the Revolutionary War.* New York: Harper, 2010.

Cowell, Benjamin. *Spirit of '76 in Rhode Island: Or Sketches of the Efforts of the Government and People in the War of the Revolution.* Boston: A. J. Wright, 1850.

Cushing, Harry Alonzo, ed. . *The Writings of Samuel Adams.* Vol. 2: 1770–1773. New York: G. P. Putnam's Sons, 1906.

Cushing, Harry Alonzo, ed. . *The Writings of Samuel Adams.* Vol. 3: 1773–1777. New York: G. P. Putnam's Sons, 1907.

Cutter, William Richard. *New England Families Genealogical and Memorial.* Vol. 2. New York: Lewis Historical Publishing, 1913.

Dalton, Cornelius. *Leading the Way. A History of the Massachusetts General Court 1629–1980.* Boston: Office of the Massachusetts Secretary of State, 1984.

Drake, Samuel Adams. *Nooks and Corners of the New England Coast.* New York: Harper and Brothers, 1875.

Duncan, Roger F. *Coastal Maine: A Maritime History.* New York: W. W. Norton, 1992.

Duncan-Page, Anne. *The Religious Culture of the Huguenots, 1660–1750.* Farnham, U.K.: Ashgate, 2006.

Federhen, Deborah A. "From Artisan to Entrepreneur: Paul Revere's Silver Shop Operation." In *Paul Revere—Artisan, Businessman, and Patriot: The Man Behind the Myth.* Edited by Nina Zannieri and Patrick M. Leehey, et al. Boston: Paul Revere Memorial Association, 1988.

Ferling, John. *A Leap in the Dark: The Struggle to Create the American Republic.* New York: Oxford University Press, 2003.

Fischer, David Hackett. *Paul Revere's Ride.* New York: Oxford University Press, 1994.

Flood, Charles Bracelen. *Rise, and Fight Again: Perilous Times Along the Road to Independence.* New York: Dodd, Mead, 1976.

Forbes, Esther. *Paul Revere and the World He Lived In.* Boston: Houghton Mifflin, 1942.

Frothingham, Richard. *History of the Siege of Boston, and of the Battles of Lexington, Concord, and Bunker Hill.* New York: Little, Brown, 1903.

Frothingham, Richard. *The Life and Times of Joseph Warren.* New York: Little, Brown, 1865.

Gardner, Frank A. "Colonel Theophilus Cotton's Regiment." *Massachusetts Magazine* 3, no. 2 (April 1910): 99–116.

Gettemy, Charles Ferris. *The True Story of Paul Revere: His Midnight Ride, His Arrest and Court-Martial, His Useful Public Services.* New York: Little, Brown, 1905.

Goodell, Abner Cheney, Jr. *The Trial and Execution for Petit Treason, of Mark and Phillis, Slaves of Capt. John Codman.* Cambridge, Mass.: John Wilson and Son, 1883.

Gordon, William, D. D. *The History of the Rise, Progress, and Establishment of the Independence of the United States of America.* New York: Printed for Samuel Campbell by John Woods, 1801.

Goss, Elbridge Henry. *The Life of Colonel Paul Revere.* 2 vols. Boston: Joseph George Cupples, 1891.

Gould, Robert Freke. *A Library of Freemasonry.* New York: John C. Yorston, 1906.

Grant, Frederick, Jr. "The Court-Martial of Paul Revere." *Boston Bar Journal* 21, no. 5 (May 1977): 5–13.

Griffin, Simon Goodell. *The History of Keene, New Hampshire.* Keene, N.H.: Sentinel, 1904.

Griffith, Samuel B. *The War for American Independence: From 1760 to the Surrender at Yorktown in 1781.* Champaign: University of Illinois Press, 2002.

Groves, Percy, *History of the 91st Princess Louise's Argyllshire Highlanders.* Edinburgh and London: W. and A. K. Johnston, 1894.

Hart, Albert Bushnell, and Edward Channing, eds. *James Otis's Speech on the Writs of Assistance, 1761.* American History Leaflets Colonial and Constitutional, no. 33. New York: Parker P. Simmons, 1912.

Harvey, Peter. *Reminiscences and Anecdotes of Daniel Webster.* New York: Little, Brown, 1878.

The Historical Magazine, and Notes and Queries Concerning the Antiquities, History and Biography of America. Vol. 3. New York: John G. Shea, February 1864.

Holland, Henry W. *William Dawes and His Ride with Paul Revere.* Boston: John Wilson and Son, 1878.

Howard, George Elliott. *The American Nation: A History.* Vol. 8, *Preliminaries of the Revolution, 1763–1775.* New York: Harper and Brothers, 1906.

Hutchinson, Peter Orlando. *The Diary and Letters of His Excellency Thomas Hutchinson, Esq.* Boston: Houghton Mifflin, 1886.

Hutchinson, Thomas. *The History of the Province of Massachusetts Bay from 1749 to 1774.* London: John Murray, 1828.

Independent Chronicle, September 9, 1779.

Jensen, Merrill. *The Founding of a Nation: A History of the American Revolution, 1763–1776.* New York: Oxford University Press, 1968; Indianapolis: Hackett, 2004.

"Journal Found on Board the *Hunter*, Continental Ship, of Eighteen Guns." In *The Historical Magazine, and Notes and Queries Concerning the Antiquities, History and Biography of America.* Vol. 8. New York: John G. Shea, February 1864.

"Journal of the Committee Who Built the Ships *Providence* and *Warren* for the United States in 1776." *Magazine of History with Notes and Queries* 8, no. 5 (1908).

Kevitt, Chester B. *General Solomon Lovell and the Penobscot Expedition.* Weymouth, Mass.: Weymouth Historical Commission, 1976.

Lamb, Martha J., ed. *Magazine of American History with Notes and Queries* 15, no. 1 (January 1886).

Leamon, James S. *Revolution Downeast: The War for American Independence in Maine.* Amherst: University of Massachusetts Press, 1993.

Leehey, Patrick M. "Reconstructing Paul Revere: An Overview of His Ancestry, Life, and Work." In *Paul Revere—Artisan, Businessman, and Patriot: The Man Behind the Myth.* Edited by Nina Zannieri and Patrick M. Leehey, et al. Boston: Paul Revere Memorial Association, 1988.

Leicester, Paul. "Some Pelham-Copley Letters." *Atlantic Monthly* 71, no. 426 (April 1893).

Longfellow, Henry Wadsworth. *Tales of a Wayside Inn.* Boston: Ticknor and Fields, 1863.

Lossing, Benson John, ed. *Harpers Encyclopedia of United States History.* New York: Harper and Brothers, 1902.

Massachusetts Archives. SC1/Series 45X, Vols. 145, 174, 175, and 201. Massachusetts Archives Collection, Boston, Massachusetts.

Massachusetts Society of the Sons of the American Revolution. *Register of Members.* Springfield, Mass.: F. A. Bassette, 1916.

Meinig, D. W. *The Shaping of America: A Geographical Perspective on 500 Years of History.* Vol. 1. New Haven: Yale University Press, 1986.

Miller, Joel J. *The Revolutionary Paul Revere.* Nashville, Tenn.: Thomas Nelson, 2010.

Moore, Frank. *Songs and Ballads of the American Revolution.* New York: D. Appleton, 1855.

Moore, James Carrick. *The Life of Lieutenant-General Sir John Moore, K.B.* Vol. 1. London: John Murray, 1833.

Morgan, Edmund S. *The Birth of the Republic 1763–89.* Chicago: University of Chicago Press, 1992.

Morgan, Edmund S. *The Challenge of the American Revolution.* New York: W. W. Norton, 1976.

Morgan, William James. *Captains to the Northward: The New England Captains in the Continental Navy.* Barre, Mass.: Barre Gazette, 1959.

Morison, Samuel Eliot. *A History of the Constitution of Massachusetts.* Boston: Wright and Potter, 1917.

Mowat, Henry. "A Relation of the Services in which Captain Henry Mowat of the Royal Navy Was Engaged in America, from 1759 to the End of the American War in 1783." *Magazine of History with Notes and Queries.* Extra issue no. 11. New York: William Abbatt, 1910.

Museum of Fine Arts. *Paul Revere's Boston: 1735–1818.* Meriden, Conn.: Meriden Gravure, 1975.

Nash, Gilbert. *The Original Journal of General Solomon Lovell, Kept During the Penobscot Expedition, 1779: With a Sketch of His Life.* Weymouth, Mass.: Weymouth Historical Society, 1881.

Navy Historical Center, *The Penobscot Expedition Archaeological Project: Field Investigations 2000 and 2001, Final Report.* Washington Navy Yard, D.C.: Navy Historical Center, fall 2003.

New-England Galaxy, May 15, 1818.

Norton, Louis Arthur. *Captains Contentious: The Dysfunctional Sons of the Brine.* Columbia: University of South Carolina Press, 2009.

Osgood, Herbert L. *The American Colonies in the Seventeenth Century.* Vol. 1. New York: Macmillan, 1904.

"Paul Revere's Deposition, Fair Copy, Circa 1775." Boston: Massachusetts Historical Society, n.d. http://www.masshist.org/database/viewer.php ?item_id=98.

Paullin, Charles Oscar. *The Navy of the American Revolution.* Chicago: University of Chicago Press, 1906.

Philbrick, Nathaniel. *Bunker Hill: A City, a Siege, a Revolution.* New York: Viking, 2013.

Phinney, Elias. *History of the Battle at Lexington, on the Morning of the 19th April, 1775.* Boston: Phelps and Farnham, 1825.

Proceedings of the Massachusetts Historical Society, 1873–1875. Cambridge, Mass.:
John Wilson and Son, 1875.

"Proclamation of June 15, 1779." *Magazine of History with Notes and Queries.*
Extra issue no. 11. New York: William Abbatt, 1910.

Quincy, Josiah. *Reports of Cases Argued and Adjudged in the Superior Court of
Judicature of the Province of Massachusetts Bay Between 1761 and 1772.* Boston:
Little, Brown, 1865.

Report on American Manuscripts in the Royal Institution of Great Britain. Vol. 1.
London: Mackie, 1904.

Report on American Manuscripts in the Royal Institution of Great Britain, Vol. 2.
Dublin: John Falconer, 1906.

Roberts, Oliver Ayer. *History of the Military Company of the Massachusetts:
Now Called the Ancient and Honorable Artillery Company of Massachusetts:
1637–1888.* Boston: Alfred Mudge and Son, 1897.

Russell, William, and James Kimball. *Orderly Book of the Regiment of Artillery
Raised for the Defence of the Town of Boston in 1776.* Essex Institute Historical
Collections. Vols. 13 and 14. Salem, Mass.: Salem Press, 1876.

Scots Magazine 41 (Edinburgh: A. Murray and J. Cochran, September 1779).

Shaw, Henry I., Jr. "Penobscot Assault –1779." *Military Affairs* 17, no. 2
(Summer 1953): 83–94.

A Short Narrative of the Horrid Massacre in Boston. Boston: Town of Boston, 1770;
John Doggett Jr., 1849.

Snow, Edward Rowe. *The Islands of Boston Harbor.* Carlisle, Mass.:
Commonwealth Editions, 1935, 1971, 2003.

Society for the Diffusion of Useful Knowledge. *A History of the American
Revolution.* Columbus, Ohio: Isaac N. Whiting, 1824.

Sparks, Jared. *The Library of American Biography.* Vol. 13. Boston: Charles C.
Little and James Brown, 1847.

Steblecki, Edith J. "Fraternity, Philanthropy, and Revolution: Paul Revere and
Freemasonry." In *Paul Revere—Artisan, Businessman, and Patriot: The Man
Behind the Myth.* Edited by Nina Zannieri and Patrick M. Leehey, et al.
Boston: Paul Revere Memorial Association, 1988.

Thacher, James. *A Military Journal During the American Revolutionary War from
1775 to 1783.* Boston: Cottons and Barnard, 1827.

Todd, Charles Burr. *The Real Benedict Arnold.* New York: A. S. Barnes, 1903.

Triber, Jayne E. *A True Republican: The Life of Paul Revere.* Amherst: University
of Massachusetts, 1998.

Tudor, William. *The Life of James Otis of Massachusetts.* Boston: Wells and Lilly,
1823.

Wadsworth, Horace Andrew. *Two Hundred and Fifty Years of the Wadsworth Family in America*. Lawrence, Mass.: Eagle Steam, 1883.

Washington Historical Quarterly. Vol. 2. Seattle: Washington University State Historical Society, October 1907–July 1908.

Waste Book and Memoranda. Revere Family Papers. Vol. 1 (1761–1783), roll 5. Massachusetts Historical Society, Boston.

Weedon, William B. *Economic and Social History of New England 1620–1789*. Boston: Houghton, Mifflin, 1899.

Wheeler, George Augustus. *History of Castine, Penobscot, and Brookville, Maine: Including the Ancient Settlement of Pentagöet*. Bangor, Maine: Burr and Robinson, 1875.

Wheeler, George Augustus. "William Hutchings' Narrative of the Siege, and Other Reminiscences." In George Augustus Wheeler, *History of Castine, Penobscot, and Brooksville, Maine: Including the Ancient Settlement of Pentagöet*. Bangor, Maine: Burr and Robinson, 1875.

Wheildon, William W. *Siege and Evacuation of Boston and Charlestown, with a Brief Account of Pre-Revolutionary Public Buildings*. Boston: Lee and Shepard, 1876.

Whittemore, Henry. *The Heroes of the American Revolution and Their Descendants*. Brooklyn, N.Y.: Heroes of the Revolution, 1897; supp. to sect. 1, 1898).

Williamson, William D. *The History of the State of Maine: From Its First Discovery, A.D. 1602, to the Separation, A.D. 1820, Inclusive*. Hallowell, Maine: Galzier, Masters and Smith, 1839.

Wilson, Susan. *Boston Sites and Insights: An Essential Guide to Historic Landmarks in and around Boston*. Boston: Beacon Press, 2004.

Winsor, Justin, ed., *The Memorial History of Boston*. Boston: Ticknor, 1881.

Wood, Gordon S. *The American Revolution: A History*. New York: Modern Library, 2002.

Index